Wind of the Spirit

A Spiritual Freedom Odyssey

E. Gene Vosseler

Wind of the Spirit

E. Gene Vosseler

© E. Gene Vosseler 2009

Published by 1stWorld Publishing
P. O. Box 2211, Fairfield, Iowa 52556
tel: 641-209-5000 • fax: 641-209-3001
web: www.1stworldpublishing.com

First Edition

LCCN: 2008938744
SoftCover ISBN: 978-1-4218-9039-5
HardCover ISBN: 978-1-4218-9038-8
eBook ISBN: 978-1-4218-9040-1

All rights reserved. No part of this publication may be reproduced or transmitted in any form or by an means electronic or mechanical, including photocopy, recording or any information storage and retrieval system now known or to be invented, without permission in writing from the author, except by a reviewer who wishes to quote brief passage in connection with a review of written for inclusion in a magazine, newspaper or broadcast.

Some materials used by kind permission of Church Universal and Triumphant®, Contact information: 63 Summit Way, Gardiner, Montana 59030. ph. 406-848-9500, email: tslinfo@tsl.org, web: www.SummitLighthouse.org, www.TSL.org.

Excerpts from the lecture, "Chuang Tzu, World Philosopher at Play" taken from *The Complete Works of Chuang Tzu* by Burton Watson, copyright © 1968 Columbia University Press are reprinted with permission of the publisher.

ACKNOWLEDGEMENTS

First, I would like to thank Michael and Kaylie Utter who have faithfully supported my freedom mission over the years and without whose assistance this book would not be possible. Also my spiritual son, Henry Kriegel, has provided invaluable editing assistance.

In a very personal way, I want to acknowledge Dr. Jeane Wolf and Dr. Margaret Paul as the counselors who gave me the unconditional love and insightful wisdom that was an essential part of my soul healing during a rough patch in my life.

And to all my friends, who are too numerous to name, I am grateful for all of the love and kindness you have shared with me along life's highway. Peace be with you.

DEDICATION

This book is first and foremost dedicated to my beloved Gurus, Elizabeth Clare and Mark L. Prophet (the ascended master Lanello). Further, it is dedicated to all of the ascended masters including Jesus, Saint Germain, El Morya, Archangel Michael, Mother Mary, and the other great masters who have blessed me and my beloved wife, Wanda, along life's journey.

And I could not express my feelings fully without speaking of my blessed Wanda. This book is a living testimony of what we have shared together over the past thirty-one years. She has been not only my loving wife and faithful companion, but also my best friend. The best part of this book is surely an expression of the love that we share.

This book is also my spiritual-freedom legacy to my children, Linda Kay, David Gene, Judith Ann, and Martin Stephen Paul, to my stepdaughter, Dayna Davidson, and also to my grandchildren, Clarlynn, Franz David, Gabriel Stephen, and Jamie.

I also dedicate this book to the souls I love in my spiritual community of the Holy Spirit, and to every earnest seeker of truth, enlightenment, Christhood and God reality in this life.

Contents

Foreword 15

1. Early Years 17
    The Path Home 18
    Stumping for Mother 20
    Fighting for Freedom 21
    Feed My Sheep 24
    Working on Alpha's Agenda 26
    Stumping for the Defense of America with the Blessings
       of Mother, Saint Germain and El Morya 30
    No Fear! 32
    Undefended: The Case for Ballistic Missile Defense .. 33
    Coming Home 35

2. Poetry and Essays (1966-1977) 37
    Wind of the Spirit 38
    The Rhythm of Life 39
    The Framework of Life 41
    The Undertone of Life 43
    The Meaning of Life 45
    The Language of Life 47
    The Creative Life 49
    The Unity of Life 51
    Song of Life 52
    The Creative Movement 54
    Love's Quest 56
    Three Little Words 58
    The Hate Peddlers 59
    From Sheep Slave to Man Christ 62
    Life's Bitters 64
    Life's Demons (Ignorance and Fear) 66
    Sea Of Life 70
    Dawn 71
    Hail To The Institution 72
    If I were in charge... Pioneers Of The Spirit 73
    Freedom Marchers 75
    The Minister's Role in Contemporary Society 77

3. **Poems and Essays of Light and Sound (1977-present)** 91
   A New Song 92
   The Christ...................................... 94
   Thoughts before Dawn 96
   Divine Wisdom 104
   I AM 105
   Light and Sound 106

4. **Poems of Love and Wisdom (1977-present)** 107
   Only Love 107
   Camelot, Jewel of Light 109
   Hope, The Wellspring of Joy 111
   Rain Drops 112
   I AM (White Light).............................. 113
   The Torch of Freedom............................ 114
   The Flame of Love............................... 116
   Freedom's Call 117
   Angels of Light 119

5. **Freedom Speeches** 121
   "The Mighty Collision of Freedom"
      World Freedom Day Speech, May 22, 1982 121
   America is the I AM Race:
      The Flame of Freedom Speaks, July 4, 1980 132
   Peace Through Strength: Countering the Nuclear
      Freeze Movement............................. 161

6. **Ban the Soviets Coalition**......................... 169
   Victory! On the Day the Soviets Announced their
      Olympic Boycott.............................. 170
   Exposing Soviet Human Rights Violations
      on ABC News, *Nightline* 174

7. **Defending America—**
   The Case for Ballistic Missile Defense 181
   The Threat is Now!—Easter Class Presentation 182
   Deploy Now! Challenging the Reagan Administration..... 201
   Working the Media to Wake-Up America: Radio
      Interview Broadcast on 400 Stations Nationwide........ 207
   Stumping for the Defense of America in a
      Nationwide Lecture and Media Tour 228
   E. Gene Vosseler, Biography 230

8. Education of the Heart: Family—
   The Spiritual Foundation for Children and Youth 243
   The Grand Design of Destiny 244
   The Law of the Circle 245
   The Nature of the Soul 246
   The Impact of Karmic Ties 247
   The Role of Father and Mother 250
   Your Children Will Wear Your Psychology 251
   The Need for Discipline in the Household 253
   Television, the Pseudo-Teacher 254
   The Role of Parent as Teacher 255
   The Value of Community 257
   Prepare Young People to Make a Difference 258

9. Taoism: Chuang Tzu, World Philosopher at Play 259

10. Defending the Church 313
    America In Deadly Peril, Advertisement,
       Thousand Oaks Chronicle 314
    Twentieth-Century Witch Hunt, Advertisement,
       Los Angeles Herald Examiner 338
    Mission Amethyst Jewel: Stumping for Saint Germain
       in the British Isles and Africa 350
    Golden Moments with Mark and Mother 356

11. The Path of Personal Christhood By Michael Utter 365
    On My Special Friendship with Brother Gene 366
    Friendship and Community on the Path 368
    Respecting Our Elders 371
    Gene's Three Biblical Quotes for Overcoming on
       the Path of Personal Christhood 375
    Inspiration for the Path of Individual Christhood 376
    A Teaching from Gene on the Path Forward
       for Our Church 380
    Saint Francis Senior Resources—
       Caring for Our Elderly 382
    Questions for Those Who Are Striving on
       the Path of the Ascension 386

12. Epilogue 389
    Thanksgiving Thoughts 390

Afterword 393
    A Testimony to My Guru
        My First Meeting with Elizabeth Clare Prophet 393

FOREWORD

When contemplating the writing of an autobiography of your journey through life, several thoughts occur almost automatically. First, does the world really need another book of a soul's lifelong struggle to figure things out and come to some resolution? Second, isn't it the height of arrogance to think that you might have something to say that could be of interest or of enduring worth to your fellow man? Hasn't everything that needs to be said already been said and probably said far better than you can communicate? So it is with some trepidation I undertake this task of sharing some basic aspects of my life in the fervent hope that they may be of some help to you, my fellow pilgrims questing for truth and God-reality in this journey through life on our darkened planet.

With these caveats made, I now feel that I can share with you primarily in poetry and essays or philosophical fragments that which I deeply believe and have experienced in this life. As I approach my eighty-second birthday, this book is my legacy to my children, grandchildren, and to all souls who have had the opportunity to incarnate on planet earth.

In this book you will see the spiritual evolution of my soul that has hungered for truth, wisdom, and God-awareness. It is not a tell-all book but simply a sharing of life's insights and truths gleamed from personal experiences and discoveries.

Some of my earlier poetry and essays reflect my awareness at that stage of life and have changed after experiencing a profounder insight garnered from study at the feet of my beloved Guru, Elizabeth Clare Prophet, and the Great Brotherhood of light.

Finally, my friends, we are all pilgrims on a path that can lead us back to the light, the soundless sound, and our eternal home from which we all came in the very beginning—the I AM THAT I AM.

Always Victory,

Gene Vosseler

1. THE EARLY YEARS

I was raised in a very traditional Lutheran-German home. The Lutheran ministry, it seems, was written in my genes and DNA. My father was a Lutheran minister as was his grandfather and also my great-grandfather on my mother's side.

My childhood was not a particularly happy one with harsh discipline and family mores dictated by life to be lived as the preacher's kid. But I found my personal fulfillment and outlet in sports, music, friendship, and school politics. My efforts were rewarded as I was elected by my peers as Senior Class President of the Class of 1944 of Hoover High School in San Diego, California.

My college years were spent in a Lutheran college (Midland) in Fermont, Nebraska. I graduated in 1948 and then went on to Western Theological Seminary, matriculating in 1951.

After being ordained as a Lutheran minister, I served parishes in British Guiana for three years, Hawaii for ten years, and finally concluded my Lutheran stint as a Campus Minister at Fresno College in 1966.

In 1966, my true spiritual quest really began. After concluding a very unhappy karmic marriage of seventeen years, yet blessed with five children, I broke free from Lutheran orthodoxy. At that time I concluded that the traditional Christian teaching of original sin was false and that a person only living one life didn't make any sense at all. I kicked the traces completely and became a very liberal Unitarian minister. In

Unitarianism, I discovered total doctrinal freedom, but for me that church proved a spiritual dry hole.

Later, I met and became close friends with a beautiful Japanese Buddhist Master, Nippo Syaku of the Nichiren sect. He taught me much about the way of the Buddha. But my soul hungered for an even more active path.

At the same time I entered a series of failed relationships, seeking answers in other human beings rather than from within, but nothing was working for me. I sought diversion in work and I helped create a series of private schools that I had cofounded in California. Despite outward success, I felt like I was losing my soul.

Over the next year, God took me through a painful, stripping action. It finally ended with my assuming the position of Director of the Placer County Community Action Council where I served for several years until I found my true spiritual path and way home in the Church Universal and Triumphant.

The Path Home

One day, a friend who I had hired as my deputy director handed me a book and said, "The book is not for me, but I feel it's very important to you." That book was entitled, *The Culture and History of the Great White Brotherhood,* by Elizabeth Clare Prophet. (The Great White Brotherhood is a spiritual order of Western and Eastern masters who have reunited with God. The word "white" refer not to race but to the aura of white light surrounding these immortals.)

As I read the book, I got very excited and my heart was filled with joy. I devoured the entire book in one sitting. The next morning I called headquarters of The Summit Lighthouse, then located in Pasadena, California, and asked, "Do you folks ever have conferences?" "Why yes, as a matter of fact we are having a conference in two days," was the reply. "Great, I'll be there," was my answer. And I was. From the moment of my arrival, amazing things began to happen.

As I walked into the conference hall, a very large auditorium, I was greeted by a very familiar, friendly face. The usher was Ben Knudsen, an Air Force pilot. Five years earlier when I was a Lutheran minister in Hawaii, I had baptized Ben, his wife, Dee, and their three children in St. Johns Lutheran Church, where I was minister. As you can imagine we had quite a joyful reunion.

At the conference that evening Elizabeth Clare Prophet announced that the next morning at 9:30 a.m she would be giving a dictation which is a message delivered through the agency of the Holy Spirit. I was chagrined because I was scheduled to pick up a girl friend at the airport the next morning at exactly the same time.

The next morning I went to the airport and arrived back at the convention hall in Pasadena at 11:30 a.m. At the moment of my arrival, the meditation music preceding the dictation began to play.

As an aside, about a year earlier I had a profound dream about something called the eighth ray. I was totally baffled. Now, much to my amazement, the first live dictation that I heard that morning was given by Archangel Uzziel on the eighth ray. And so I had an outer confirmation of an inner experience—I knew I was home. I had found my Guru and my spiritual family, my community of light. I dissolved into great tears of joy.

Another surprising feature of my first conference of The Summit Lighthouse was my meeting of this beautiful lady who came up and introduced herself to me. There was a deep feeling of recognition and soul knowing. Though we had just met, it felt like we were old friends.

Later this wonderful lady was to become my wife and faithful companion. She has shared with me life, testings, joys, and tribulations for the past thirty years. But I'll let her share that story in a book that I am encouraging her to write.

Wanda and I were wed in September 1977. That fall we attended Archangel Gabriel's quarter at Summit University, the educational arm of The Summit Lighthouse.

Stumping for Mother

We joined staff in January 1978 and our spiritual disciplines really began in earnest. My first assignment was to do radio, television, and newspaper interviews preceding Elizabeth Clare Prophet's stump lectures and to prepare the way for her coming. My wife Wanda's assignment was to work in the world while at the same time to serve on Mrs. Prophet's permanent staff. For the first four years of our marriage Wanda and I were like ships passing in the night. That was our first major test together as a couple, but not the last.

Also during that period I was afforded the privilege of delivering Mother's stump lecture widely in the United States, Canada, and overseas, particularly in Ireland, Wales, Scotland, and England. We called Mrs. Prophet "Mother" because of her devotion to God as Mother. Those were glorious days, and our team felt the presence of the Holy Spirit, our blessed Guru, and the ascended masters overshadowing us.

In February 1982, this cycle abruptly ended and I was sent by Mother off of staff and into the world to "polish my skills," as she said. Within two days I secured employment as an economic development consultant with my dear friend, Michael Utter. Michael and I were to work together in a variety of assignments helping to provide education, teach vocational skills, and create jobs for a variety of refugee communities. Many of these refugee communities immigrated to the United States from countries that had suffered under Communist oppression.

Fighting for Freedom

However, in March 1982, while in Washington, D.C., I suffered a stroke and was hospitalized for two days. After being released I returned home to California where my wife nursed me back to health. Then my freedom action cycles began. I was very concerned about the nuclear freeze issue orchestrated by the Kremlin in Moscow and embraced in California by the liberals and leftists as Proposition 13. The nuclear freeze initiative had little opposition and was 45 percent ahead in the polls.

One day I was having breakfast with my freedom fighter friend from Hungary, an architect named John Dolinsky. "John," I said, "this nuclear freeze issue has to be fought and no one is doing it. Let's take it on." John agreed and together we organized Californians for a Strong America. We utilized the captive nations groups in Los Angeles as our support base.

The proponents of Proposition 13 had twenty-six full-time staff in Los Angeles and a $2 million budget. We had John's secretary part time and me as the only full-time person working on it. Every night I was debating in the media left-wing lawyers and retired former military personnel, including a former assistant secretary of defense and a retired admiral.

A few months into the campaign, I picked up the phone and Charlton Heston was on the line. He was infuriated over a pro-freeze commercial done by Paul Newman and Jack Lemmon and wanted to know what he could do to help. I told him we could really use a good commercial, since we were given equal and free television time under the Fairness Doctrine.

Heston agreed and we went to his house and filmed a great commercial—very presidential—that was good for at least 10 to 15 points in the polls. A consummate professional, Heston read our script once, asked if he could make some minor changes, and cut the commercial in one take. I also did a thirty-minute rebuttal to Paul Newman on the Merv Griffin Celebrity Show. The upshot of our efforts was that we came from 45 points behind in the polls and were barely beaten 52-48. But the real victory was this: we stopped the nuclear freeze movement in its tracks and it became a dead issue.

The next freedom issue that I got involved with was the Los Angeles Olympics in 1984. The freedom issue was triggered by the Soviet Union's shooting down of an unarmed, commercial Korean Airlines Boeing jet (KAL-007) that had strayed across the Soviet border. This Soviet outrage killed 269 passengers including 60 Americans, among them U.S. Congressman Larry McDonald. While the Soviets claimed KAL-007 was a fighter jet, the Soviet pilot who was instructed to shoot down the plane was told to lie about the encounter. According to an interview published in the *New York Times*, Lt. Colonel Gennadi Osipovich said that although he knew he was firing at a commercial plane, he thought it was being used for spying. Osipovich voiced no regrets, but complained that he didn't receive a great bonus from the Soviet Army for completing this mission.[1] The United State's limp-wristed response, which was essentially to do nothing, was infuriating to say the least.

I got together with two freedom-fighter friends, David

---

[1] Michael Gordon, "Ex-Soviet Pilot Still Insists KAL 007 Was Spying," *New York Times*, December 9, 1996.

Balsiger and Tony Muzeika, and we decided to take action. Our goal was to block the Soviet Union from participating in the U.S. Olympics. This "Ban the Soviets" activity allowed us a bully pulpit and base of operations. If we failed in that public relations endeavor, we declared we would mount a campaign to encourage defections from the Soviet Union and their satellite countries during the Olympics. At the very least, we would use this opportunity to expose Soviet atrocities to the world through the media. We organized our captive nations base once again and formed the group, "Ban the Soviets Coalition." We also secured endorsements from 158 conservative organizations across America.

We then launched a nationwide public relations campaign consisting of press conferences, radio and TV interviews, and boycotts picketing actions that received wide media attention. It also caught the attention of the Soviet leadership. The Soviets responded, through their official propaganda organs, *Pravda* and *Itzvestia*, both of which were regime-controlled newspapers. They attacked our coalition as a group of right-wing-extremist thugs who were going to kidnap and drug their athletes and force them to defect, a classic example of psychological projection as these were the very methods used by the Soviet KGB in their gulags, which our small group could not and would never even contemplate. The more the Soviets attacked us, the more media coverage we got. Finally at the last minute, the Soviet Union pulled out of the Olympics and blamed our Ban the Soviets Coalition for their decision.

We never needed the safe houses for defecting athletes or the large billboard signs in German, Russian, or English telling athletes how to defect. I remember doing a show on CNN called "Crossfire" where I told Ron Nessen and Tom Braden that we had plans for a colossal sized billboard that said, "Defect Now. Avoid the Rush."

After the Soviet pullout, I was contacted by ABC News Nightline, a top-rated television talk show, and Ted Koppel, its host, for an interview. Koppel, like many others, accused us of trying to disrupt the Olympics and punish the athletes.

As a footnote to this victory for the voice of freedom, shortly afterwards, the *Los Angeles Times,* who fought us each step of the way, published what could be construed as a backhanded compliment about our efforts in an article, "Anti-Soviet Coalition Quickly Grew into a Mouse that Roared." This reporter had previously tried to break my relationship with my two freedom fighter colleagues by telling them that I was a member of a cult, only to be strongly rebuffed by both of them. She ended the article by attacking me and my relationship to my Church and my spiritual teacher, Elizabeth Clare Prophet. At least the reporter quoted me accurately, a rare occurrence with the *Los Angeles Times*. She wrote, "'What you're all about is slime,' said Vosseler."

Feed My Sheep

Later in 1985, I received a phone call from my beloved Guru inviting me to stump New England with her. We would both lecture separately during the week and join together for weekend seminars. Of course my answer was yes, and I was thrilled with the invitation.

While doing a weekend seminar in Washington, D.C., a most unusual event occurred. Mother asked me, to go down and do an interview with Fox television, which then covered most of New England. I got to the station and was briefed and preinterviewed. They wanted me to do ten devotionals, each of them five minutes in length, from the Holy Scriptures. There would be a two-minute break between each devotional with the music, "Eternal Father Strong to Save" coming on at each five-minute interval.

When I got the picture, I made some intense calls to Jesus to overshadow and inspire me and to the Holy Spirit. Now I must confess that I didn't have a good sense of timing. But, by God's grace, I taught the teachings of the ascended masters in ten five-minute segments and each concluded as the music was coming on—perfect timing. The TV station liked them and used them to conclude their evening broadcasting four times over a period of a year. Thus we had given to us two hundred free minutes of television time on the largest independent TV station in America. (Years later during a lecture I was giving at Summit University, one of the students raised her hand and spoke of the time when she was half-awake viewing that very television segment. She became so intrigued by the content that it ultimately led her to our Church.)

For the next two years, I had the privilege of serving as Director of the Office of National Coordinator for the Church, working with study groups and teaching centers.

Early in 1987, Wanda and I moved to Montana and the Inner Retreat. In April I was feeling the strong inner prompting that I needed to get involved in strengthening our national defense against intercontinental ballistic missiles carrying warheads of mass destruction. I talked to Mother about what I was feeling. She told me that she would get back to me in several days.

Several days later, Mother told me that she had had a message from Jesus for me and it was, "Feed my sheep." For the next few months, I was involved in an intense counseling cycle with many chelas, i.e. devoted students of the masters.

Working on Alpha's Agenda

On July 4, 1987, Alpha, the master who personifies the God flame as Father spelled out his agenda in a dictation delivered by the messenger. Here are some of the critical comments from Alpha that have helped to guide my freedom work. Alpha said:

> …*There are, beloved, conditions upon which earth and her evolutions might be saved. The areas of greatest urgency which present themselves are for the final binding and judgment of fallen angels who have positioned themselves in the economies and the governments of the nations and in the banking houses to exercise absolute control over the people.*
>
> *Beloved ones, for earth to be saved, World Communism with all of its supporters, agents and tools must go down. I raise my right hand and the fire does flow to turn it back upon itself…*
>
> *Of the greatest urgent necessity, therefore, as you have heard our presence through the Messenger and all ideas discussed, is the physical defense of the physical continent of America. Thus, the greatest urgency is to defeat World Communism in its present attempt to take over this planet, to defeat it in every area where it is making inroads into systems and into the minds of the people, and simultaneously to raise up the defense…*
>
> *I charge you to go to all upon this planet who have taken their stand against World Communism and for defense and a strong strategic defense. Go to them…*[2]

---

[2] Alpha and Omega, "Alpha's Agenda," delivered July 5, 1987, published in *Pearls of Wisdom,* vol. 30, no. 38, (Gardiner, Mont.: Summit University Press, September 20, 1987) pp. 382, 383, 387.

After the dictation Mother commented on the urgency to deploy strategic defense and said, "We are entrusted and summoned [by Alpha] to awaken America to deploy immediately our defenses—our strategic defense, all that is necessary—and to defeat World Communism."

Again I felt the prompting to take this issue up and asked Mother. I waited patiently. In August, I received a phone call from Mother telling me that it was time for my mission.

Several days later, I was ready to embark on my mission. Wanda and I were celebrating her birthday over dinner at the Four Winds Restaurant. Mother came in and invited us to join her in her vehicle for a private conversation. She told us that four ascended masters were sponsoring my mission. This gave great consolation to Wanda to know about that blessing, since I was leaving the next day or two.

When I arrived in Los Angeles, I had the privilege of meeting the champion of ballistic missile defense, then known as SDI (the Strategic Defense Initiative), Lt. Gen. Daniel Graham. Some time later I reached Washington, D.C., and I decided to check out Gen. Graham's operation at High Frontier, his nonprofit organization promoting a strong defense for America.

As an aside, I started my missile defense tour on a financial shoestring—a little money from several dear friends including Michael Utter.

Now, in Gen. Graham's office, a most unusual event occurred. Danny said to me, "How would you like to work for me, doing lecture tours and radio and television shows?" I was shocked by the offer but managed to blurt out, "That would be interesting but I would need a salary and some expense money." After giving him what I considered a fair, low-ball figure, he literally jumped out of his chair, grabbed my hand, and said, "Done!"

For the next twenty months I worked for this great patriot and freedom fighter. My financial concerns were addressed by Gen. Graham. By conservative estimates and figures, I contacted sixty million people with a strong message urging the deployment of ballistic missile defense. Done largely through the media, I spoke to the heart of Americans on television super stations and large syndicated shows hosted by talk radio leaders including: Jim Bohannon, syndicated on 400 stations; Barry Farber, syndicated out of New York to 105 stations; Bob Grant, syndicated on 100 stations; and many others. Additionally, at every lecture stop in the U.S. we made sure to secure as much local and regional media as possible.

Mother commented on my work while teaching Summit University. She said:

> *Gene Vosseler was here and sometime in 1987 I agreed that he could go forth and deliver his message, the message of Saint Germain on prophecy …He joined Danny Graham, he went lecturing for him. He's interacting with, on a daily basis, all the people that are for defense, the people in the military, the conservative movement, the people in Congress. He has arrived in all circles. He is on his third tour and has gone to cities all over the country. Now he's going to 36 colleges and universities.*
>
> *He's been on hundreds of talk shows, shows that are syndicated where he gets interviewed by the key talk show hosts and it's heard on radio stations all over the country, debating the scientists and all the people that are anti-defense.*[3]

In July 1988, Danny Graham did a Summit University Forum with us in Montana. He was overwhelmed with the

---

[3] Elizabeth Clare Prophet, "Teaching on the Process of Surrender of Inordinate Desire," (lecture presented to Summit University Level 1, Corwin Springs, MT, November 8, 1988.)

number of people in attendance at the Heart of the Inner Retreat, a mountain-top retreat center, when he drove past the thousands who participated in our Fourth of July Parade of Nations. Henry Kriegel and I memorialized this great patriot in a foreword to the booklet, *Undefended: The Case for Ballistic Missile Defense.*

"[Gene] has done what everybody would like to do. He has taken that message to the airwaves, he has taken it on television, and he has taken it to the newspapers."

—Elizabeth Clare Prophet, Nov. 8. 1988

But as many of you know, cycles change. One day as I was just completing a national lecture tour, I received a phone call from Mother. She told me that I was to return to the Inner Retreat one day after the completion of my lecture tour on missile defense. I was obedient. I had a dinner meeting with twelve of my freedom fighter friends and passed the torch to them and then returned home to Montana to resume my chelaship and spiritual service at the Inner Retreat.

My new assignment was to work at the business office in Glastonbury during Saint Germain's call for physical and spiritual preparedenss know also as the "shelter cycle." It was a great experience working primarily on a physical level mowing lawns, chopping weeds, and, in the winter, shoveling sand on icy hills. My coworkers and I became great friends and we had a good time.

Stumping for the Defense of America with the Blessings of Mother, Saint Germain, and El Morya

During this time, I developed an experimental project with detailed program descriptions and budgets for regional ministers. Mother liked the idea but she had another project in mind for me—teaching three levels of Summit University. She asked me to teach courses on the Old Testament, New Testament, Taoism, and Tibetan Buddhism and to team-teach with her, "The Art and Science of Preaching."

> "We commend our representative Reverend Gene Vosseler and his beloved Wanda for their great service to us and to America... What they have done, you can join them and do also."
>
> —Saint Germain, January 2, 1997

This assignment was challenging, exciting, and brought great joy to my life. This, along with Stumping for Mother, was the fulfillment of my reason for being. I knew it.

However, there was still one aching void in my life. At a soul level, I knew that I had not completed my mission to help get our nation defended from ballistic missiles carrying warheads of mass destruction that could be launched by accident or design. In 1995, I began to feel the urgency of the inner call to complete this mission. This call was confirmed by the masters El Morya and Saint Germain:

Look, then, to the nations. Look to the [former] Soviet Union—amply prepared for nuclear war, not too prepared in their armies but, nevertheless, having tremendous potential to destroy this nation.

As you know, many missiles have been removed in this country and therefore America the vulnerable is still America the vulnerable. Thus, Gene Vosseler and others have gone forth and will continue to go forth to make the statement that America is not protected.

Blessed ones, serious issues are at hand...[4]

—El Morya, October 14, 1996

We commend our representative Reverend Gene Vosseler and his beloved Wanda for their great service to us and to America. We ask you to multiply that action by your prayers, by your decrees, by the wonderment of God and know that what they have done, you can join them and do also. You can go and canvass the nation, beloved, and bring the realization of the threats upon this nation to those who are the youth, those who may be older, those who are college students and those who are the ancient patriots from long ago come again.

Now you understand, beloved, that our focus and my main focus in this hour must be for you, throughout these three years, the reversing of the tide of all attempts of those foreign governments and foreign military establishments to move against the United States, to do so with nuclear weapons, to do so with nuclear submarines. All of this can come to pass or all of this will be defeated.[5]

—Saint Germain, January 2, 1997

---

[4] El Morya, "It Is Time for the Victory, Part 1," October 14, 1996, in *Pearls of Wisdom*, vol. 46, no. 7, (Gardiner, Mont.: Summit University Press, February 16, 2003) p. 54.

With the public endorsement of our mission by Saint Germain and El Morya, Wanda and I launched out for Washington, D.C., in a 1987 Astro van with a couple of lamps and our wardrobe. We had less than $1,000 in cash but we felt totally confident that God would supply all of our needs for housing, transportation, and food, which of course he did—as always in the past.

No Fear!

"No fear!" That was our motto, because we both knew it was a God-ordained mission. For the four years it took us to complete the mission, we always had enough, generously given by our freedom fighter friends, to supply all of our needs.

For the first time my beloved Wanda was able to accompany me on my lecture tours to America's greatest universities. It was wonderful. My lectures not only dealt with the need for ballistic missile defense, they exposed the power elite and the military technology transfers being made to Red China and the Soviet Union. Of course, the Marxist professors were still there to debate me.

I also became a member of the Republican Senatorial Inner Circle, which gave me access to key senators like Trent Lott, John Ashcroft, and Strom Thurmond. This got me plugged in to the high-level conference calls on many key issues. It also gave us great opportunities to lobby key senators on BMD (ballistic missile defense).

One of my great experiences in Washington, D.C., was speaking before two thousand people at the Conservative

---

[5] Saint Germain, "There Will Never Be a Greater Opportunity, Part 1," *Pearls of Wisdom,* vol. 45 no. 39, (Gardiner, Mont.: Summit University Press, September, 29, 2002) p. 279.

Political Action Conference on BMD. Previously, I had engaged the head of the U.S. Arms Control and Disarmament Agency, Kenneth Adelman, in a debate on the need to deploy BMD now. My points were well received and it paved the way for the later invitation to give a major speech on the subject.

Undefended: The Case for Ballistic Missile Defense

As many of you may know, President Ronald Reagan and Lady Thatcher of Great Britain were fellow freedom fighters and they were great friends to each other. There was a dedication of a painting of the two of them together in one of the Congressional office buildings. Wanda and I attended. I told Wanda to get a copy of our booklet, *Undefended: The Case for Ballistic Missile Defense*, to Lady Thatcher. The place was jam-packed but Wanda made a call to the angels for help. When she opened her eyes she was standing right before Lady Thatcher. Wanda gave her the book and Lady Thatcher quickly glanced at it saying, "You tell Gene he is to get this book to everyone."

So at every major conference that we attended, Wanda made certain that everyone in attendance got a copy of our book, *Undefended*.

At a CPAC conference, a man came up to our table and made an interesting comment. He shook my hand and said, "You and I are soul brothers." Holding up our book, *Undefended*, he said, "This is the best thing I've ever read on defense." The man was Sven Kraemer, a member of President Reagan's National Security Team. Sven then invited us to a concert by his wife, who was an accomplished pianist. It was our pleasure to attend.

One meeting in Washington, D.C., that Wanda and I regularly attended on a weekly basis was held at Grover Norquist's meeting room. Congressmen, staff, candidates for office, heads of political action committees, and non-profit activist groups attended, and I fairly often gave briefings on missile defense, as did Frank Gaffney from the Center for Security Policy.

At one meeting, a woman representing Phyllis Schlafly's Eagle Forum was in attendance. Wanda gave her our book, *Undefended*. The woman said, "I can't believe this because Phyllis Schlafly told me to find Gene Vosseler because she wanted Gene to speak and no one else." She then said, "I don't know how to find him." Wanda then said, "He's right here sitting next to me." By God's grace, I did give that speech on BMD to over 150 students from all over the country at as part of an Eagle Forum conference. As the only non-Congressman who spoke, my speech was very well received. My wife (who is somewhat prejudiced in this matter) said it was the best speech I ever gave.

In my opinion, Phyllis Schlafly is one of the greatest American patriots who has ever lived. She and her very articulate, well-informed Eagle Forum ladies are a major force to be reckoned with. When they descend on Capitol Hill to educate on a freedom issue, they are effective, they know how to turn up the political heat, and they get results. In the words of late Senator Everett Dirksen, "When I feel the heat, I see the light." Eagle Forum women knew how to turn up the thermostat.

A major turning point in the battle to get a ballistic missile defense deployed came when North Korea fired a missile that landed in the Pacific Ocean. This was the wake-up call from a rogue state that motivated Congress to vote overwhelmingly to deploy. Reports that North Korean missiles could soon reach Alaska and Hawaii galvanized a lethargic Congress into taking action. At that point, I knew our action cycle in Washington, D.C., was over. Today a partial shield is deployed over Israel and on various Naval vessels. BMD is progressing, but more slowly than we had hoped.

Coming Home

As a result, Wanda and I headed back to Montana and the Inner Retreat. After stopping for a brief vacation with our dear friend Judy Freeman and her sister Dee Dee, I assumed the position of ministerial counselor for students studying in our ministerial training program. After two years of service in that capacity, I accepted a position as minister for Region V, serving seven states including Texas, Oklahoma, New Mexico, Louisiana, Colorado, and Arkansas. Wanda and I did spring and fall lecture tours of all seven states that resulted in our being on the road for eight months out of the year.

By God's grace, I was privileged to serve on the Board of Directors of the Church, the Council of Elders, and the Ministerial Council during a time of difficult transition for the Church.

Also I completed my service as a regional minister and am currently serving on the Church Stewardship Team located at Church headquarters.

In the fall of 2007, I joined Michael Utter in founding a non-profit service corporation—St. Francis Senior Resources, Inc., dedicated to developing and funding senior resource programs including low-income housing, transportation, nutrition, and other services. Michael, in my opinion, has a rare genius in developing great programs and writing and securing grant money to fund them. Exciting days are ahead!

This concludes Part I and a brief autobiographical picture of my spiritual and action odyssey in this life.

2. POETRY AND ESSAYS (1966-1977)

In 1966, when I left the Lutheran Church, I went through a period of deep inner reflection, contemplation, and meditation. Then one day without warning, I began to write out of the depths of my being a series of brief essays or philosophical fragments and poetry that were my own personal insights about life and living. Penned between the years 1966 and 1977, before I found my home in Church Universal and Triumphant, I have entitled them "Wind of the Spirit," poems and essays of light and sound.

Wind of the Spirit

Wind of the Spirit
    Fanning creative spark
        In origin mysterious
            Yet yielding deep secrets
                To the searching heart.

Wind of the Spirit
    On love's quest for earth,
        Impassioned sculpting of mountains and valleys,
            Caressing fingertip touch on downy vale,
                Whispering endearments of love.
Wind of the Spirit
    Crying out for fulfillment
        In union achieving enraptured completeness—
        The drama of man!

The Rhythm of Life

There is an ebb and flow to life—
   A time for living and a time for dying,
      A time to laugh and a time to weep,
         A time to love and a time to hate,
            A time for steely hardness and a time for compassion,
               A time for action and a time for reflection,
                  A time for fellowship and a time for solitude.
For life is motion and movement. It is variety and change. It is never stationary—even in sleep or repose.
Life is full of contradictions. I am many things to many people.
To exist means
   To live out life honestly
      To be true to my inner being,
         To be what I am before God and my brother.
To live in harmony with the rhythm of life is to really live. It means tuning in with those around me. To be open and accepting—or to be closed and inaccessible as the occasion demand.
I am a part of everyman and everyman is a part of me.
   When one suffers—I suffer!
      When one is hurt—I feel pain!
         When one laughs—I rejoice!
            When one weeps—I too feel sadness!
Life is spontaneity and creativity.
   To respond without thinking,
      To react intuitively,
         To feel instinctively,
This is creativity.
There is beauty as well as pathos in life.
   There is dignity in the most shattered life of God's creation.
      There is calm in the eye of the fiercest storm.
         In the onrushing darkness—a myriad of stars.

What then shall I do with my life? How shall I cope with life's paradoxes?
    I must die in order to live.
        I must suffer in order to feel compassion.
            I must be tested before I can give out.
For to resist life's rhythms is to fight God—Who is Life!
To yield to life's rhythm is to know God and Being.
It means really living now—and in eternity

The Framework of Life

The framework of life and existence is the world. The world is big, dirty, ugly and beautiful. The beauty is clearly seen in the glory of creation. A Master Artist has painted the canvas of the world with the full spectrum of color. The Designer of the Universe has structured creation with harmony and order—even in the tiniest atom.

The majesty of the heavens,
    The ceaseless rolling roar of the surf,
        The caress of the whispering wind,
            The sweet smell of the earth after a gentle rain—
All testify to the handiwork of a loving creator.
But there is a dark side to life in this world.
    Beneficent nature can be cold, harsh, and unyielding.
        Quiet seas can be distorted by the fury of an angry storm.
            Gentle breezes can turn into a hurricane of devastating destruction.
The fingerprints of God are on creation. But they are smudged and blurry.
Nature is an imperfect mask. The Creator is still obscured and hidden.
And what of man—the one placed by the Creator at the center of the universe?
Man created in the image of god is like nature—an imperfect, distorted mask of the Source of life.
Man desires to be God.
    He is proud, rebellious and lonely.
        He is anxious, insecure and afraid.
And underlying all existence is the certainty of death.
The lost soul reaches out desperately to contact those around him —only to discover that he manipulates, exploits and destroys the ones he should love. The cruel reality is the world, the flesh and the devil will have their way-------unless?
To one who faces the paradoxes of life in the framework of a cold, unrelenting world—there is only one hope—to become related to the Source of life.

The ultimate reality alone gives
    Strength to meet life's crushing blows,
        Insight that transcends doubt and despair,
            Love that heals and liberates the fellow pilgrim.

The Undertone of Life

Life begins with a crisis—birth!
    Life ends with a crisis—death!
        Between these two poles man lives in the tension of existence.
To exist means—
    To live,
        to be,
            to become.
But beneath the surface of life is a swift cold current—the coursing undertone of all life.
    Man is a creature—
        Finite and mortal,
            Subject to decay and death.
Death is the last enemy that every man must face along the corridor of time.
Death is the end
    To man's highest hopes,
        His cherished aspirations,
            His intense struggles,
                His pressing ambitions,
                      His fondest dreams.
Death is the opposite of life and a visitor to every man!
How can I face this reality?
    I must become aware of my predicament.
        I must see life as it is.
            I must face self with courage and honesty.
                I must seek the answer to the riddle of existence
                with every fiber of my being.
The old moth-eaten dogmas,
    The rigid propositional stereotypes,
        The endless metaphysical speculations,
            The vagaries of philosophical thought—none of these
        answer my questing pilgrimage.

I must experience!
    I must live!
        I must feel life!
I desire not concept or abstract thought but life in its fullest sense
—to be related to the Source of my being.
Without this relationship life is
    A dead end street
        A futile journey into the abyss.

The Meaning of Life

On the basis of objective evidence, there is little or no meaning to life.
From the viewpoint of reason and the intellect—life is confusing and irrational.
Every attempt to systematize life is shattered.
For life is not—
    A system of thought,
        A standard of values,
            A group of ethical universals,
                A body of principles.
Life is relationship and commitment.
    Life is experience—
        irrational,
            contradictory,
                and paradoxical.
There is no rhyme or reason to existence.
    "Man
born of a woman is like a flower...
    Reason will stumble at life's paradoxes.
        Intellect will be offended by life's contradictions.
For life is faith and faith is—
    relationship not concept,
active not passive,
radical not conservative,
                expensive not cheap
                    transforming not conforming,
                      experience not performance.

The relationship of faith is an encounter—
    open,
        sensitive,
            and feeling.

The essence of faith is love—
   unconditional,
      freely offered,
         and reciprocal in action.
As one appropriates the gift, he willingly extends the gift to another. To receive the gift is to know life. To know life places one under obligation to share life. This is commitment—to give oneself as an instrument of love and healing in a hostile, rejecting world.
Who will pay the price?

The Language of Life

There is an inexpressible sadness to life—intangible but real.
    It is our heart-hunger for love.
        It is a deep, relentless, compelling force.
            It is by nature—physical, emotional and spiritual.
The hunger for love propels us out of the cocoon of self into the world of people and relationships.
It is expressed in many ways—
    The infant nursing at the mother's breast,
        The child seeking parental approval,
            The adult entering a one flesh relationship with the beloved.
We are created for love. We find our true being in relationship with one who cares. Our need for love is expressed in many little ways,
    A wistful smile,
        A searching look,
           A warm hand clasp,
                An anxious glance.
The unspoken question is always the same.
    Do you love me?
        Do you really love me?
And there is desperate urgency in the silent plea.
We all live in order to be fulfilled. It is the deprived, the unloved, the rejected who take the strange byways that lead to despair and death—
    The rigid moralist,
        The mechanical prostitute,
            The calloused degenerate,
                The mentally disturbed—
All are victims of a hostile, unloving world.
For love is a fragile thing. Feelings are dangerous and highly combustible. One can be tragically hurt. The one you love may not love you.
    To love—is to become vulnerable.
        To be open—to invite hurt.
            To give of self—means to suffer.

The healers of our time are those with the capacity
   To love,
      To suffer,
         To endure.
Grounded in God's love through Christ, their love is
   A balm for heartache,
      The cure for loneliness,
         An antidote for pain.
They are the courageous ones!
   They confront the stark reality of a cruel and loveless world.
      They twinkle with laughter even though their hearts are breaking.
They meet life head on!
   They are bloodied but not defeated.
      They are knocked down but not out.
         They endure hurt—but quietly.
      They possess resiliency and strength.
They know the language of life—the essential reality—the meaning of love.
   In giving—they receive.
      In suffering—they mature.
      In dying—they live.

To know one who loves is to know life. It is undefinably sweet. It is inexplicably sad. For the one who loves, frees the beloved. The one who is liberated, in turn, becomes an instrument of love. Set free by love, he willingly assumes the burden of suffering! Christ becomes real! To love is to suffer! This is the meaning of the Cross.
We are in tune with the Infinite.

The Creative Life

Deep in the heart of every man,
Dwells a core of truth and beauty.
In primal splendor glowing
Illuminating life and sacred duty.

Deep in the heart of every man
Burns creative fire that fashions
A work of art—all dross removed,
Forged in the flame of holy passion.

Deep in the heart of every man
Is a great and yearning need
The hunger for life's fulfillment
Found in the ethereal seed.

Deep in the heart of every man
Is the relentless quest for new birth,
Intense as man's hunger
For women, or God's spirit
Embracing the earth.

Deep in the heart of every man
Strains the pull of opposite surges,
When body and soul are united
The genius of self emerges.

When conscious and unconscious are
Blended, and thought and feeling
Combine and immortal creator
Emerges—A poet, composer, or
Sculptor sublime.

Or perchance in wisdom eternal
A rare flower appears among
Creations,
The sun-kissed towering spirit,
Creative in love and human
Relations.

For God in His infinite purpose
Hath made man greater than clay,
And waits man's creative awakening
To hasten His glorious day.
Creation is an act of the Spirit,

No law to guide or to kill—
Man in freedom exalting
His destiny elects to fulfill.

There are no scriptures to lead him
In his struggle toward life's destination
The God-man dwells and moves in spirit.
And lives out his own revelation.

It is not God's intention for men to
Wait passively, the highest road is not
Obedience, but to live life creatively.

To live a full creative life
Requires a courageous daring,
Leaving the safe and chartered course
New grief and fresh burdens bearing.

For one who would share in creation
Discovers the truth is long—
That all of God's world is groaning
And suffering the keynote of song.

The law and cross are but stages
In the spiritual pilgrimage of man,
For after death comes resurrection,
Creative new life is God's plan.

The call of creative spirit
Cries out to everyman—soul
Look not to the things external,
Truth flames in the inner whole.

The Unity of Life

The unity of life is expressed in the inner-relationship of opposites. God created—
  Earth and sea,
    Night and day,
      Male and female,
        Thought and feeling,
          Pain and pleasure,
            Joy and sorrow,
              Life and death.
Creative energy is the result of the fusion of opposites. Uniformity breeds monotony and death. Variety breathes change and life.
The unity of opposites is always in flux. Tension never ceases. And yet it is precisely this tension that creates a creative work of strength, dignity and beauty.
There are many underlying strains to the music of life—but only one central theme. For unity is at the heart of life's composition. The delicate tonal shadings and varying rhythm of life enhance the beauty of the theme.
The tragic is accentuated by the comic.
  Harmony is enriched by a discord.
    Art is illuminated by contrast and shadow.
      Joy is made creative by suffering and pathos.
        Courage is ennobled through the realism of fear.
The unity of life is expressed individually and collectively. As in integral being, I am part of a cosmic whole. The movement of history is toward at-one-ness. Past, present and future are merging into a coherent unity with the author of our being in the stream consciousness.

Song of Life

Life is like a stormy sea
By raging passions tossed
Upon the sharp defiant rocks
Or hidden shoals bemossed.

The crashing surf destroys life
That fights cascading foam
Man to live must breast the waves
Through perilous water lone.

Life is like an ocean tide
With ceaseless ebb and flow
And one who swims in its rhythms
The secret of life will know.

Life is instinct and passion
And the surge of wild pounding surf
Is like the warm embrace of two lovers
Or water that permeates earth.

When man and woman have union
Like the earth embracing the sea
A lush fruit of beauty emerges
Nature's gift from love's ecstasy.

The fruit of life's deepest fusion
Spanning the eons of time
Is a new and glorious creation
An immortal soul—yea, divine.

For even as the sea needs sunshine
The wind and the life giving rain
God needs man and woman
To merge in the life-giving flame.

For God is not known in the ether
Nor in the wind, or rain, or the surf
God knows us as we know him
In life that is lived out on earth.

This is God's world; He made it
The sea and the sky-vaulted dome
And the nourishing breasts of warm mother earth
God gave it to man as his own.

Man is like nature symphonic
With diverse and melodious strains
When all parts are organically blended
Life sings our harmonious refrains.

And if perchance there's an "off-note"
Discording the music of life
Existence is dull without contrast
Would we ever know peace without strife?

The climax of symphonic creation
Ascending in triumphant song-poem
Is praise to Alpha and Omega
In love's union eternal—our home.

The Creative Movement

There is a core of creative energy called life at the center of every being. It is primal and generative in origin and function. It is the fiery point where the finite and the infinite fuse into a timeless moment. The flaming core of creativity cannot be consciously commanded, but is at the mercy of the Spirit that animates life. There is a lot of living and dying before the creative moment occurs. The elemental passions of life must be intensely experienced before creation takes place. All of the stuff of life becomes a fuel for the creative fire. When the blood reaches the boiling point, the inner being erupts the flaming lava of inspiration from the unfathomed depths of human existence. There is a deep surge of primal feeling and wisdom. Then the spirit begins the creative act, coursing with tremendous energy through the human vessel. To be inspired is to be in touch with the Source of life. We can only handle inspiration in limited amounts or else be consumed by its fiery intensity. Inspiration is like a refining fire consuming all dross and impurities. It is a pure flame of love, beauty, and truth creating compositions of priceless value in art, music, and poetry.

In human relationship the creative force of inspiration is translated into a deep, timeless love for all of life…an acceptance of all that is and all of one's inner being is to really know life with its diverse moods and many faces. In a creative, liberating love, the act of creation reaches the zenith of life lived out on earth.

During the creative moment, the limitations of time and space are transcended in a moment of spontaneous freedom. The moment of creation is ultimate freedom. It is the explosive fusion of all the elements of life in a triumphant release.

The long climb is over and all feelings are released in a blinding moment of ecstatic bliss—then peace!

We have shared in creation with God!

Love's Quest

Life without love is a desert
Sterile and barren and bleak,
We all need love in fulfilling
The oneness we desperately seek.

Each soul cries out for expression
For unlived life is a crime,
Only when hearts beat in rhythm
Is there joy and rapture sublime.

The secret of love can't be hidden
It sings a song through the eyes,
Though lips may stammer and stutter
Love shines like the sun in the skies.

Eyes may be restless and yearning
Crying out with an eloquent plea,
For response in the deeps of a lover
As the tide embraces the sea.

Love is life's core and center—
Without it the rich man is poor,
While the beggar who finds joy in loving
With the wings of an angel does soar.

Courage is the mother of true love
To be really yourself is the test
And few there be who pass muster
In a life that is fully expressed.

My dimensions are high as the heavens
With depths as deep as the sea,
And only the woman who feels this
Will rest in my arms comfortably.

Wind of the Spirit

One must be constantly growing
In life that is lived out on earth,
Our goal is to share in creation
To give our old world a new birth.

To create is an act of the Spirit
Fed by a life-giving stream,
And nurtured with life's glowing embers
Fulfilling our lost inner-dream.

The creator stands shoulders above men
In freedom exerting his powers
In living life true to his feeling
His genius takes root and flowers.

Only the creator is a free man
Spontaneous and fresh in his thrust,
Transcending his fears about sinning
His own inner being must trust.

The saint is ensnared in his own webb
Though pious his struggles with sin,
He never becomes a full—free man
His strength is all bottled within.

This is my song to the world, love,
Tell no man what he should be
Let each man discover his freedom
And live out his own destiny.

For life on this earth's a shadow
A flickering moment in time
And many on earth never know love
In their life—no reason or rhyme.

Marriage is not made in heaven
But in life lived out here on earth,
True love is known only by equals
In communion bestowing new birth.

Three Little Words

Three little words—"I love You!"
    Words encompassing the secret of the universe,
        For the mystery of life is love.
Love is the mother of the creative act—
    In art, music, and poetry.
        Beauty finds its highest expression in love.
Without love the creator dies.
    Life turns to ashes, rubble, and ruin.
        People exist but do not live without love.
To love means to love with ones whole being.
    Reaching to the heavens and plumbing the depths of the sea.
    Love embraces all humanity.
Only in love is our destiny fulfilled.
    The bird was made to sing.
        The flower was made to bloom.
            The heart was made to love.
Pure love is at the soul's center.
    It is pristine with incandescent glow.
        But most men do not know their soul.
True love is rare.
    It involves a communion of spirit.
        When two souls kiss—love is born.

The Hate Peddlers

There's a cancer malignant
In America's blood-stream,
'Tis the peddlers of hate
Whose views are extreme.

Suspicions their tool
And division their goal,
With malicious intent
They seize a man's soul.

With a blood-stirring slogan
And high sounding phrase,
They promise to lead
The sheep through the maze.

Those who would fight
Their deceptive half-truths,
Are labeled and cursed
As pro-Communist dupes.

No matter how complex,
The problems men face,
Hate peddlers spout answers
In rapid-fire pace.

They shoot from the hip
Without taking aim,
And scatter their buckshot
To cripple and maim.

For fear is essential
In fulfilling their plan
Of democracy's demise—
A new slavery of man.

"Impeach the Chief Justice—
He's a liberal skunk.
Send troops into Cuba
And show 'em our spunk."

"Spurn talks with Russia—
Withdraw recognition!
Threaten with H-bombs—
Send 'em to perdition."

"Down with all Niggers
And Catholics and Jews,"
State's rights forever—
Is used as a ruse.

The extremist must crush
All strong men who think,
By smearing the label,
"He's a Communist pinko."

The sheep shout in rhythm,
"Our hero's so grand;
He's slaying the dragons
Infesting our land."

"Hail to our leader—
We blindly will follow;
For he has the word
That all men must swallow."

"For those who refuse
Our call to enlist—
We will crush and destroy
Their will to resist."

The weapons employed
To break a man's will
Are the tools of a tyrant
Who freedom would still.

Phone threats of violence
Ring through the night—
One of hate's weapons
Employed in the fight.

Anonymous letters
With phrases obscene,
Play a big roll
In the hate-monger's scheme.

American—wake up
Before it's too late!
The forces of hatred
Would take over the state.

Freedom is lost
By men unaware,
Deep in their sleep
In a soft easy-chair.

Freedom's maintained
By men wide-awake—
Who consciously know
All that's at stake,

With strength and awareness
The free men will win
The battle for freedom
With tyranny's sin.

Hatred and fear
Cannot stand the light,
For courage and truth
Will put them to flight.

From Sheep Slave to Man Christ

With eloquent words and fine gestures,
The divinely anointed declaims;
In phrases of sweet flowing honey
Binding men's souls in silk chains.

The priest-king today is more subtle
Than blustering Church-lords of yore
In exploiting the credulous convert
And milking the gullible poor.

Sheep-slave bleats for a shepherd
A beguiling, flattering priest
One who will whisper sweet nothings
While keeping their wool neatly fleeced.

Don't think—don't question too freely
Accept things just as they are
For god has made me your teacher
Don't carry reflection too far.

The sheep-slaves lapse into silence
In blind acceptance of fate.
The priest-king entrenches
more firmly
And strengthens his growing estate.

And what is true of religion
Is true of commerce and state,
The tyrant rules by convincing
Each man of his sheep-slave fate.

Freedom's too precious to squander
On the child-like masses of men.
It is better that we bear it for them."
A theme from the Inquisitor Grand.

The laws we make are for your sake,
As leader above you—we're free.
We have no need to obey rules
Our destiny above you to be.

But freedom's urge is inherent
Though blinded, fettered and bound
Slave-sheep eventually rise up
To cast tyrant down to the ground.

And then in history's strange pattern
A great mockery of life is repeated
The sheep can't handle their freedom
A new shepherd is sorely entreated.

O God, will man ever grow up?
Will he ever have courage to be
Mature in spontaneous freedom?
Fulfilling his life's destiny?

The drama of life is a journey
Beginning and ending in God
Who needs our creative endeavors
Before we can rest neath the sod.

God in His infinite patience
Is waiting for man's liberation
In body-soul's union achieving
The fusion of life's integration

God, like man, desires union
In freedom exalting his tryst,
But true life is only for equals
God waits for the advent of man-Christ.

Life's Bitters

There is no heartbreak or sorrow
In the earthly saga of man
Alikened to feeling lonely
Experience in mortal timespan.

For some the load is o'erwhelming
No glimmer of light do they see
Hurt deeply and badly exploited
From life they desperately flee.

In a world of icy indifference
Where heartache and pain is ignored
Without the balm of love's healing
By life they are fatally gored.

A part of them dies e'en daily
And life becomes futile and dark
Only the touch of an infinite love
Rekindles dead hope with its spark.

Life's pleasures, escapes, and evasions
Become sterile, tasteless, and dry
Only the warm flame of compassion
Can light up their cloudy-night sky.

We are made for each other
In the harmony of cosmos we see
A portent of union together
Fulfilling our life's destiny.

The harlot, the thief, and the drunkard
By this world shunned and despised
Are my family—my brother and sister
For them Christ suffered and died.

The lost, despairing, and shattered
Are chewed in the grinder of pain
Yet each contains in his essence
A spark of the original flame

For man is made in God's image
No matter how lost it may be
The divine self burns as potential
Though only the rubbish we see.

To you who are inwardly weeping
Alone in your anguish and grief
My heart leaps out to embrace you
In a soul kiss of rapturous release.

Look deep into my eyes, O brother
View well the mirror of your soul
And learn that all heartache is fleeting
A cosmology joyful—our goal.

This life with all of its bitters
Is a brief movement—eternities nod
And those who suffer like Lazarus
Will rest in the bosom of God.

Life's Demons

(Ignorance and Fear)

The demons of life
Are something—not new;
The scourges that kill
Are really just two.

The demons that curse
And wither a life
Are ignorance and fear;
The cause of all strife.

Man is reluctant
To enter the fray
And fight the twin demons
That govern his day.

In blindness and sleep
Man lives out his days,
Not trusting his spirit
To lead through the maze.

Man is the victim
Of tyranny's rule
By denying his vision
And becoming a tool.

Exploited and milked
Of his precious humanity,
He dribbles away life
Or retreats in insanity.

The tyrant lives well
By sucking his prey
Who gradually weaken
Till death steals away.

The man is a tyrant
Who rules by suppressing
The instincts of others
Their full life expressing.

But energy's a force
That can't be restrained
Exploding with fury
Leaving crippled and maimed.

Who are the exploited
And credulous dupes
Who feed tyrants hunger
With boot-licking stoops?

The victims are slaves
Of their ignorance and fear
"Give bread and fringe benefits
And lots of free beer.

"Let us be children
We're too blind to see
That man must mature
To meet destiny."

"Let us be sheep!
Lead to the slaughter
We will even be passive
When tyrant rapes daughter."

"Kill off our sons
In stupidities war
Don't give us a good reason'
To think is a bore.

For man is so passive,
So blind and so weak,
That one who is free
Is regarded a freak.

The man who emerges
Above the herd's level
Is clawed at and cursed
Like an incarnate devil…

Or if one should stumble
Below the mass level
The herd tramples him
In dust and the gravel.

The battle of life
Is not fought with evil,
But with tyrant's forces
That make man a weevil.

The life force is sacred
And can't be contained;
Life must be lived out
And creativity sustained.

God didn't make man
His foot-kissing slave;
He made man in freedom
To rise from his grave.

From torporing slumber
And sterility's sleep,
From groveling obeisance
And bleating like sheep.

God give man courage
To stand head held high,
With feet planted on earth
And his eyes in the sky.

God give man courage
To look squarely within
To face with serenity
What tyrants call sin.

God give man courage
To be honest and free
To taste of the fruit
Of Divinity's tree.

True knowledge is insight
And gives vision clear.
It heightens perception
And takes away fear.

As man's vision expands
In widening circles,
Dark becomes light
And waves turn to ripples

For those who have courage
To be true to life's plan
Will hear history's verdict—
"God, there lived a man."

Sea Of Life

Sea of life—
   Frigid, arctic water or balmy, tropic
   Blue; murky rays piercing unfathomed
   Deeps,
   Dancing foam on sandy shallows,
      Playful, gentle swells and
         Boiling, roaring surf,
Speak to the soul of man!
Mother of water—
     Fountains bubbling source,
     Journey's mysterious end,
     Racing silvery brook
     Mighty silt-darkened river,
        Swelling, turbulent eddies
           Vagrant, meandering stream,
Speak to me of life!
Keeper of mysteries—
       Witness of creation,
       Infinite expanse,
       Eternity's companion
         Bountiful giver,
           Constant rhythm,
              Flowing movement,
Tell me your secret!
Music of the sea—
        Insistent surge begetting life,
        Crashing billows,
        Stormy passions,
          Harmonious, quiet water,
            Meditative calm,
               Ebb and flow—death and birth,
The mirror of life!

Dawn

Silver lined black clouds race across
    The horizon
The sky is heavy except for a sliver
    Of sunlight blue.
Large rain drops splatter on leafy
    Giants.
Branches sing and sway in subtle
    Rhythm to the shifting wind.
Far below my hilltop, the corrugated
    Waters of the lake
Become placid in protected coves.
Suddenly a shaft of ethereal light
    Illuminates the heavens–
Piercing the small fluffy cumulus and
    The somber black–
Revealing the impenetrable blue.
The mystery of life is revealed
    In the magic of dawn.
Reality lies deep within, and
    Paradoxically, far beyond.
The scent of life is in the morning
    Air.
All things become new.
It is dawn!

Hail To The Institution

Hail to the institution
Oh Mother Church of all
Beguiling souls of children
Exhorting weak—"Stand Tall."

The souls of men are fodder
Ground up as grist for the mill
And eaten up by mother
Her own needs to fulfill.

For one who is truly mother
Will set her children free
To live, and love and suffer
And serve creatively.

If mother becomes the "end all"
And binds her child in chains
The light of life is darkened
The soul goes up in flames.

The following editorial appeared in the *Sacramento Bee* editorial page, Sunday, July 11, 1976.

If I were in charge...
Pioneers Of The Spirit

IN THIS BICENTENNIAL year, I would invite and challenge the American people to become pioneers of the spirit. The new frontiers are within the realm of inner space. The clarion call must resound throughout the land. Wake up, America, assume responsibility for freedom. Realize your true identity as sons and daughters of God. Utilize your God-given potential to create and breathe new life into our weary world. Discard outmoded models and patterns. Reform existing institutions that are salvageable. Help build a world where man is free to be truly human.

For modern man has mastered his environment, but lost his soul. He is rich in material possessions, but poverty-stricken in spirit. Man has conquered the worlds of outer space, but remains an earthbound slave to vanity, greed, lust, anger, and attachment.

Concentration, meditation, and contemplation are needed to balance the outer expressions of life. Self-realized individuals, operating spontaneously out of the center of being, can give our world a new birth.

A new revolution is needed where men and women will:

Accept the inherent dignity of each individual and his right to grow and develop his full potential as a human being.

Affirm the rule of law based on equal justice for all men—not only for the rich and powerful, but also for the oppressed, the exploited, the prisoner, and the slave.

Acknowledge the family of man as the basis for economic security for all, social interaction between groups, and the valuing of each human life.

Commit themselves to work for equality of opportunity and the equitable distribution of wealth and resources until the specter of poverty and its attendant evils of hunger, disease, and hovels are banished from the face of the earth.

Pledge themselves to resist—until death—any tyranny over mind and body and brutal crushing of the human spirit.

Recognize that the real enemies of man are ignorance concerning the true nature of life, the fear of confronting oneself, and the dread of the unknown.

Challenge the hearts and minds of all free men to do battle with the forces of economic and cultural imperialism, racism, nationalism, militarism, and every other ism or system that degrades our humanity and does violence to the soul of man; in order that men of goodwill can burst the "mind-forged manacles" and unite in creating a society in which all men will be free to stand tall, with human dignity, as befits the sons of God.

ONLY THEN will man realize his destiny in that fleeting instant called life here on planet earth.

Freedom Marchers

Processions of hope wind slowly
Through sunny streets in the south
Downtrodden men are awakening
Revealed in the set line of each mouth.

One group walks through the streets of Greenville
Heckling jeers and mocking catcalls greet
"The farmer takes a wife—a Nigger wife"
Derisive laughter echoes up and down the street.

There are no answering insults
From the freedom-marching throng
But a note of suffering sadness
As they take up haunting song.

"The Lord is on our side." "The Lord is on our side."
Is their answer to curse and derision
Their detractors become strangely silent
Truth's knife cuts a deep incision.

For the spirit of those who are marching
Is the spirit of something—not new
Reminiscent of a cry from Calvary's hill
"Father forgive them they know not what they do."

Love and truth are the answers
To ignorance, prejudice, and fear,
Each man has the right to freedom
And his essential dignity – so dear.

For with all of our marvelous advancement
In science, technology, and space
When it comes to the realm of the spirit
We haven't begun to keep pace.

O God, how You must suffer
As You view man's cruelty and hate
Or even worse the calloused indifference
To the plight of our black brothers' fate.

O Lord, stir up the fires of compassion
In the deeps of every man's soul
To the truth that all men are brothers
In fulfilling eternity's goal.

And lest we become smug and self-righteous
Pointing fingers of scorn at "the others"
Give us the courage to examine ourselves
"Do we treat all men as our brothers?"

The Minister's Role in Contemporary Society

During the period of time when I had kicked the traces of orthodox Lutheranism in 1966, I wrote this article, "The Minister's Role in Contemporary Society." Much of this I have written is still applicable today with the possible exception of the very last section of the article, which, in my current thinking, would undergo some revision.

There appears to be much confusion in our culture concerning the role of the minister in our fast-moving, complex society.

The minister's image, in the popular mind, is in the tradition of Norman Vincent Peale—a rather unctuous, smiling, paternalistic bearer of sweetness and light, a defender of the status quo and a protector of morality and civic virtue; one whose chief role is to make people feel good.

To modern man, trained in the scientific method, the minister is often considered an anachronism, a superstitious throwback to the dark ages; one who exploits the credulity, ignorance, and fear of the sheep herd. I must confess that in my opinion, most of what parades under the guise of organized religion fits the picture all too well. The hucksters of the spirit have been running a protection racket by programming fear and guilt into the masses and then charging a price for absolution and the guarantee of celestial realms above.

But what, if any, is the role of the minister in contemporary society? Is there a valid ministry to be performed or has the minister outlived his usefulness? Let me give a general philosophical statement to serve as the framework for my views. I feel that there is room for a valid ministry that embraces a redemptive community of concerned individuals. The ministry is a gut-level concern dealing with "real people" with "real problems" living in a "real world." More than sterile intellectualizing, it is marked by a deep caring for each other, a sharing of burdens in a climate of healing, liberating love. It is marked by openness and sensitivity on all levels of human need and awareness.

With this context in mind let us consider:

I. The minister as a person

II. The minister and the religious community

III. The minister and the world

I have a number of strong feelings about the minister as a person. I believe that every minister worth his salt is first a person and second a minister. The individuality of the man determines the role rather than vice versa. There are many ministers of my acquaintance who have completely submerged their identity in the role they play. As a result there is no reality in their relationships. You never meet the real person but a bewildering variety of masks. This type of minister is a blind leader of the blind. He is like the actor who puts himself so completely into a role that he promptly loses touch with his own reality.

Pet Peeves about Ministers

At this point let me state some of my "pet peeves" about ministers in general. I react negatively to ministers who feel that their image is more important then their substance or reality. They are the phonies. A real bore is the minister who patronizingly dispenses the quintessence of the obvious. There are others who are guilty of what Churchill called "terminological inexactitudes." They are lying down their throats.

Then there are the cobweb spinners who give a beautiful blend of abstruse metaphysical and philosophical speculations. Dazzling men with their eloquence—all of which signifies nothing.

The "party-liners" are another group who know all of the right words. They play the game with monotonous deadness. They never come out with an original idea and are tedious to say the least.

Then there are the "qualifiers." In their passionate attempts to remain detached, objective, and uncommitted, they qualify and qualify and qualify until by the time they hit the idea, you, as a listener, couldn't care less.

The "twittering bird" type is another offender. They are so enamored with their vocabulary that "how they say it" is more important than "what they say." Consequently they say little, but say it beautifully.

Finally there are the "name-droppers." They are desperate to let you know how well informed and avant-garde they are. They are perennial quoters and never have courage to express ideas forged in the crucible of their own experience. When they preach, you are fed a diet of warmed-over hash.

Varieties of Ministerial Leaders

At this point let me say something about the minister as a leader. There are four types of leaders, as I see it, with infinite variations of each type. First is what I call the hard-boiled dictator. He runs a tight ship. He knows what he wants and he gets it regardless of tactics employed and the sensibilities involved. He is a tyrant and everyone knows it. At least the hard-boiled dictator is honest about who he is and everyone is aware of it.

Second is the benevolent autocrat. This is the manipulator type. He knows how to use people, play on their fears, ignorance, and prejudice to achieve his aims. He is as arbitrary and autocratic as the hard-boiled dictator; however, he is a slicker operator in using people to get his way.

Third is the laissez-faire leader. He doesn't take a stand on anything but generally lets everything run itself—like a ship without a helmsman. Like the chameleon, he changes color to fit the situation, preferring to operate in the vacuum of indecision and non-involvement.

The fourth and last kind of leader is the democratic leader. This kind of leadership involves a high degree of maturity. He seeks to get all points of view, weigh all the alternatives, and give guidance and direction to the enterprise. Essentially he sees the art of leadership as a team process and he knows how to draw out all the strengths and skills of the participants. This type of leader will stand on principle, fighting tyranny or injustice whenever he encounters it, because he understands the meaning of the words integrity and courage. Needless to say, this type of leadership is rare.

Affirmation of Life

But what do I affirm concerning the identity, qualities, and values of the minister as a person? First let me say that I affirm life with all of its rhythms, polarities, and nuances; its joy and sorrow; its blood, sweat, and tears. Life to me is a process of growth—a becoming aware on all levels of human existence. Each of us must choose our stance—either to be open or defensive, to choose life or death, growth or retrogression. To me, the challenge of life is to become fully human, to break through to my own identity, to possess my own inner authority, to trust my vision and spirit, to tap into the wellspring of my own wisdom and creativity, to battle the demons of fear and ignorance in my own life, to be intellectually curious and critically discerning. In short, to be a human being with all that involves in strength and weakness. I feel strongly about the dignity and integrity of each individual. Each man is called to make his own quest for values and to walk his own road of life. For only the man who has a sense of his own identity is ready for mature community. There is no need for the games of one-upmanship or scapegoating. When a man is secure within himself he doesn't need to be in control of every situation. He has no need to project his frustrations, guilt, and fear on others. It is the fearful and insecure who present the greatest test of love and maturity to a religious community. They are the vindictive neurotics who oscillate between individuality and conformity. Since they lack knowledge of who they are, they usually project their conflict against the minister as the authority figure. Symbolically, they are not willing to assume the responsibility of becoming their own mother and father. These unhappy people are the nitpickers who want to take pot shots at authority but lack the courage to grow up and accept the responsibility for their actions. They are in a state of perennial adolescent rebellion and lack courage to break through and make a full affirmation of life and their own individuality. The vindictive neurotic is a great test of the patience of a society in general and the minister in particular. Their number in organized religion is legion.

Proclaiming "His Truth"

Another aspect of the minister as a person is the personal conviction that every man could proclaim "his truth" processed by and through his own life. Witnessing out of the matrix of his own subjective authority—he proclaims life at the level of his awareness. This kind of proclamation out of the womb of being has the taste, touch, sound, and smell of life. There is a prophetic element in the message and not just a feeble echo of society. This is the cutting edge that knifes through the hypocrisy and deceit of "mass-man" society and values. For in the final analysis, it's not what we say, not even what we do (we do many good things for wrong reasons) but what we are, really are, that speaks more eloquently than a thousand words.

My view of the minister as a person is idealistic, admittedly. To become a self-actualizer, mature and possessing the attitudes and qualities I have previously outlined is a tall order and there are probably very few who achieve it. But the challenge for the minister is to become fully human, a free spirit, possessing his own inner authority. Only then will he realize the inner security that will enable him to relate to the society in a mature way.

The Minister and the Religious Community

Let us turn now to the relationship between the minister and the religious community. Does the minister have a specialized role? The demarcation lines of the ministerial role vary from tradition to tradition. Some religious communities have a strongly centralized authority pattern with Herr Pastor holding the reins or ruling the roost as a benevolent or autocratic dictator. In the more liberal traditions the role of the minister is more sharply defined into the category of "spiritual concerns." My own feeling is that the minister is called to preach (in the best sense of the word) from a free pulpit, without fear of favor, his witness to life as processed through his own experience. He is not able, in the final analysis, to give anyone the word. Individuals must get it for themselves. But an effective message is one that stirs the thinking and feeling of a congregation. As a minister cuts down through the levels of life he hits the great universal truths of human experience which call for a resonant response in his listeners. As a sort of gadfly the minister is existentially involved in dialogue with the religious community and speaks truth as he sees it. I feel that there is room for honest passion in the pulpit. In contrast, a state of cold, detached objectivity has all the appeal of cold mashed potatoes. The minister is also a counselor, a group leader, administrator, educator; one who ministers to people from the cradle to the grave. At this point, a warning: the minister is always in danger of spreading himself too thin. Dr. Sitler speaks of the "maceration of the ministers, or being chopped into bits." The minister needs time for solitude and reflection, for reading and meditation, for renewing his inner life.

Another aspect of the relationship between the minister and religious community is the mutual ministering to each other. There are times when the minister is down and needs a helping hand. "The mantle of infallibility" (I speak facetiously) rests heavily upon him. There is a two-way street, a partnership, a mutual sharing and caring in a climate of freedom and acceptance. The goal is to grow in awareness, to expand consciousness both individually and corporately on all levels of being.

Commitment to Each Other

In a vital community there is real commitment to each other—not just a token involvement, but a deep caring and giving of self to each other. The test of any relationship is what both parties are willing to invest in it. The acid test is always—do we really give a damn?

The test of maturity in our life together is can we tolerate and accept each other's anger? Can we live with each other's faults? This is not to imply a doormat approach when differences arise but an honest exchange of feeling. The problem is not only to love your enemies but conversely to at times hate your friends. The deep human needs of life are universal and can best be summed up by what I call:

The Language of Life

For there is an inexpressible sadness to life—intangible but real.
   It is our heart-hunger for love.
      It is a deep, relentless, compelling force.
         It is by nature—physical, emotional and spiritual.
The hunger for love propels us out of the cocoon of self into the world of people and relationships.
   It is expressed in many ways—
      The infant nursing at the mother's breast,
         The child seeking parental approval,
            The adult entering a one flesh relationship with the beloved.
We are created for love. We find our true being in relationship with one who cares. Our need for love is expressing in many little ways,

A wistful smile,
    A searching look,
        A warm hand clasp,
            An anxious glance.
The unspoken question is always the same.
    Do you love <u>me</u>?
        Do you love me?
            Do you *really love* me?
And there is desperate urgency in that silent plea.
We all need love in order to be fulfilled. It is the deprived, the unloved, the rejected who take the strange byways that lead to despair and death—
The rigid moralist,
    The mechanical prostitute,
        The calloused degenerate,
            The mentally disturbed—
All are victims of a hostile, unloving world.
For love is a fragile thing. Feelings are dangerous and highly combustible. One can be tragically hurt. The one you love may not love you.
    To love—is to become vulnerable.
        To be open—is to invite hurt.
            To give of self—means to suffer.
The healers of our time are those with the capacity
    To love
        To suffer,
            To endure.
Their love is
    A balm for heartache,
        The cure for loneliness,
            An antidote for pain.
They are the courageous ones!
    They confront the stark reality of a cruel and loveless world.
        They twinkle with laughter even though their hearts are breaking.
They meet life head on!
    They are bloodied but not defeated.

> They are knocked down but not out.
>> They endure hurt—but quietly.
>>> They possess resiliency and strength.
>
> They know the language of life—the essential reality—the meaning of love.
>> In giving—they receive.
>>> In suffering—they mature.
>>>> In dying—they live.

To know one who loves is to know life. It is indefinably sweet. It is inexplicably sad. For the one who loves, frees the beloved. The one, who is liberated, in turn, becomes an instrument of love. Set free by love, he willingly assumes the burden of suffering! Life becomes real! To love is to suffer! This is the meaning of the Cross.

We are in tune with the Infinite.

Carl Jung sums up what I've been saying in a memorable sentence: "The more we love, the more exquisitely we suffer, and the more we suffer, the more we love."

In a day when dehumanizing forces contribute to deep feelings of loneliness, alienation, anxiety and despair, the fellowship has a need to be a healing community. There is need for small groups where individuals are free to relate to each other in the problem areas of life, to share their feelings and be reaffirmed by each other in a deep caring way.

Summarizing, the relationship between the minister and the religious community is a mutual ministering to each other on the levels of deepest need, intellectually, spiritually and on the feeling level. It is accomplished in a climate of freedom and acceptance that encourages the fullest possible growth as human beings.

Minister and the World

Turning to our last point, what is the relationship of the minister to the world? I can answer in two words—involvement and commitment. I don't know much about the next world, but I can see, feel, and react to the needs of this one. The minister is called to speak out what he believes on the critical social issues of our time—peace, race, social justice—making his voice heard. He is responsible for becoming involved in the power struggle, or to paraphrase Oliver Wendell Holmes, be judged not to have lived. The minister and the religious community have a duty as part of the power structures of society to be responsible and creative. This involves the resistance of tyranny and injustice wherever it is encountered. It involves the building of bridges between hostile and contentious groups. It means battling the forces of fear and ignorance that reduce men to sheep-slaves. There are tremendous new frontiers that are opening up that call for creative imagination in the psychic, economic, social, political, and education spheres. Our world is in need of fresh creative energy. This can only be given by individuals who have the courage to tackle the problems confronting man. It is easier to stand on the sidelines rather than become involved. Cowardice and love of security keep many liberals from speaking out in areas where their voices should be heard. We need a new "aristocracy of service," a commitment to the brotherhood of man which transcends parochialism and the chauvinistic nationalism that characterizes life today. "My country, right or wrong" is the theme. I don't buy that! Every man is my brother! Most people, to use Thoreau's phrase, live "lives of quiet desperation," lives full of banality and superficiality—because they have sold their souls for mammon and the security of the sheep herd.

I have been somewhat general. Now let me be quite specific in one area where I feel informed. Liberals should be making their voices heard. The issue is Vietnam and all that it symbolizes for us as a people.

When I was a boy, my nature was convulsed when I saw Mussolini's planes strafing Ethiopian peasants. As a young man, my inner being wept when I saw the atrocities of Dachau, Buchenwald, and Bergen-Belsen. I thought, "How cruel, how inhumane, is man's inhumanity to man." Now, under the guise of a "holy crusade" against Communism, we are slaughtering innocent peasants in Vietnam. We will save them from Communism even if we have to kill them to do it. Our fighting men complain, "We can't tell who is the enemy." Our planes make a navigational error. Bombs are dropped on a friendly village. Forty lives are lost. "Sorry about that."

It has been said that old men make wars and young men fight and die in them even before they are allowed to vote as citizens. They have no political lobbies like labor and medicine that spend millions to fight their causes. It is any wonder that they take to the street to protest the senseless slaughter in Vietnam? Our youth must depend on the awakened sensitivity and protest of those who know and see through the ignorance, greed, and lust for power that causes war.

Our leaders have been less than candid with the American people and have shrouded their actions under a mantle of secrecy. Peace feelers by the enemy go unreported. "God," "Mother," and "Uncle Sam" have been involved to whip up a war psychology. Under the guise of defending South Vietnamese from Communist aggression, we are supporting another military dictator in a long series of puppets, this one an avowed admirer of Adolph Hitler. Premier Ky's recent stand of executing suspected black market profiteers, without trial, indicates that he also approves of Hitler's methods.

As Americans we have failed to realize a basic axiom that there is no lasting rule without the consent of the governed. Tyranny, by nature, contains the seeds of its own destruction. We cannot give the people of Vietnam freedom. They must achieve it themselves. Democracy is a highly sophisticated form of government demanding a high level of consciousness on the part of the electorate. In backward countries, any attempt to impose democracy is certain to fail. New strongmen will seize power and simply use the new labels.

* * *

The beat and tempo of war drums is increasing. Is the curtain rising on the last act? Today, we sow the wind—tomorrow we reap the whirlwind. Weep now for your children and children's children, for in my mind's eye, I see miles of burned-out rubble and a prevailing silence too deep for tears.

Gene Vosseler

Spring 1966

3. POEMS AND ESSAYS OF LIGHT AND SOUND (1977-PRESENT)

These poems of light and sound were written after I found the ascended master teachings and my beloved Guru and teacher, Elizabeth Clare Prophet, in April of 1977.

These love ruminations from the depths of my soul I give to you, my treasured reader.

A New Song

Life has no meaning,
    Without a new song.
The words are quite simple,
    And not very long.
    I've got to be free in my heart—
    Free in me.
    I want to be free in my heart—
    Free in me.
Life's sweet, passing pleasures
    Will soon fade away.
Space—times a shadow,
    And night follows day.
    I've got to be free in my heart—
    Free in me.
    I want to be free in my heart
    Free in me.
Only the GURU
    Can light the night sky.
The God-man incarnate
    Will teach me to fly.
    I've got to be free in my heart
    Free in me.
    I want to be free in my heart
    Free in me.
The Path of pure Spirit,
    And love is It's way;
To guide the lost traveler
    Into a new day.
    I've got to be free in my heart—
    Free in me.
    I want to be free in my heart—
    Free in me.

The way of the Victory
    By the chela is found.
"Just be" that pure spirit,
      The light and the sound.
      For It makes me free in my heart—
      Free in me.
      What makes me free in my heart?
      It's free in me.

The Christ

Out of the womb of Being,
  timeless and eternal,
Flows the life essence of the Source.
The Christ is the immortal flame of pure Spirit,
  an illuminating light,
  a refining fire.
The music of the soul is a freedom song
  of celestial sound,
  creative energy,
  and liberating power.
The wind of the Spirit is the light and sound-
The voice of the Christ expressing itself in all of life.
  It is the source of every
  great composition,
  work of art,
  or ode to beauty.
  It is the author of all
  noble truths,
  intuitive insights,
  and divine wisdom.
It speaks in
  the whispering of the wind,
  the roar of the sea,
  the warmth of the sun,
  and the patter of a spring rain.
  It is seen in
  the snow on the mountain top,
  the green of the forest,
  the colors of a rainbow.
  the magic of dawn.

For God is life, and life is reality.
We are that reality,
pure Spirit,
light and sound,
one with it,
all that is,
immortal souls,
sons and daughters of the Most High God.

Thoughts before Dawn

1. The inner movement of the spirit is subtle and exceedingly fine.

2. The inner sound of the spirit can be elusive to the beginner in his pursuit of God.

3. Old habit patterns, thought formation, and reflexive reaction are broken up by the liberating power of the Spirit of God.

4. Only the refining fire of the spirit can cleanse and heal an oftimes fatal disease—hardness of heart.

5. Trust, patience, and humility are the fruits of the spirit.

6. Only the pure fire of the holy can destroy the calcified, defensive layers that encase the soul of man.

7. The soul of modern man is in chains. He has forgotten his true identity.

8. It's not easy to swim against the worldly tide of convention, conformity, and mediocrity.

9. At first, it's difficult to trust the Guru. The world has been replete with saviors and savants from its inception. They have promised much, but delivered so little.

10. Experience of the Guru's presence on the inner planes is a gift of the spirit. Expectant receptivity is the attitude that opens the window of heaven for soul's return to the Source of life.

11. The pride and vanity of man resists the idea of needing help or assistance from anyone.

12. We find that we are able to scale the heights of the sumit of Being only when we each the end of our own rope.

13. Pure consciousness is a state of being. We each choose our state of awareness. It's all a matter of where we place our attention. Why settle for baubles and trinkets of the transient world? The soul's longing for home is rooted in eternity.
14. The true wisdom of spirit is the light illuminating the darkness of this world.
15. The Soundless sound is the music and wind of the spirit animating all of life. It's regenerative in function and liberating in purpose.
16. Soul in its pure, natural state is always living in a state of at-one-ment with its Christ Self. Christ is pristine, pure, and possesses total awareness of all that is. Soul is an expression of the formless spirit that flows out of the womb of being.
17. Soul is the bridge between the I AM nameless world of pure spirit and the world of soul's creation, the physical universe of space-time, matter, and energy.
18. Pure being expresses itself in the acts of creation and the dance of life. Death is only an illusion. The play of opposites is only a paradox of the mind. Space and time are mental constructs to measure mass and movement.
19. Soul created all the lower worlds and then became enamored and attached to its creation. It identified with the physical—the world of matter—rather than with itself the creator. Awareness of soul's true identification with its Source was forgotten. The author became caught up with the lower-world script it had written and forgot itself as the source of creative energy and power.
20. The key to breaking attachment to the human condition is to break free and detach from the lower world consciousness. Soul must get in touch with its true center by cutting

through illusion, duality and the passions of the mind.

21. Soul is potentially a perfect microcosm containing all that is. The only limitation for soul is what it places on itself in ignorance of its true identity.

22. Soul is potentially omnipresent, omnipotent and omniscient—existent everywhere, all powerful, and all knowing. That is our true heritage as sons and daughters of God. The Christ consciousness is soul's true nature.

23. The living Guru is soul's guide on the inner who will lead it to that total awareness. The impersonal love of the I AM is the essence of being and permeates all that is.

24. Soul is realistically divine love, eternal truth, and creative energy. It has never been limited; it only thinks it has.

25. There is no wisdom on the earth plane—only knowledge of observable data to the senses, categories of thought, analytical reason, and metaphysical religious speculation.

26. True wisdom is soul wisdom drawn from the heart of the eternal Source of all life and being. It is timeless and formless, infinite and limitless, intuitive and free.

27. You and I as pure Spirit—are Alpha and Omega without beginning or ending, living manifestations of the one pure Spirit—"all that is."

28. All objects and things exist in relationship to the mind that perceives them. Seeing with spiritual eyes, all of space—time—matter is non-existent. No thing exists. Reality is in the eye of the beholder in the spirit-matter worlds. All is illusion, projected on the screen of nothingness by the universal mind. The tragedy is to take life on the earth plane seriously. Physical life is but a dream—a play—a dance. To see through appearance and form, maya and illusion—is to become free.

29. There is only one thinker; there is only one consciousness; there is only one playwright, one producer, one actor, one audience; there is only the one—the Source of all life, one pure being, one pure Spirit that manifests throughout all its creations.

30. When soul remembers its true identity—when it wearies of its play in the enchanting worlds of the senses, emotion, and mind—it will realize Its true nature in God-reality.

31. Soul's Journey
    Original essence
      Of transparent light
        Descending into the gloom
          Of opaque illusion
            And darkest night.
    The master's voice
      Melodious and clear
        Calls soul from the shadows
          Of pure Being, saying;
            "JUST BE AS THE SUN AT MIDDAY."

32. Joy is soul experiencing itself.

33. The ego is a construct of the mind. It is a creation not the creator.

34. The passions of the mind are like the tentacles of an octopus. If one cuts off a tentacle or an aberration, five more tentacles or aberrations spring up to take their place.

35. The lower worlds of duality and negativity are conquered and left behind only when soul recognizes itself as a free spirit.

36. The conflict of the opposites in man reaches its highest intensity just before resolution and transcendence in self-realization.

37. Unconditional surrender to God and the masters seem

like the ultimate defeat. Paradoxically, it is the prerequisite for experiencing the ultimate victory of God-realization.

38. The ego always goes down to defeat struggling and kicking.

39. Life is like a school. Some lessons are very hard to learn. Ego (small I) blames its problems on the teacher (God), the subject matter (life), or surrounding environment (world). The problem really lies with the student who resists growing up and taking responsibility as a free spirit for his thoughts, words, and actions.

40. Life is organic and whole.

41. Without the help of the Guru, man is always stuck in the mire. The more he struggles, the deeper he sinks. Only the living Guru can help raise soul out of the mud of lower consciousness and guide it to the high ground of pure Spirit.

42. One would never venture to climb Mt. Everest without proper preparation and an experienced guide who knows the way. For soul to scale the heights of the far country, the spiritual exercises are the preparation and the Guru is the guide to the highest God worlds.

43. God is
    God is all
    God is all that Is
    This I am!

44. Only God exists! All else is illusion and the play of maya.

45. There is only one consciousness.

46. God manifests as individual beings in the lower worlds of duality and illusion.

47. There is one consciousness manifesting itself in infinite wisdom, creative power, divine love, and perfect freedom.

Soul is that one consciousness.

48. The world of duality exists only in the mind of man.
49. Man's outer circumstances are the reflection of his inner awareness.
50. The old Adam (ego) is a delusional construct of the mind. After the ego dies, life in the spirit becomes real.
51. Soul unaware on planet earth is like a butterfly trapped in its cocoon.
52. To become fully aware of life soul must burst the cocoon of illusion and experience the joy of perfect freedom.
53. To speak of God in the ultimate sense, is to become silent.
54. God-realization is total awareness. It cannot be reduced to words. God-realization is here and now—complete and available to all who have eyes to see and ears to hear. It is our birthright—ours to reclaim as the sons and daughters of God. Man needs to wake up from torporing slumber and remember his true God-identity.
55. God is! Soul is it.
56. The sun at mid-day is a symbol of the universal consciousness.
57. All of life is numinous.
58. Out of darkness comes the light. For the awakened consciousness, there is only light.
59. The light of spirit is universal truth and divine wisdom illuminating all of the universes of the Ancient One.
60. The sound of spirit is the primal power and universal energy of divine love that animates all life and sustains all creation.
61. There is only life—universal consciousness—the Christ. All else is illusion.

62. The true nature of soul is the Christ consciousness. It is omnipotent, omniscient, and omnipresent. To realize this fully is God-realization.

63. Every step in growing awareness is accomplished through the death of an old self-limiting idea and the birth of a new insight.

64. Life is a struggle as long as we view life dualistically.

65. All evil is in the eye of the beholder. Universal consciousness perceives perfection in all that is.

66. There is no death—only a shift or change in consciousness. And even that apparent change of consciousness is an illusion.

67. Ignorance and fear are illusions. They are the products of ego, which is itself a construct of the mind.

68. Awakened soul knows no fear.

69. Soul is potentially free, unlimited and eternal.

70. Only God Is!
    All life is a reflection of it.

71. There is only God.
    What do we have to fear?

72. All souls are potentially it!

73. To the fully awakened soul existing in perfect freedom, life is pure Spirit, a primal essence of love, wisdom and power, manifesting in light and sound, radiating the fire and energy of the Christ consciousness as it proceeds out to the Womb of Being, the Source of all life—the divine Godhead.

74. Soul is pure spirit
    Soul is pure
    Soul is

75. I am one with God
    I am one
    I am

76. God is all in all
    　　God is all
    　　　　God is

77. It is,
    　　And
    　　　I
    　　　　Am
    　　　　　It.

78. Soul is God manifesting on earth as individual being.

79. Soul's inner vision sees through form and appearances. It perceives God in everyone and everything.

80. My world is perfect as it is.

81. Soul is universal consciousness
    Soul is universal
    　　Soul is.

Divine Wisdom

There is no wisdom on the earth plane—only knowledge of observable data to the senses, categories of thought and analytical reason, and metaphysical religious speculation.

True wisdom is soul wisdom drawn from the heart of the eternal Source of all life and being. It is,

Timeless and formless,

Infinite and limitless,

Intuitive and free.

It is,

All knowing,

All seeing,

Existing everywhere

In everything.

It is the Christ manifesting the pure being of the Eternal One on all planes of consciousness. You and I are pure spirit—are that Eternal One—without beginning or ending, living manifestations of the Source of life.

I AM

I am a body, the temple of God
I am the mind, a channel of light
I am the heart, a seat of pure love,
I am a soul, the source of the dove.
        I AM
      Heart, mind, body
          and
          soul!
        I AM all,

          and
        All is One.

Light and Sound

Original essence of transparent light
Vibrating in harmony with celestial sound
Descends into darkness of soul's darkest night
A slave of illusion and struggle profound.

Then at the moment of deepest despair
The Master's voice beckons, melodious and clear.
"Awaken, O soul in captivity bound,
Remember soul's source, the light and the sound."

Soul soars from the shadows of earth's darkened plain
On wings of the light and the sound,
The love of the God flame envelops the soul
For paradise lost has been found.
    The message is clear—
    To all who will hear
    "Just Be, as the sun at midday."

4. POEMS OF LOVE AND WISDOM (1977-PRESENT)

Only Love

O lovers of life, and lovers of man,
O lovers of God, and nature's pure plan!
Hear ye my song of hope, joy, and love,
Sent from God's heart on the wings of the dove.

Love opens the door and sets men free;
In God's love eternal, is life's cosmic key.
Only in love is the seal of God's plan,
A life lived in love is the goal of God-man.

Love's tie alone unites all men's hearts,
Pure flame of truth to all life imparts
The joy and the hope answering life's deepest need
With a spark of pure love in the ethereal seed;

The source of all life in the heart of the rose,
Divine spark in the star fire in the galaxy glows,
A light of pure joy in the smile of a child,
Seedpod of the oak in the primeval wild.

For love is the spark in life's center and core;
Love is the pole-star to which we all soar.
In moments of freedom our hearts are inspired
By God's Holy Spirit our beings are fired

With freedom and hope and courage and joy,
transformed by love's rays in gold flame alloy.
Only love, then, is our clarion call,
O lovers of light, rally ye all!

Proclaim to the world with heart flames aglow,
The joy of new birth, love's victory bestow.
Arise, arise, O lovers of life!
Put to the torch your burden and strife.

Love's victory is waiting, your crown now to win,
In love is your freedom, a new life to begin
Of channeling light and energies shower,
Redeeming all life with love's flaming flower;

The white lotus of truth, love, wisdom, and power
Sealing all hearts in eternity's hour.
When all life shall sing in glorious refrain "Thank God,
I AM free! I AM home once again."

Camelot, Jewel of Light

O Camelot, thou jewel of light
Born from the heart of God
Light up the darkness of night,
Bring all 'neath heaven's rod.

Blaze, O blaze Excalibur
Thou torch of living flame,
Recall to all the sons of light
Their cosmic I AM name.

Sing of Merlin, freedom's friend,
And of his love for all.
Exalt his gift—the violet flame
That transmutes human pall.

Hail Guru Ma, sweet Guinevere
Thou great and noble beauty,
Supreme light of the Mother ray,
God flame of holy duty.

O, sing ye sons of Lancelot
Staunch knight and friend of old,
Who gave his life in sacred trust
And held his vision bold

That earth would claim her final goal—
A freedom star to be,
Where man would live as pure God-soul
Throughout eternity.

Sing of Arthur! O, Morya dear,
Your perfect love casts out all fear.
We march to battle in your flame,
Linked arm in arm with Saint Germain,

With Lancelot and Mother too—
For we have cosmic work to do;
Challenging evil and invoking the light,
Confronting the fallen, putting foe to flight,

Piercing the gloom of the energy veil,
Quickening men's hearts to search for the Grail.
For the God star of Light is buried within,
Ever triumphant in it's battle with sin.

Camelot, gem of white fire beauty,
Awake in man his sacred duty,
To be a fiery orb of love,
A source of light, the snow white dove

That draws the knights and ladies home
Into the sacred fires of Om,
Where soul fulfills its cosmic plan—
Reunion with its Great I AM.

At last the crown, love's victory won,
God flame eternal, a bright new sun.

Hope, The Wellspring of Joy

O radiant grace, transcendent wonder
O blazing light, let all men ponder
The hope that soars on wings of joy
Freeing all souls from sin's alloy.

From fear and doubt and darkest night
The joy of hope puts fear to flight
And anchors the soul in joy supreme
Of life's lost vision—the inner dream.

Awake my soul, the truth to see
The heart of my life infinity
A blazing orb of light and power
Expressing beauty in the tiny flower.

This is my plea, for all to see
That the secret of life, and destiny
Is found in words that set men free;
"I AM That I AM" eternity.

Rain Drops

Tiny gentle rain drops
Caressing window pane
Feeding myriad grassy shoots
Restoring life to barren plain

Budding flowers drink deeply
Of heavenly nectars draught
And flood the air with perfume
Sweet fragrance can't be bought

Sensitive, glistening raindrops
Sparkling on mother earth
Share your hidden meaning
To give your story birth.

It may console thee spirit
To know earth's weeping too
Lamenting her departed lover
With pearl like tears of dew

All life awaits on tiptoe
With breathless expectancy
Will spirit and earth be united
Fulfilling divine destiny?

Will heaven and earth get together
As spirit and body combine
And in radiant rapture fusing
Create a new vision sublime?

I AM (White Light)

"I AM" pure white light
   a snow-white dove
   lighting the night
   on wings of love.

"I AM" pure white light
   ablaze with truth
   lighting the night
   with eternal youth.

"I AM" pure white light
   sending hope and peace
   lighting the night
   and sorrow's cease.

"I AM" pure white light
   singing freedom's call
   lighting the night
   bringing joy to all.

"I AM" pure white light
   with wisdom's ray
   lighting the night
   on your ascension day.

"I AM" pure white light
   a snow-white dove
   lighting the night
   with cosmic love.

There is no death, I know, it's
True, for God's pure white light
Is the eternal you.

The Torch of Freedom

O freedom touch of light sublime,
Blaze within this heart of mine.
Casting out all doubt and fear,
A flaming sign of victory dear.

Freedom's warriors ablaze with light
Transcending gloom and darkest night;
Attack, attack in God's own name,
Holding aloft, love's freedom flame.

The forces of tyranny that bow men down
Are minions of night wearing Lucifer's crown.
Rebellion's their tool and seduction the measure
"All things are yours, enjoy your full pleasure."

Awake, awake O Children of Light!
Force into retreat the sons of the night.
Armed in your armor of blazing white light
God's warriors victorious, put foe to flight.

There are no neutrals in life's freedom fight,
Choose ye this day, Sons and Daughters of Light.
> Hold high the flame
> Of blest Saint Germain.
> In the power of light
> Conquer the night.
> With courage to win.
> The battle with sin.

The warriors immortal are tried, brave, and true,
With courage and strength your life will imbue.
For they covet your victory of life's crown to gain,
God-realized in freedom through the violet flame.

The final fulfillment of your eternal life plan
Of the ascent into freedom of your mighty "I AM"
So come all ye warriors of blest St. Germain,
With music triumphant sing Victory's refrain;
And join the immortals who their victory have won
In a love feast of joy in the Great Central Sun.

The Flame of Love

I AM pink flame of love divine
Transcending light of space and time
Aglow with fire and burning zeal
The heart of God to all reveal.

I AM the flame, the fiery core
a loving touch and spirits soar.
The breath of healing on love's wings,
The joy of life creation sings.

I AM the mighty flame of love
The Source of life, the snow white dove.
My heart sings out with cosmic power
Of life revealed in nature's flower.

I AM the love of all that's true,
the torch of freedom passed to you,
God-spark of purity burning bright,
Sings out the glory—I AM Light.

Come, come, come now sacred fire
with holy love our souls inspire.
As lovers of God and man we run,
For we are one with the Central Sun.

Let us each day our voices raise,
Hymns of joy, and love and praise.
As life flows to its final goal
Of Alpha and Omega, our one God-soul.

Freedom's Call

O flame of freedom, burning bright
A blazing torch of pure white light
Dispersing shadows and darkest night
Symbol of hope to the planet's blight.

Of defeat, despair and death's dark tomb
Awakening men's souls to resurrection's bloom
A flaming star piercing the gloom
Exposing the lies of the prophets of doom

Who spread their poison of doubt and fear
Crushing men down so that none may dare
Challenge the lie that man's a slave
In earth's cradle of freedom the home of the brave

Gird up your loins prepare for the fight
With the forces of tyranny, O Sons of the Light.
Too long have you slept in ignorant sleep.
Awake to the roll of freedom's drum beat

With vision and courage, a new course to plot
For the age of Aquarius—a new Camelot
Where honor and truth will live once again
In the heart and the souls of the planet's free men.

And power will be tempered by wisdom and love
In the chalice of purity, a snow white dove,
And liberty's torch will blaze in new light
To illumine all shadows and chase away night.

The joy flame will fill all hearts with its glow
in our heaven on earth, God's blessings will flow.
    and men will sing praises
        to the saints and the sages
            who down through the ages
                kept truth alive
                    with freedom's sweet call
                        those prophets of hope
                            who transcended
                              the fall.

And wherever men honor love's freedom's flame
A toast will be raised to blest St. Germain.
From Camelot, to Malta, to America's shore
This fighter for freedom has opened the door
In the hearts of all souls to eternity's plan
Of life's final freedom in their mighty "I AM."

Angels of Light

From realms of pure light, angelic hosts came
to the shadowy light of earth's darkened plain,
Love's message of hope, to all men proclaim,
Of the victory of light in God's "I AM" name.

Wave after wave of the angels of light
blazed down to earth armed with the might
of Michael's blue sword and Gabriel's white rays
following their leader, the Ancient of Days.

All heaven sang out with music celestial,
saluting God's mission to the planet terrestrial.
The dangers were great—no sure guarantee
that sin-blinded man would choose to be free.

The battle raged fiercely down through the ages
so God sent His Sons, the saints and the sages;
Masters and avatars, all sons of the Light,
to awaken man's spirit and put fear to flight.

Lord Buddha's wisdom awakened the earth,
kindling men's hearts with the joy of new birth,
quickening man's vision of life's final goal
of ascent into freedom of his one God-soul.

Then, at the dawn of the Piscean age,
the heart flame of Jesus blazed on earth's stage.
Christ showed forth the truth that men can be free
by slaying his ego; God's real image be.

Through balancing karma and being pure light
mankind will recapture their God-given sight;
that sees with the vision of God-victory won
our earth bathed in freedom, a brilliant new sun.

O chelas of Morya and blest Saint Germain,
O angels of Gabriel and Michael's blue flame,
Arise, arise to all life impart
A soul kiss of love to each trembling heart.

Salute all ye hearts with soul fire ablaze
Lord Sanat Kumara, the Ancient of Days.
Hail to all lightbearers, who in God's Holy Name,
are invoking the light of the violet flame.

The victory is ours, a gold crown to gain,
our birthright of freedom with blest Saint Germain.
O Sons of Germanus, alchemy's sage,
Come gather together, bring in the New Age,

Creating a new order in the city foursquare
for the twelve tribes of Israel are gathering there.
The vanguard of light is preparing the stage
for the hierarch of earth of the new Golden Age;
when all men shall live in accord with God's plan,
in full conscious awareness of their mighty "I AM."

We are all pilgrims on earth united in our humanity and our divinity, learning life's lessons as we forge the bands of unity in the oneness of God and all life.
We are all one in the great mandala of life and its experiences. We contain all that exists, all that is real. Our destiny is our God-reality where all shadows disappear and there is only light.

5. FREEDOM SPEECHES

Editor's Note: Among the many of Gene's inspiring freedom messages, here are two of the best.

"The Mighty Collision of Freedom"
World Freedom Day Speech, May 22, 1982

According to many U.S. government defense experts, America is vulnerable to either a nuclear first strike or nuclear blackmail. Either option might pose an irresistible temptation for the Soviet Union. Friends of Freedom Foundation is dedicated to awakening the American people to the threat of a Soviet first strike and to the realization that peace can only be achieved and maintained through strength. A true peace is more than a mere absence of war. The real battle today is for men's minds and hearts; the issue is tyranny versus freedom, for there is no true peace without liberty. Gene Vosseler, founder and first president of Friends of Freedom Foundation delivered the following message on World Freedom Day, May 22, 1982, at City Hall Los Angeles, California.

Friends of freedom, of late we've read a lot in the newspapers and we've watched on television and we've seen a movement getting off the ground in America called the Nuclear Freeze Movement. We've seen graphically illustrated for us the horrors of nuclear war and what would take place in a nuclear holocaust. It looks like the Communist-backed peace movement that swept Europe with massive peace rallies has finally reached the shores of America. There has been an all-out push from such tired retreads as McGeorge Bundy, George Keenan, and Robert McNamara who have now put out a new statement that appeared in the Foreign Affairs magazine backing nuclear freeze. And the Foreign Affairs magazine, of course, as you know is sponsored by the Council on Foreign Relations headed up by David Rockefeller. Rockefeller also contributed nearly $300,000 of initial funds to make sure that the nuclear freeze movement was well oiled to get off the ground. We now have what we call a born-again "Ban the Bomb" movement that's sweeping across America. This movement will call for a nuclear freeze no matter what our current relative strength is in relationship to the Soviet Union.

America is Vulnerable

The fact is we are now in a position of military inferiority. According to the U.S. Defense Department records and records in the Library of Congress, we are now faced with the fact that the military strength of the Soviet Union has reached the point where we are vulnerable to a preemptive first strike. The real scenario may not be a nuclear holocaust; it may be something entirely else. Imagine this. It's Sunday afternoon and you're sitting down watching your favorite program on television, when all of a sudden there is an interruption for an important message from the President of the United States. The image of the president in somber voice and tones makes his point. He says:

> *The U.S. government has just received an ultimatum from the Soviet Union. In order to prevent nuclear destruction of the United States our government has decided to accede to Soviet demands. Within the hour Soviet troops will begin landing at airports around the country. All citizens are urged to cooperate, to remain calm, and to obey fully the instructions of the Soviet officers.*

Fiction? Fantasy? Is nuclear blackmail a real and present threat? The tragic reality is that America is becoming increasingly vulnerable to this scenario. It's conceivable that our allies in Europe, seeing the handwriting on the wall, might strike their own deal with the Soviets and we would be left to face the Kremlin alone. We are and have moved into that window of vulnerability testified to by none other than Henry Kissinger. The apostle of detente, Henry Kissinger has pointed out this danger in testimony before Congress. He says we are facing the 80s with weapon systems designed for the 60s. That reality is before us and you need to take a hard look at it.

The US-Soviet Strategic Nuclear Imbalance

Just take one issue of strategic military defense weapons. We have a grand total of 309 defense interceptor fighter planes. The Soviets have 2,600 interceptors. They have 1,200 anti-ballistic launchers. We have zero. They have 64 anti-ballistic missiles; we have none. They have a grand total of 14,600 strategic defense weapons to our 309. When you consider our Navy fleet, you are faced with the reality that we have scrapped half of our fleet in the past ten years. They now have a two-to-one advantage in combat ships and submarines. They have 4.8 million troops compared to our 2.1 million. We have 435 strategic bombers, 200 of which are B-52s that are in the graveyard and are completely inoperable. The Soviets have 650 strategic long-range bombers. Then you become aware of what the odds of victory or defeat are.

This background on our strategic nuclear imbalance gives us sense and meaning to what the president is trying to do in building up our defense. We should have learned a long time ago that you do not deal with a world bully from a position of weakness. The schoolyard should have taught us that. When you are confronted with a school bully, the only thing the bully respected was strength. Well we have a world bully on the scene that has gobbled up fifty-seven countries since 1917. This world bully, the Soviet Union, has been nourished and fed by money, technology, and resources. As many as one thousand turnkey factories built by United States multinational corporations were given to the Soviets. We have literally created, developed, and built up the Soviet machine that is currently threatening to destroy us. Now I don't know what you think, but I don't think that is very smart.

I also don't like the idea that the Soviet-backed military junta in Poland can move into action and imprison five thousand leaders of Solidarity including Lech Walesa. In response, the U.S. put a few impotent sanctions up against them. We threaten more if they don't ease up and they haven't eased up and we haven't done anymore. And a few weeks later we discover the Polish government cannot pay its debts to American banks. What does the United States government do? In order to keep the Poles from defaulting, the American government picks up the interest tab. You and I, the taxpayers, make good on the loans made by American bankers that nourish the beast that they created and developed in the first place. It simply does not make sense. I don't know about you but I do not like the idea of my tax dollars going to support the Soviet repressive tyrannical slave state. It does not make sense.

Peace Through Strength

We are all for peace but we are for peace with freedom. We do not believe that you achieve peace through weakness. World War II and Nazi Germany taught us that lesson. We believe in "peace through strength," where you can sit down at the table from a position of strength. When you have the doctrine of Mutual Assured Destruction, of MAD, which was the basis of American defense policy for the last twenty or thirty years, you are operating from a position of weakness. MAD is based on the false belief that the Russians will never push the button to destroy our cities because we would retaliate and destroy theirs. MAD contends that we will never push the button because it will mean the destruction of their cities and they would retaliate and destroy ours. The Soviet Union never believed in MAD for a moment. They've been preparing since 1961—from the time they were forced to back down at that Cuban Missile Crisis—for fighting a nuclear war and surviving it. We, on the other hand, have not done the same.

Did you know that the Soviet Union has built 1,500 bomb shelters at the cost of $500 million a piece? These massive bomb shelters are located under the major cities in the Soviet Union. What kind of civil defense program does the American government have for you and for me? What kind of safety is there? The answer is—nothing.

Once you begin to understand the name of the game you realize how we as people have been lead down the primrose path of a false peace, and I am speaking for America because I represent an American group. But in one sense we're all Americans. The refugees who founded this country were the early Americans. But this country has been built on the backs and on the strength, the brains and the creativity of its refugee population. That's who built this country. Believe me when I tell you that only an alliance of the oppressed people of the world, with an awakened America, can stop the Soviet threat. It's that kind of an alliance that's got to be made. That's what Alexander Solzhenitsyn said.

A Soviet First-Strike

Let me pose a few questions. Is nuclear freeze the best assurance against the insane threat of a nuclear war? Possibly, but only if all the governments who had the weapons could be trusted to keep the faith. The Soviets continued their massive military build up while we were reducing our arms. In the West, a nuclear war is unthinkable. Is this true of the Soviet Union? Not at all—Soviet psychology is very different, greatly misunderstood by most westerners. To the Soviets, a nuclear war is not only survivable, but it's winnable. And that explains their enormous civil defense efforts that I talked about.

Are the Soviets planning a nuclear war? Certainly they are planning for such a contingency. However, conventional war appears to be their present course of action. They have invaded Afghanistan, committing genocide. We are very ill-prepared from a defense standpoint, from a weapons standpoint. The Afghan freedom fighters have brought that Soviet juggernaut to a screeching halt. It's a tribute to their love of the flame of freedom that beats in the hearts of the Afghans that they are willing to stand up, this small nation, to the full power and might of the Soviet Union.

What has the West done? Sadly, very little. What did the West do when Hungary was invaded by Soviet tanks in 1956? Or when, in 1968, they invaded Czechoslovakia twelve years later? We did a little bit of jawboning but barely raised a whimper, but nothing from a strategic military standpoint even though the Hungarians and the Czechs were begging for us to help! When people cry out for help and for assistance and the West does not respond, we may face the same threat on our own front door and no one may be there to help us.

Can the Soviets be trusted to keep a nuclear freeze treaty? No. Whereas the United States has honored SALT I (Strategic Arms Limitation Treaty) and used diplomacy as a means to end the arms race, the Soviets used diplomacy as time to build and expand their military might. They abrogated SALT I with twenty-six major violations. Armand Hammer told Nixon that he went over as a doctor visiting the countryside and saw starving children. He went back and told Lenin about that and he said tears came to Lenin's eyes. Hammer went on to say that the Soviets have abided by SALT I and turned to Kissinger and asked, "Isn't that right Henry?" Henry Kissinger said, "Yes that's right, the Soviets have kept SALT I." Armand Hammer's whole pitch was a blurring of distinctions, a promotion of the idea of convergence, that we have all these common interests and common investments that multinational corporations and banking interests like Chase Manhattan have vested interests in both countries. David Rockefeller has 175 banks overseas and he is going to protect those investments if at all possible. Rockefeller bragged he opened the first bank in Moscow and he had the first bank in Peking.

Would a nuclear freeze and a ban on testing, development, and deployment be verifiable? Only in the West! The Soviet Union is a closed society. They have consistently refused to permit such verification in the past.

What would happen to the leaders and supporters of a ground zero or nuclear freeze movement in the Soviet Union? They would be arrested, imprisoned, or placed in Soviet psychiatric hospitals for mental rehabilitation. A grassroots movement such as we have in America would be crushed before it began.

Why wasn't nuclear freeze an issue when the United States had a clear nuclear superiority? The Soviets wouldn't back that ploy until they had a decisive nuclear military edge. Now it's full steam ahead and KGB agents have been at the forefront of the European nuclear freeze movement. They even funded the peace rallies. The Soviets are concerned that America will neutralize their newfound superiority with the defense build-up under President Reagan.

> "Communism is a failure. If the West would stop supplying food, money, and technology, their war machine would grind to a screeching halt."

Upon what basis can a nation like America deal with the Soviet Union? Only military, industrial, economic, and spiritual strength and a desire to stand for freedom against all tyranny of the slave state can defeat them.

Maybe you've asked yourself the question, why has the Soviet Union built such a massive, military machine? What is their goal? Nikita Khrushchev, the former Soviet Premier said it in four words, "we will bury you." Now in the face of such a massive Soviet military build up, can we conclude that only war would prevent them from their goal? Absolutely not! Communism is a failure. If the West would stop supplying food, money, and technology, their war machine would grind to a screeching halt.

The people of the oppressed nations of the world are restless. They have seen the failure of communism. They know it first hand. If we did that, if we had total economic sanctions upon these Soviet Bloc nations of the world, we could bring that house of cards crumbling to the earth in no time.

Is a conventional military force outmoded in the face of nuclear power? No. Although the Soviets have nuclear power, they used conventional and chemical weapons in Afghanistan including yellow rain, a very deadly form of chemical warfare. However, the Soviets do not hesitate to use the threat of thermonuclear blackmail; they don't even have to state it. It's implicit in their strength and power.

What can be done about the threat of a nuclear holocaust? We can institute a massive economic boycott, cutting off the Soviet war-making capability, grinding that machine to a halt. We can stop our bankers from providing low-interest loans, many of which are guaranteed by American taxpayers. Doesn't it bother you that we are picking up the tab for those cancelled loans? It bothers me. We can crack down on the flood of KGB agents who weaken our free press with disinformation. Soviet agents steal or borrow sophisticated technology to use against us. Let's end this vicious cycle of being forced to spend billions of dollars developing newer and more sophisticated technology to counter the sabotage of our own national defense. We can back President Reagan in his urging and his plea for defense buildup and we can also build an antinuclear military ballistic missile system to nullify their threat. It was Aleksandr Solzhenitsyn who said Communism is unregenerate; it will always present a danger to mankind. It's like an infection in the world's organism. It may lie dormant but it will inevitably attack with a crippling disease.

China, Our Next Threat

In expectation of World War III, the West again seeks cover and finds Communist China as an ally. This is another betrayal, not only of Taiwan but of the entire oppressed Chinese people. Moreover it is a sad, mad, suicidal policy having supplied billion-strong China with American arms. The West will defeat the USSR, but thereafter no force on earth will restrain Communist China from World Communism. Solzhenitsyn goes on to say, "Communism stops only when it encounters a wall even if it is only a wall of resolve. The West cannot avoid erecting such a wall in what is already an hour of extremity." Meanwhile, however, twenty possible allies have fallen to Communism since World War II. Western technology has helped develop the terrifying military power of the Communist world. The wall will have to be erected with what strength remains. The present generations of westerners will have to make a stand on the road from which its predecessors have so thoughtlessly retreated for the last sixty years.

The Flame of Freedom

Solzhenitsyn is a true prophet. He does not gild the lily; he does not sugarcoat the truth. The hour is late; the time to act is urgent. The example has been set by every fiber of freedom, by every friend of freedom around this world, particularly the Poles and the Afghans at the present time. They have set that flame, that spark of freedom, which I hope will ignite the fire of freedom throughout the world. For peace without freedom, without truth, without justice, without honor, is no peace at all but the slow death of the human spirit and all that is creative and real.

> "There will always be a glow within us and what is that glow? It's the flame of freedom…the fire that burns in the heart of everyone who believes in freedom and who is opposed to tyranny."
>
> —Lech Walesa[6]

Lech Walesa says, "There will always be a glow within us and what is that glow? It's the flame of freedom. What is that flame of freedom? It's the fire that burns in the heart of everyone who believes in freedom and who is opposed to tyranny of the slavery of the Communist system."

We're a handful here this morning, but believe me right here in Los Angeles this can be the spot where a handful of dedicated freedom fighters can ignite that spark of freedom to sweep across America, to awaken our sleeping American brothers to the cause of freedom and to the nature of the threat.

I am going to give you the word that the Poles have given us because it spells it all out. Solzhenitsyn was right when he said that it's a collision of the oppressed people of the world with the American people of the West that is going to be the answer. The decisive force is the freedom fighters of East and West linking arms in that magnificent word given meaning by our gallant friends, Solidarność, Solidarity, Union. We are one in the flame of liberty. The flame of liberty is that fire that will unite the hearts of the American people to once more stand up for freedom even as our forefathers did.

Let me leave with you the words of a very great patriot, Thomas Jefferson. He said, "I have sworn on the altar of almighty God eternal hostility to every form of tyranny over the minds of men." To ensure that victory you and I must band together in a collision, a mighty collision of freedom. We are one; we are one. We are one in the flame of liberty. Thank you.

---

[6] Lech Walesa was the leader of Poland's Solidarity (Solidarność), the Soviet bloc's first independent trade union. Walesa, a charismatic yet humble man, was a devout Catholic and a key player in contributing to the fall of Polish communist regime. Walesa won the Nobel Peace Prize in 1983, and served as President of Poland after the fall of the communist regime in 1990 until 1995.

America is the I AM Race: The Flame of Freedom Speaks, July 4, 1980

Delivered by Rev. Gene Vosseler at Swan Lake, Camelot in Malibu, California

> *Editor's Note: This freedom message, is as relevant in many ways today as it was the day it was given. Gene discusses the history of freedom of America and the I AM race as well as many of the threats to our liberty we still experience today.*

The subject of my lecture is "America the I AM Race: The Flame of Freedom Speaks." Most of us have had an awareness that America is indeed a unique nation—a noble experiment in the history of civilization, the history of cultures—of diverse ethnic, cultural, and racial backgrounds, and a pluralistic society; and yet, despite these differences, we have managed somehow to forge a great national identity.

Despite inept and compromising leadership of our nation, despite the lethargy and the slumbering complacency of many of the American people, we still have a land richly blessed with the virtues of God's blessing and love. We know that the blazing fire of freedom can quicken and awaken in the hearts and souls of all the true lovers of God, the true lovers of light, and the true lovers of freedom. This spark can then be kindled into a blazing fire that will sweep away all ignorance, all miasma, and all illusion.

America is the I AM Race. We have a cosmic destiny. The very word America itself has contained within it, I AM Race. Our national identity is based on the fact that we are the children of the sun, we are the sons and daughters of God, and the crown of God's blessing rests upon us as long as we are obedient to God's most perfect will and God's most perfect laws. America, home of the brave and home of the free, can be a springboard for a great revolution in higher consciousness as we, the children of the light, march under the banner of the ascended masters, our beloved Mother of the Flame and our beloved Saint Germain.

It's in this context that I wish to share with you the flame of freedom, the fiery flame that burns within my heart and, as I know, burns within your hearts as well. I thank God that we are all here at the right place, at the right time, under the mantle of the Great White Brotherhood.

We have waited, yeah; we have waited for lo thousands of years for these days, for these moments, and for these hours to roll back the darkness of the fallen ones, to challenge the darkness and evil of their ways, those exploiters, those spoilers, those destroyers, and those perverters of life. And by the power of love, and only love, to expose the unreality, not only of our own carnal minds, but to realize the Christ mind where we will realize our victory as being of The Lord Our Righteousness.

God Intends Man to Be Free

God intends man to be free. God intends man to be free to love, to create, to build a world of beauty and truth, to become the full expression of the Christic light, of that Buddhic awareness and finally to realize our glorious ascension in the light. To make known to all men that they can become the Christ, that they can be free, not only in their souls, but free to create a society where all men can stand tall and erect with dignity that befits the sons and daughters of God.

And so I am grateful this day. I am grateful to the hosts of the Lord, the great saints robed in white, to beloved Kuthumi, Archangels Michael and Gabriel, Mother Mary and Jesus, Morya and Saint Germain, for the privilege of speaking to you on this great day which we dedicate in our hearts to the blazing flame of our beloved Saint Germain and the Mother.

The Great Betrayal of America

There are three areas that I would like to cover with you in my message today. I would like to speak briefly of our freedom heritage as Americans. I would like to talk a little about the betrayal of America, the great betrayal of America by the power elite. Then I would like to issue a call to action, a call to wake up America.

My message is directed to all those who can read the handwriting on the wall, who believe that there is hope, that we can have the victory, that we can defeat the forces of tyranny and the mechanistic concept that the Great Divine Director speaks about that would reduce life to the level of the robot creation, to clones, to another *Animal Farm* or to Huxley's *Brave New World.* Big Brother in *1984* may be just around the corner, but the fallen ones have not bargained for the mighty Lady with the Lamp and the children of the Sun, who have learned how to use the power of the spoken Word to invoke the light, to roll back every bit of darkness that rests on this planetary body and bring in that great golden age under our beloved Saint Germain.

And so we know that as we are walking hand in hand, arm in arm, it will make this planet a mighty orb of crystal fire where the light of God will descend and where the ascended masters will step through the veil and once again we will talk with them in the flame, in the love that unites us and makes us one in the Father-Mother God. And so today we pledge to our beloved Sanat Kumara the full power of our lifestreams and by the power and radiance of the Holy Spirit we pledge the victory, the victory of the light for the age of Aquarius. We consecrate our minds, our hearts, our bodies, our souls to that victory and we willingly lay all on the altar of the Great White Brotherhood and our beloved Mother and our beloved Lanello.

One of the fascinating things about the teachings of the masters is that when you are reading other books you come across all sorts of verification, whether it be books of science, literature, or archeology, you find the verification of the teachings of the ascended masters. And it's always a beautiful experience to have that. We all know, for example, we read and traced the history of the fallen ones in the book *The Twelfth Planet*. Those of us who have seen *Star Wars* and *The Empire Strikes Back* know that it is a portrayal of Armageddon, the battle between absolute evil and absolute light and goodness.[7]

---

[7] To learn more about the ascended masters, please see *The Masters and Their Retreats*, by Mark L. and Elizabeth Clare Prophet (Gardiner, Mont.: Summit University Press, 2003).

The Twelfth Planet, by Zecharia Sitchin, discusses the Nephilim, referred to also as "giants" in the book of Genisis, their arrival on planet Earth and their co-mingling with the daughters of men. The Nephilim are also considered by many to be the original fallen angels who fell with Lucifer, and who had superhuman powers but were wicked. Their wickedness earned them the wrath of God and was thought to cause the Great Flood. In *Fallen Angels and the Origins of Evil,* Elizabeth Clare Prophet goes further in discussing what fallen angels first incarnated in human bodies and the proceeding primordial drama of Good and Evil. She also examines the controversy surrounding the *Book of Enoch,* a text cherished by the Essenes, early Jews, and Christians, but later condemned by rabbis and Church Fathers and ultimately banned. *Fallen Angels and the Origins of Evil* is available through The Summit Lighthouse, www.tsl.org.

Columbus, a Man of Destiny

In a very recent book entitled *Light and the Glory* by Yale graduates, Peter Marshall, son of the late, great Peter Marshall, who was a chaplain of the United States Senate, and his colleague David Manuel, the authors researched very carefully a number of old extinct documents. One of documents contained a hitherto unpublished record of Columbus and a statement that he made. Most of us from our history books learned the lesson, or thought we learned the lesson: the discovery of America was a mistake, that actually Columbus was looking for a trade route to the Indies. And that's been taught in our history books all through the ages. But let me give you a quote from the voyages of Christopher Columbus. These are the words of Christopher Columbus who, as we all know, was embodied at that time; he is none other than our beloved Saint Germain who had the destiny and the fire to discover this land.

> *No one would fear to undertake any task in the name of our savior if it is a just one and if the intention is purely for his holy service. The working out of all things has been assigned to each person by our Lord but it all happens according to his sovereign will even though He gives advice. He lacks nothing that it is in the power of men to give him. Oh what a gracious Lord that desires that people should perform for him those things for which he holds himself responsible, day and night, moment by moment, everyone should express their most devoted gratitude to him.*

Columbus was a man of faith, a man of vision, a man with a sense of destiny. He felt that his life's mission was a direct hand from God and the Holy Spirit guided him every league of the way. The hand of God was placed on this country early in its inception and it was sealed in the light by beloved Saint Germain from the very beginning. It's in that flame that you and I celebrate this day, the Fourth of July, the flame of freedom when the great Declaration of Independence was signed in Independence Hall in Philadelphia.

That sense of God destiny and God freedom is firmly anchored in the hearts in all the true sons and daughters of God, for all those who love freedom, and for all those who love the light. When you look at the lives of those early individuals, those early patriots, our founding fathers, they had a keen sense of not only their identity but a keen sense of what they were doing. John Adams, our second president, penned these words to his wife, Abigail, several hours after the signing of the Declaration of Independence: "I am well aware of the toil and the blood and the treasure that it cost us to maintain this declaration to support and defend these states, yet through all the gloom I see rays of ravishing light and glory. I see the end is worth more than all of the means."

Freedom is Our Heritage

Our heritage illustrates that great drive for freedom for new frontiers that actually founded this country, America. The early pilgrims and forefathers, for the most part, were fleeing from religious and secular oppression so they founded this noble experiment, the thirteen states indicative of the twelve tribes and the Christ at the center. They had a vision of a new life, a life where men could be free, where children could be raised in the sun and the light of freedom without fear. With that vision this country was founded.

These early colonists were also faced with a threat and the tyranny of King George III, including excessive taxes on sugar, basic commodities, and other necessities of life and revenue stamps. We were people who were subjected to taxation without representation and this fueled the fires of rebellion against the tyranny of George the III—a rebellion that culminated in the Boston Tea Party. I was on a stumping tour through the northeast and had the opportunity to stand in the Old South Meeting House[8] where Samuel Adams stood forth and addressed the souls of light. When he dropped his arm, all the individuals jumped off the balcony dressed as Mohawk Indians and made their way quickly to the Boston harbor, where they had a tea party of a little different nature than the kind we are ordinarily accustomed to. They plunged all of that tea into the sea as an act of defiance and rebellion, as an act of freedom. Later, of course, we had fighting breaking out in Lexington and Concord and Paul Revere made his famous ride warning the colonialists that "The British are coming."

The thirteen colonies blessed by God forged a union, a union to fight a common enemy. George Washington, John Adams, Ben Franklin, and the list of those great patriots, many of whom have become immortal, all of them pledged their lives, their fortune, and their sacred honor.

They were all willing to embrace the fight in the battle for freedom. Now we know that if they had failed, their fate would have been at the end of a hangman's noose.

After a bitter struggle that included starvation, severe cold, disease, and all sorts of hardship and deprivation at Valley Forge, the American cause culminated in victory. We remember the scene of our beloved Godfrey, who at that time was embodied as George Washington, kneeling in prayer in Valley Forge. We also remember that when he was in his tent he had the vision given to him by the hosts of light, of three great tests of American life, American culture, and American freedom. Our founding fathers were men of God. They were inspired; they hammered out a divinely inspired document of the Constitution and the Bill of Rights. It's a beautiful model of checks and balances, and if we truly followed it closely we

---

[8] Built in 1729, the Old South Meeting House was the largest building in colonial Boston and provided a stage for the American Revolution.

would have a model government today. Unfortunately, that is not the case as certain branches of the government, the judicial branch for example has usurped certain powers of the executive and legislative branch. And, of course, the executive branch usurped a considerable amount of powers only delegated to Congress. And Congress sits back with its 535 members, quite relaxed and willing to give the power away to the judicial and executive branches. Today we no longer have the checks and balances that the early patriots envisioned for this country.

This country was built on four sacred freedoms: freedom of speech, freedom of worship, freedom of assembly, and freedom of the press. But now I would like to take you, in a flash, back in time. As we heard last night during the beautiful dictation and message concerning Philadelphia and the new teaching center located there, I would like to take you back to July 4, 1776, to the signing of the Declaration of Independence in Independence Hall. On that day, in the Old State House in Philadelphia, a group of patriotic men were gathered together for the solemn purpose of signing the Declaration of Independence, a bold statement that declared that the entire thirteen American colonies were now separate and independent from England.

'Sign That Document!'

From the letters of Thomas Jefferson, which are preserved in the Library of Congress, there has been gathered considerable data concerning that portentous event. In reconstructing the scene it is well to remember that if the Revolutionary War had failed they would have been signing their death warrants for high treason. It's also well to remember that these delegates represented thirteen different states, thirteen different colonies, and they were not all of one mind concerning the policies which would dominate the new nation. There were several speeches. In the balconies, patriotic citizens crowded all available space and listened attentively to the proceedings. Jefferson expressed with great vigor. John Adams, of Boston, spoke with great strength and clarity. Benjamin Franklin, quiet and calm, spoke his mind with will and chosen words and the delegates hovered between sympathy and uncertainty. When you stop and think about it, when you consider the contemplation of your life and the lives of countless others, life gets pretty sweet. That's what these men were beginning to wrestle with. Should they or should they not sign? Should they lay it all on the line? In fact, there was a period of considerable uncertainty as to whether they would sign the document or not. According to Jefferson it was very late in the afternoon before the delegates gathered their courage to actually deal with the signatures. The talk was about axes, gibbets, and the hangman's noose when suddenly a strong, bold voice sounded. It was an old man who gave a passionate speech and thundered out, "Sign that document!"

That is the flame of freedom. We recognize that flame and the voice of the master, of our beloved Saint Germain who was that unknown speaker. I definitely know he deserves a big hand. We certainly take inspiration from our early founding fathers who had the courage to put it all on the line. It's going to take all of us to put it all on the line for freedom, for America, for the teachings of the masters to pull off the victory of the light. We can follow in the footsteps of our founding fathers and the great masters, our elder brothers and sisters who walked the earth, and we will have that victory. The fact that our early forefathers, with thirteen small, divided, struggling colonies, were able to stand up against the might of imperial Great Britain at that time is a tribute to their God determination and to the reality that God had a mission and a plan for America.

Unity in Freedom

Now this union of states based on the principle of unity in freedom was tested to the utmost in the mid 1800s. It seems rather incongruous that a nation based on freedom and equality should be divided over the issue of slavery. Slaves were used primarily for economic reasons, but it became apparent to certain pioneers of the spirit that there was something incongruous about 25 percent of the nation walking the earth as slaves. And so God raised up a prophet and a statesman in the person of Abraham Lincoln who challenged the evil of slavery in his Emancipation Proclamation. Our nation was split down the middle and the test would be as a nation united we'd stand or if divided we'd be conquered like many other nations which have experimented with freedom in the past. Thus the battle for preservation of freedom and unity was fought and won. Our beloved Abraham Lincoln was vilified and cut down by an assassin's bullet, but the union had been saved. America had survived its greatest test. Lincoln, the patriot, reflects the true love of freedom and also possesses the spirit of reconciliation. If he had lived, our country would not have experienced the reconstruction era, the era of the carpetbaggers and the various humiliations imposed upon the South by certain vengeful politicians in the North.

The next hundred years in America saw the expansion of America to the west, the Industrial Revolution and the age of science and technology. It was a tremendous acceleration in advancement as we moved from horse and buggy to jet planes to traveling at supersonic speed. We have now placed a man on the moon and we've had revolutions in communications and technology. America as a nation has scientifically come of age. Unfortunately we cannot say as much in the realm of the spirit.

"We Will Pay Any Price"

Then there was that shining light appearing as John F. Kennedy. I remember the day of Kennedy's assassination; I was in Hawaii at the time. I also remember the tears that flowed without ceasing as I contemplated this great lifestream and his contribution to America and to freedom. He breathed the message of hope, light, and freedom in a world that was tired and worn out with doctrinal ideas. I remember the feelings in my soul, and I remember going back to the Lutheran church, where I was a minister at that time, and preaching a four-page eulogy sermon on John F. Kennedy, what he meant to this nation and to this people and to this land. The courage of vision, the ability to transcend secular or religious prejudice, the courage of his convictions, and the ability to see far into the future with God vision and God determination. This shining meteor across the stage of history flashed only too quickly to the world weary of aging politicians. He was truly a breath of fresh air.

He was a warrior in World War II. His PT boat was sunk and although he was badly injured he swam all night, towing one of his injured crewmember's mates along to safety. In the face of the bluster and the bullying of the Soviet Union during the Cuban Missile Crisis, his nerve never faltered and the Communists were forced back. What a tragedy, what a loss for this nation when he was gunned down by assassins' bullets in Dallas. John F. Kennedy is a modern example of what we look for in our leaders—his freedom flame, his vision, his courage, his compassion, his patriotism, and his love of freedom. He lived and walked in the tradition of our founding fathers, the true patriots of America. His life to me was immortalized in a never forgotten inaugural address:

Let the word go forth from this time and place to friend and foe alike that the torch has been passed to a new generation of Americans born in a century tempered by war, disciplined by a hard and bitter peace, proud of our ancient heritage and unwilling to permit the slow undoing of those human rights to which this nation has always been committed. Let every nation know whether it wishes us well or ill that we will pay any price, bare any burden, meet any hardship, support any friend, oppose any foe, to assure the survival and the success of liberty.

That is our freedom heritage as Americans. That is the substance of our forefathers.

Today's Challenges are Greater Than Our Forefathers'

Today, we face even greater challenges than they faced. What about America today? What is the state of our leadership? How about President Carter? What is the state of our defense, our government, and our economy? What is the condition of the soul of America this day? What are the prospects for the 1980s? We find the great cosmic keys given to us in Mother's manifestos, these great statements of eternal principles that will literally set this world afire if we get the message out to the people. The message of the eternal God is revealed in our beloved messenger's words that come from the hosts of light. They are immortal, they are timeless, they are powerful, and they cut to the very soul of man's being. It's up to us as the children of the light, the sons and daughters of God to run with this message across this land to confront the sons and daughter of light caught up in the rock and drug culture, psychic phenomenon, or any of the other basic world trips that the world has to offer.

I remember when I first picked up the book, *The Prophecy for the 1980s: The Handwriting on the Wall* by Elizabeth Clare

Prophet, the joy and the elation that I felt that now we are going to take it to them. Now we are going to challenge the fallen ones in all of their evil and nefarious ways. Now we are going to challenge the darkness, that now we are going to bring forth the light of freedom that will raise this country to its true God-destiny, its freedom, and its victory in the light.

I remember reading the introduction to that book, done succinctly and concisely, and I thought it was great. I would like to draw a couple facts from that introduction. It talked about the 1980s and said a lot can happen in a few days or in a few months. President Carter placed an embargo on fifteen million tons of grain and high technology sales to the Soviet Union. The longshoremen expanded that administrative policy by refusing to load the 3.4 metric tons of U.S. corn that was already sold to the Soviet Union. Soviet tanks in Kabul, Afghanistan destroyed detente. The cold war returned with a vengeance. The threat of a hot war hung heavy in the air. The Carter Administration announced the U.S. boycott of the Moscow Olympics. And the Afghanistan crisis brought the greatest threat to world peace the world has known since World War II.

Pot, which once enjoyed a widespread reputation as a harmless intoxicant with –a –mistakenly bad reputation, suddenly came under fire. Angry parents and persistent scientists' research demonstrated that the weed, far from harmless, is dangerous; this made even *Time* magazine.

Inflation skyrocketed, recession played hide-and-seek with the economists, chilly discussions and the draft came back. Congress agreed with a no-longer-somnambulistic president that the nation had to spend more on defense or that the wild Soviet bear would be soon tampering with our oil lines in the Middle East. The events of the first few months in 1980 show that a common sense energy policy is desperately needed. Oil profits soared, gas prices followed suit, and the Middle East looked like the site of a future war.

The energy policy worsened. Our energy policy, as usual, was in shambles and was placed on the back burner. Thirty-five Moslem states issued a united condemnation of the Soviet invasion of Afghanistan. The Soviets turned a covetous eye toward Yugoslavia. The "brave new world" became less of a cliché and more of a possible reality as genetic engineering loomed as a major growth industry. Patents for genetic engineering were set up. The news of sperm banks surfaced once more and some of us saw the movie of Aldous Huxley's *Brave New World*, which after two years of being in the dark room and not being shown was suddenly and mysteriously brought forth before the face of the American public.

The pace of international terrorism picked up and started moving closer to home. U.S. Custom Service intercepted a letter alleged to be circulating among the Muslim community instructing the faithful of their duty for terrorist action in the event America took any military action to release the hostages in Iran. We recall the attempt to free the fifty hostages in Iran by military action failed dismally. American prestige and influence with its allies sank to a new low. France and Great Britain, our close allies, both decided to send teams to the Olympics and Moscow.

America and the Free World are in Deadly Peril

The 60s was a decade of revolution, the 70s, one of confusion, and the 80s, a decade of reckoning and destiny. The buried and seemingly unrelated events of the 80s are emerging rapidly. As we analyze the many seemingly unrelated events we see clearly the challenge of world tyranny to freedom. America and the free world are in deadly peril. The tide of totalitarian power is rising, seventeen nations taken up and seized in the last decade, fifty-seven nations swallowed up by the beast of the totalitarian state of World Communism since the inception of the revolution in 1917. There is an all-out assault on world freedom today, as well as religious liberty. We see freedom of religion under attack and how you and I respond will determine whether our children will live as slaves or free men.

But what is freedom? What is freedom? Freedom is a flame. It cannot be confined to the realm of politics, religion, or philosophy. It encompasses all. It burns as a mighty fire in your heart. It means that you can never accept any tyranny of any sort. Throughout the centuries men have discovered the truth that Jesus talked about, the truth that sets men free, the realization of their Christ identity, walking the path of initiation with the hosts of the Lord to their victory in the light. This flame of freedom is a blazing spirit of God. It compels man to oppose all tyranny of conscience, heart, and mind.

The lovers of freedom will damn a tyrant's lies to his face. The friend of freedom is a devotee of truth. He is armed with a crystal sword of truth. There is no compromise with dishonor. There is no compromise with entrenched evil. There is no breaking of bread or making of treaties with totalitarian states. Above all, the friend of freedom is not stupid nor is he calculating. He will not give arms, food, and technology to slave states that have threatened to bury him. The flame of freedom, then, is a patriotic fire. It burns in the hearts of all men with eternal principles, eternal values, and eternal truths. He believes in Armageddon, this patriot of freedom. He knows that we are in a struggle between light and darkness. He judges men and nations by their actions, not just by what they say. He knows that where there is freedom of speech, freedom of the press, freedom of assembly, freedom of religion there will be creativity, joy, beauty, and a free society. Where there are slave states and slaves of people, there is sterility, apathy, death, and a brutal crushing of the human spirit that produces the ant-hill society.

In this time of great peril, the call of Camelot and the call of the ascended masters is to wake up, to come alive, and to look at the threat that faces us today as we look at the great betrayal of America by the power elite. The American people, when the truth is revealed, when they realize how they've been betrayed and manipulated by the power elite, their fury will have a reckoning. The sons and daughters of God do not take to betrayal lightly. We have the betrayal of the American people by the power elite and the monopolistic capitalism linking arms hand-in-hand with the government.

We see all sorts of alliances and strange votes taking place and we know that they've been aided and abetted by the controlled media, controlled for the most part by the power elite. *The New York Times* and the *Los Angeles Times*—some of the greatest newspapers of our land—simply write and put down the line that is given by the men who control this country at the present time. We also have the picture of academia, where scholars in our university campuses sell the line of Socialism. They write the lines that the power elite want to have implemented in our government. They write the lines that you and I read in our newspapers. The brainwashing takes place at almost every level, whether on television, the radio, or in the mass media.

The tragic part of it is that most people in America continue to sleep. Caught up in the pleasure cult and the cult of materialism, they sleep the sleep of death, saying to themselves on some level, "Don't bother me with the facts." We have the escapism of the entertainment media that keeps people half drugged, half asleep not knowing what's going on and not knowing how freedom is being betrayed. It's a constant source of amazement to me that the world is on fire, freedom is threatened at every hand, and yet the American people sleep on.

Where are the prophets in religion? Where are the spokesmen of God in government? Where are the statesmen of God? When they rise up, if they rise up, it will be from the lightbearers, it will be from you. We need those statesmen in government; we need ministers of God who are not afraid, who are not currying the favor of their congregation, who do not preach sweetness and light when there is no sweetness and light and who do not say, "Peace, peace," like the false prophets of Jeremiah's time, "when there is no peace."

We've got to wake up! We've got to have a passion for freedom! We have to have a passion for God and a passion for life! Our day and our age are even lacking passion in their sins. Though it's unfortunate, but you look at it, it's a mediocre society where the line of mediocrity, the lowest common denominator is what is elevated to the heights of praise and the great heroes are the rock drug stars and superathletes. People look to the athletes for words of truth about what's going on in the world. You and I are amazed as to how our world can continue to sleep, knowing what we know and knowing what I am going to share with you in a few minutes about the true state of affairs.

Richard Wurmbrand, who spent eleven years in a Soviet concentration camp, has written a number of magnificent books. He described what took place in the secularized civil religion of Romania when Soviet Union took over:

> *In Romania when the Communist took over they convened a congress of all Christian bodies in their parliament building. Four thousand priests, pastors and ministers gathered to pay homage to their conquerors and to elect Joseph Stalin as honorary president. Almost without exception, the bishops and pastors declared that Christianity and Communism were fundamentally the same and could coexist. Deputy Bishop Rapp of the Romanian Lutheran Church*

began to teach in the theological seminary that God had given three revelations: one through Moses, one through Jesus and the third revelation through Stalin.

America has developed a secularized civil religion. That is why you do not hear the prophetic voice in America's churches today. Many of the ministers I know and have known personally have long since quieted their voice of truth and they have settled for security and easy sinecure and for advance in the religious establishment. As a result, we have a civil secularized religion today where the word of truth, the word of the Lord in the prophet tradition is lacking.

You and I, when we sit in the chapel of the Holy Grail and we hear the living flame of the Holy Spirit and it comes down and pours through our messenger, Elizabeth Clare Prophet, we know we hear the truth, we know we're in the light, we know because we feel the fire and the flame of the Holy Spirit as it flows through her being, illuminating the darkness of our own worlds with the light of the ascended masters' octaves. You will not hear that voice anywhere else; I guarantee it. Because we have a beloved messenger who stands on the point of hierarchy for the deliverance of the fire, the fire of truth, the fire of freedom, and the fire of the word of the living God that will exult all souls and catapult us into a golden age under Saint Germain.

We've finally come to the third and last point of what I speak, and I promise it's much shorter than the other two. It is the theme of our survival conference, *America—Wake Up and Survive.* There are two prophets. Mother, I see two great prophets on the scene in contemporary history now. I see our beloved messenger, Elizabeth Clare Prophet, as a leading prophet of our time. In the tradition of the Old Testament prophet, she speaks with the force of the Lord when she says, "Thus saith the Lord;" you know the Lord is speaking through her.

Solzhenitsyn: The Fight for Our Planet... is a Fight of Cosmic Proportions

There is another great prophet of our time; actually beloved Lanello, beloved Mark, loves this man dearly. That man is Aleksandr Solzhenitsyn, who is a prophet to both East and West. Solzhenitsyn was a man who got his education the hard way with the hard knocks in the Soviet concentration camp at the gulag. I am about two-thirds through his latest book called *The Calf and the Oak,* a powerful, magnificent testimony to the power of the free-loving human spirit. If you get a chance pick it up, it's a story of his last ten years before he comes to America, before they released him. It's a game of cat and mouse that he plays with the KGB, after he's been released and how his publications were released in the West. You see this indomitable freedom fighter with a flaming love of God and his flaming love of freedom in every page you read. He went to deliver a speech at Harvard, the citadel of the Nephilim that cultivated the great businessmen, the great economists, and the great lawyers. Before Harvard he delivers a message of ringing freedom. He challenged the floppiness of American statecraft, the materialism of our age, our loss of nerve, and the deep sleep in America. His truth is a word of truth that stings and it's a little unpalatable in certain circles, but it is the living truth for our age:

> *A decline in courage may be the most striking feature which an outside observer notices in the West in our days. The Western world has lost its civil courage, both as a whole and separately in each country, in each government, in each political party and of course the United Nations. Such a decline in courage is particularly noticed among the ruling groups and the intellectual elite causing the impression of the loss of courage by the entire society.*
>
> *From the ancient times the decline in courage has been*

considered to be the beginning of the end. But the fight for our planet, physical and spiritual, is a fight of cosmic proportions (Solzhenitsyn knew about Armageddon), not a vague matter of the future. It is already started, the forces of evil have begun their fight, their decisive defensive, and you can feel the pressure. Yet your screens and your publications are full of prescribed smiles and raised glasses. What is all the joy about? Very well-known representatives of society, such as George Kennan (who used to be our ambassador to the Soviet Union), say: "We cannot apply moral criteria to politics." What criteria do you apply then? Expediency? Cowardice? Evil? Lack of integrity? Compromise with the dark forces? If you cannot set moral criteria to politics what may I ask may you set as criteria to politics? Thus we mix good and evil, right and wrong, and we make space for the absolute triumphant of absolute evil in the world. On the contrary, only moral criteria can help the West against Communism's well-planned world strategy. There are no other criteria. Practical or occasional considerations of any kind will be inevitably swept away by strategy. After a certain level of the problem has been reached, legalistic thinking produces paralysis. It prevents one from seeing the size and meaning of events.

And yet no weapons, no matter how powerful, can help the West until it can overcome its loss of willpower. In a state of psychological weakness weapons become a burden for the capitulating side. To defend oneself one must also be ready to die. There is little readiness in this society, raised in the cult of material well-being. Nothing is left then but concessions, attempts to gain time, and betrayal.

That is telling it like it is from a true prophet. It's time, time for the American people to wake up out of their slumbering sleep, time to recapture that love of freedom and to challenge all tyranny and to know that the power elite are paper tigers. When you expose them you will find there is no core, no substance, only darkness because light is real. Light is eternal. They have little or no light. When we invoke the dynamic decrees of the power of Almighty God and we bring in the light of beloved Mighty Astrea and we call to beloved El Morya for the Mercury diamond-shining mind of God, you know that nothing that is of the darkness and nothing that is unreal can stand up to the reality of Almighty God and the hosts of the Lord and our beloved messenger, Elizabeth Clare Prophet.

It's Up to You and Me

My friends, it's you and I. It's going to be up to us to take it on. We can't expect Mother to do it all. God bless her, she's got such courage. God bless her lifestream. She stands on the line of the clock in the true tradition of the prophets of the Lord and I am always amazed. I am amazed and yet I am not amazed. Her lifestream has been a lifestream of beauty down through the ages, a complete dedication and love of God. With our beloved Lanello, hand-in-hand they walk through the streams of history and they've guided nations and the destinies of people and they have always been faithful to the light. In the final analysis their commitment is to the light.

It's going to be up to you and me. It's going to be up to us to take on the world, to take on the fallen ones, to challenge the rock drug culture, to do the exposures. It's going to be up to us to challenge the evil of abortion, the slaughtering of the holy innocents. It's going to be up to us without fear of favor, without compromise, to give the pure undiluted truth. We don't have time to cushion the message. We don't have time to play games. We don't have time to compromise the word. It's got to be straight. With Pallas Athena's crystal sword of truth, with her helmet of crystal and with her shield of crystal, we can tackle the fallen ones and bring them to their knees under the light of the living God.

This talk will not be complete without referring to Saint Germain. Mother said in a Freedom Class in Higher Consciousness in June 30, 1976:

> *Saint Germain came to give a dictation on March 7, 1976 with great concern lest America drop the torch of freedom. This was 1976, the time of our two-hundred-year bicentennial celebration. I remember a day and I will never forget this. I was with Mark when he was with us in his office in Colorado Springs. He was seated at his desk and I was at his side and Saint Germain entered the room with a purity of freedom, with a light and a determination and energy for the defense of America as the Mother Flame. He was speaking about the tremendous sale of grain and technology and computers and science to the Soviet Union, which in turn would be used against America. And with a thrust of his fist and a mighty will he said, "These resources were not intended to be exported, they were not intended to be given away to the enemy." I saw an ascended master, the fury in the defense of freedom, and I saw him looking for individuals with whom he could work. I saw him helpless because the issues were not clearly drawn and where would he go, where would he turn the tide of this insanity of preserving the enemy.*
>
> *If some of you do not know history I can assure you that America's been the sustaining force of the Russian revolution since its inception. We provide the personnel, the money, the funds, the backing, the food, and the supply. When at any point the entire revolution, the subsequent five-year plan would have collapsed without the aid of the United States. This is an amazing fact of history but I would not tell it to you if I have not researched it again and again because this*

is what has concerned me in this life. What to do about the world from the standpoint of the centuries, not a few years of enjoying life and leaving.

Saint Germain came that day and Mother saw him come again and again at conferences, dictating Pearls of Wisdom. He came again March 7, 1980, and he said:

The great barrier to the bringing in of the golden age in America and in Terra is human selfishness...

You must be the nation centered in selflessness, which gives forth the light, the protection, the perfection of the defense of freedom in every nation upon earth where freedom is threatened by the dragon of World Communism. Who are the fallen ones who have invaded the levels of government where decisions are being made to desert Angola, to desert this and that nation, to walk out and to leave behind the flame of freedom to be tended by those who know not how to tend the flame?

America, do you see what your leaders are doing to you? They are allowing this earth to be eaten up, bite by bite, by the fallen ones and the laggard generation. They are allowing the seed of the Serpent and of the dragon to be spawned. And their plot is to ring in the United States of America until every nation, great and small, is under World Communism and all of the peoples of the world are forced to march in the armies of the dragon.

And then they will march, and then their planes will fly and their bombs will be sent. And where will you be? Will you point the finger and say, "Our leaders have led us to this brink of destruction"? Will you blame your leaders, who are the blind, whom you already know are the blind? Heaven will not allow you to blame your leaders, for those who follow the blind leaders are themselves to blame.[9]

Our beloved Saint Germain lays it straight on the line. The responsibility is where?—with us because we know the truth. When you know the truth and you do not speak the truth, when you permit injustice to continue to reign, then we are responsible. In the flame of Saint Germain when he makes the call to Camelot, and the call to freedom, the true patriots will respond. They feel his flame; we feel his flame. We know he is calling us to do the job. He is counting on us to get it done. For that freedom flame is a fire that burns in our hearts, consuming all darkness, all ignorance, all fear, all doubt. As we challenge the forces in the battle of Armageddon for the souls of light, we bring the children home to the community of the Holy Spirit and to the mandala of the World Mother. That is our goal. That is our task. We willingly accept it. We hail you Saint Germain in your freedom flame as we walk in your light and in the joy of your presence and in your love this day.

This freedom cannot be denied. It's for all men; it's for all people to bring in a golden age of culture, of art, of literature. That is our task. That is our challenge. That's what we've been waiting for. We live in a time of a transition and change and we've made it to this point. God willing, we'll be true and faithful to the vow that we have given to the hosts of the Lord. We stand for the truth. We stand for the light. We would bring in the golden age and we would see that seventh root race incarnate and bring about the mastery and the victory of the light on this planetary body.

This freedom then is a blazing fire, which I hope is igniting our hearts this day as we feel the fire and the flame of Saint Germain and beloved Lanello. What is the answer to the mechanization of man and the mass consciousness? It's freedom! What is the answer to the dark forces? It's the light of

---

[9] Saint Germain, "The Meaning of Self-Sacrifice, Part 1," March 7, 1976, in *Pearls of Wisdom*, vol. 20, no. 48, (Gardiner, Mont.: The Summit Lighthouse, November 27, 1977) p. 232.

God that never fails and the mighty I AM Presence is that light. You and I are called now to accelerate our consciousness on the path of initiation, to quit our dillydallying, to quit tolerating our little indulgences, to get with it. You are on a mission. We are in war and this means that everyone, every soul, every son and daughter of God needs to be in a wartime basis with his or her discipline. Now is the time to forget some of those things that you think that you must do for your lifestream. Now is the time to commit your soul, your heart, your mind, your body to Saint Germain and to the hosts of the Lord. Now is the time to lay it on the line for the Masters and say, "Lord, here I am, use me." If we believe that then we will do it.

I can't conclude this without giving some words of Lanello. I've got to share Lanello. As many of you know I have a Buddha on my heart, it's a Lanello Buddha. I feel his love and his flame every day. He's the ever-present Guru and although I didn't know him in physical embodiment, I know his soul. I have just got to share this statement he made on freedom. Of course we know he was embodied as Longfellow and the true poetry and the true flame and his love of freedom comes through these words that he gave to us:

Freedom is more than a word. Freedom is more than an idea. Freedom is a spirit; it is a spirit which we must capture. It is our immortal birthright. It is a germinal seed. As we enshrine the germ of the seed of freedom within ourselves we shall assist it in being enshrined in the hearts of our fellow man. And so the seed shall sprout and grow and it shall flourish and it shall cover the earth and tyranny shall be out stamped. As Jefferson said long ago, "I have sworn on the altar of Almighty God, eternal hostility to every form of tyranny over the mind of men." Freedom is a flame. It cannot be confined to the realms of politics, religion, or philosophy; it encompasses all. Burning within the heart of men and nations can be found the unquenchable fires of freedom. Throughout the centuries seekers have discovered the way of freedom, the freedom of which Jesus spoke when he said, ye shall know the truth and the truth shall make you free.

We the children of the light gather here to answer the call of Camelot and our beloved Mother, march in the flame of Lanello and Saint Germain and the hosts of the Lord on to the victory in the light. We march in the name and under the banner of Almighty God to challenge the darkness of this planet.

Now I'd like to sum up. Mother, I've got a poem that's for you. It's called "The Call of Camelot."

The Call of Camelot, Jewel of Light

Oh Camelot, Jewel of Light
Born from the heart of God
Light up the darkness of the night
Bring all neath heaven's rod

Blaze o blaze Excalibur thou torch of living flame
Recall to all the sons of light their Mighty I AM name
Sing of Merlin freedom's friend and of his love for all
Exalt his gift, the violet flame that transmutes human pall

Hail, Guru Ma, sweet Guinevere
Thou great and noble beauty,
Supreme light of the mother ray
God flame of holy duty

Oh sing ye sons of Lancelot
Staunch knight and friend of old
Who gave his life in sacred trust
And held his vision bold

That earth would claim her final goal
Of freedom star to be
Where man would live as pure God-soul
Throughout eternity

Sing of Arthur, O Morya dear
Your perfect love casts out all fear
We march to battle in your flame
Linked arm in arm with Saint Germain,

With Lancelot and Mother too
For we have cosmic work to do
Challenging evil and invoking the light
Confronting the fallen and putting foe to flight

Piercing the gloom of the energy veil
Quickening men's hearts to search for the grail
For the God star of light is buried within
Ever triumphant in its battle with sin

O, Camelot, gem of white fire beauty
Awaken man to his sacred duty
To be a fiery orb of love
A source of light, a snow white dove

That draw the knights and ladies home
Into the sacred fires of Om.
Where soul fulfills its cosmic plan
Reunion with its great I AM

At last the crown, love's victory won
God flame eternal, a bright new sun.

Praise the Presence, thank you Mother.

(Mother commented immediately following the lecture.)

Mother: I'm telling Gene, that was a talk worthy of Lanello.

Gene: I felt his flame.

Mother: Gene speaks from his heart, and that is the

essential quality of Mark as we knew him, speaking from his heart, going direct to the heart of every issue, human and divine.

We are grateful to the Holy Spirit and the hosts of the Lord encamped with us. We are grateful that Almighty God has given us this land and this freedom to speak our minds and hearts and to yet rally. I am grateful for your precious words to me and your precious love to me. Truly only God is worthy of such love and devotion, and I only pray that we together may continue to be somewhat a transparency for his love. I would tell you that the burden of the Lord that he has placed upon me for his people, as I wear the mantle of the prophet and the shepherd, is the very intense concern for the survival of souls and of the physical body, our persons.

We have come together on the basis and foundation of the very message that Gene has brought forth. We have come for more; we've come for "The Call of Camelot" to determine what we will do about these issues and these situations. Saint Germain has been speaking about them. He laid upon my heart to call his seminar following this conference "Save America and Survive!" It is what God has placed upon me for the protection and the shepherding of his people.

I have looked over this nation, I have seen you betrayed by your leaders who care not for your safety, your survival, your health, your bodies, your minds, or your souls. There is no defense of the children of God by the leaders of this country today and so I have seen the jeopardy, whether it's an absence of armed forces or defense of freedom or civil defense. Where will you go in this time of trouble prophesied by Daniel? And so, we need practical alternatives that we can pursue together at the same time that we are relentless in the saving of this nation.

This will be the subject of our seven-day seminar beginning

Monday morning. I invite all of you to attend as we commune together continuing through the week on what the Holy Spirit and Saint Germain have provided for us and for all people of God who will listen to the message, who will run with it, and who realize that we are in a perilous hour, personally, in our nation, and on a planetary scale.

"That was a talk worthy of Lanello."

—Mother

I believe the ascended masters have answers and I will give you those answers and lay them before you so that you can be responsible shepherds and leaders of your families and communities. I think the need is dire. I think the answers are here and we must bind together as one body, as the Goddess of Liberty has told us, in her Fourth of July message concluded just before midnight last night. She has told us we must survive together, we can survive together, and that now is the hour to do so.

Peace Through Strength: Countering the Nuclear Freeze Movement

A transcript of one of the many media interviews
PBS Television
The Merv Griffin Show with guest Gene Vosseler

Can the U.S. Trust the Russians? Californians for a Strong America, Summer 1982

GRIFFIN: We had Paul Newman on this show last week who was very articulate on a lot of things. Today we thought we'd invite a gentleman with an opposing viewpoint because it would be interesting. So would you welcome the director of Californians for a Strong America, E. Gene Vosseler? Gene, you've heard evidently some of the statements that Paul Newman made.

VOSSELER: That is correct Merv.

GRIFFIN: Then before we start can I just play you thirty seconds of a portion of his interview and then see what you have to say about it. OK, roll that tape. This is from last week.

NEWMAN: President Reagan has never said anything about not trusting the Russians because whether you have a freeze or whether you get into the discussion of arms reduction you will, in either case, still have to trust that the other side will comply. There's not been one peep out of the Defense Department, the Pentagon, or the White House that said, "Well the big stumbling block is that we don't trust the Russians because ultimately after we build up our arsenal and we get all these first strike preemptive delivery systems in [place] that then we will trust the Russians." [It] doesn't work that way. So the Administration [and] the Pentagon, ultimately ask that you do the same thing with the people in the freeze, that is instruct your treaties, that the history has been that the Soviets have complied as well as we have.

GRIFFIN: Now Paul claimed that the Russians would honor their treaties. Can they be trusted Gene?

VOSSELER: It's not really the Russians that can't be trusted. It's the Soviet leadership that can't be trusted. They have historically a record of violating and breaking their treaties. For example we listed thirty-five major violations of SALT I (Strategic Arms Limitations Treaty)[10] alone. Now those breaking of those particular treaties of SALT I was resolved simply by accepting the violation. That's what Paul Nitze, a U.S. member at the SALT talks said when he spoke in Geneva.

GRIFFIN: Did we violate…

VOSSELER: No, not that I know of.

GRIFFIN: …the treaties?

VOSSELER: I've never seen any recorded statement. I hear that broadside statement from Paul and I think he's misinformed. Because of the people I work with, the Poles, the Afghans, the Hungarians, the Vietnamese, and the Cubans,

---

[10] SALT I is the acronym for the Strategic Arms Limitation Treaty Agreement. SALT I was intended to freeze the number of strategic ballistic missile launchers at existing levels and provided for the addition of new submarine-launched ballistic missile (SLBM) launchers only after the same number of older intercontinental ballistic missile (ICBM) and SLBM launchers had been dismantled. One clause of the treaty required both countries to limit the sites protected by an anti-ballistic missile (ABM) system to one. The Soviet Union had deployed such an ABM system around Moscow in 1966 and the United States announced an ABM program to protect twelve ICBM sites in 1967. Critics claim that the Soviets never complied to the arms reductions and also point out the Soviets' extensive ABM and civil defense system. Leonid Brezhnev and Gerald Ford are signing joint communiqué on the SALT treaty in Vladivostok, November 23, 1974. SALT I paved the way for the signing of the Anti-Ballistic Missile Treaty on May 26, 1972, in Moscow by Richard Nixon and Leonid Brezhnev. These treaties helped "normalize" relations between the two countries while putting the United States in a competitive nuclear disadvantage.

they've got a different story. If you ask them whether you can trust the Soviet Union to keep a freeze, they will give a different message. The Afghan people have now been invaded by the Soviet Union. There was formerly a peace treaty signed for example with Afghanistan of non-aggression and so to actually sign a peace treaty or even a freeze statement is sure to be violated. It may be kept by us but it won't be kept by them. When you sign a peace treaty with the Soviets, it's like getting a white rose from the Mafia.

GRIFFIN: I cited to him Afghanistan and Poland—those two. And he sighted back to me our involvement in El Salvador.

VOSSELER: Well, there again, I don't know of any treaty violation in El Salvador. It's very interesting, the pro-freeze people are very strong in the criticism of America and very little criticism on the Soviet Union which in view of what's happening in the world, in view of the Soviets' expansionism and in view of their most massive military build-up, it's sort of incredible to me because here we have been more or less unilaterally freezing for the last ten or twelve years. We haven't been building up a lot of weaponry, we have actually cancelled the B-1 bomber, cancelled the Trident submarine, cancelled the neutron bomb, closed ICBM deployment, you know, production lines.

At the same time, the Soviets engage this massive military build up. They now actually have a first strike capability which could destroy our retaliatory power. Now they may never use it, but on the other hand, the temptation is to use it to bully and nuclear blackmail and intimidate and this is what we are dealing with right now. Soviet expansionism has been fed by the fact that we've been lingering under the abuse of détente and SALT I. We think that everything's going to be rosy and under the doctrine of MAD, Mutual Assured Destruction, we have simply let down our guard.

We've got to keep America strong in order to simply deal with the Soviet Union, which is a slave state, which has actually killed millions of its own citizens in the past, and if you are a deserter you can find yourself in prison very quickly or in a Soviet psychiatric hospital getting shot full of dope. So you know when you get right down to it, in their gut, the American people do not trust the Soviet leadership. I mean how can you trust a nation that made a deal with Hitler in World War II to split up Poland, which was one of the triggers of World War II? I mean the leadership of the Soviet Union would make Hitler, by comparison in terms of what they've done, look like a cream puff.[11]

GRIFFIN: Most of our nuclear warheads are in submarines.

VOSSELER: We have considerable numbers in submarines. You need to know, however, that the Soviets actually have a three to one [advantage] in nuclear-powered subs with long-range missile capability. That's a very interesting thing, they have seventy-four, we have thirty-one. We were actually allowed forty-four under SALT I but we've actually cut back to thirty-one. Most people don't even know, Merv, that we've scrapped half of our fleet in the last ten years. They now outgun us in combat ships two to one.

GRIFFIN: Would a nuclear freeze be desirable for the Soviet Union?

VOSSELER: That is my impression as why [Soviet leader Leonid] Brezhnev backs it. You know, Brezhnev is backing this freeze. And there's a very interesting article in the October

---

[11] Depending on the sources, the Soviet Union has killed a range of 25-60 million since its inception in 1917. This includes the seven million Ukrainians who were killed in the Soviet-led forced famine of 1932-1933 in the Ukraine, formerly the bread-basket of Europe.

Reader's Digest about the KGB connection and the magical war on peace. People simply need to dig deeper than the simplistic answers that are being given by various components. If we've learned one lesson out of WWII, you have to be strong when you are dealing with a world bully. And in that particular case we've weakened ourselves, we were not strong; WWII came upon us, we tried a freeze then with the Kellogg-Briand Pact.[12] We actually tried to cut back weaponry and that time was a time when Hitler built up strength.

GRIFFIN: Let me if I may now, Mr. Vosseler, another clip of Paul Newman talking about parity, equality with the Russians. Roll that clip would you?

NEWMAN: On a freeze you gotta' stop it now. If the Soviets have an advantage in one area that's fine, we have the same advantage in some other area. Freeze all of the advantages and disadvantages because we have basic parity and then you will allow the political process to arrive at the same place as the technological explosion.

VOSSELER: We've been freezing for the last ten or twelve years like I said before. Now the Soviets have the most massive military build-up known to man. And they now have this first-strike capability which can move in on our Triad, chances are we will never have to use it—if they get to the place where they can simply blackmail us under the table. But, for example, if it were to happen, we have 273 fighter interceptors, they have 2,600 fighter interceptors—defensive weapons we are talking about now. They've got 12,000 surface-to-air missiles, we have none. They have 64 intercontinental ballistic missiles launchers, we have none. What I am saying is that if they fire, there is nothing to stop it. Whereas our B-52s are twenty-five

---

[12] The Kellogg-Briand Pact, also known as the Pact of Paris, after the city where it was signed on August 27, 1928, was an international treaty "providing for the renunciation of war as an instrument of national policy."

years old, it would be like a turkey shoot. They would never even be able to penetrate that border. And they have developed these heavy-duty missiles that actually can bust our silos before our missiles can get out. They estimate 90 percent loss.

If you figure half of your subs and half of your ships are in port at any given time and then the president is faced with a decision. "What do I do? I've got this order coming from Moscow that they are threatening us with a preemptive first strike." Well maybe they just do it. Now actually Leonid Brezhnev said [the Soviets would] never do a first strike. But you know Brezhnev lies. That's a problem when dealing with Brezhnev. And two, three days later they do a total first strike; operationally practice one. Can anyone tell why, for example if you are concerned about the defense of your country, you would build missiles with four times the mega-tons that can destroy silos and missiles in silos if you are just concerned with defense. That's an offensive first-strike capability, whereas our Minutemen III, our ICBMs, do not have a silo-busting capability. So when you come right down to it we are extremely vulnerable.

GRIFFIN: What's the alternative then, Gene?

VOSSELER: I think the alternative, Merv, is very simply this, peace through strength. We've got to be strong. There's an anti-ballistic missile defense system that has been promoted by High Frontiers which has a beautiful prospect for the defense of America.

GRIFFIN: Is that where you put the platform up into space?

VOSSELER: Right.

GRIFFIN: Well, I asked Paul Newman about that because the General had been on who was advocating that.

VOSSELER: Daniel Graham.

GRIFFIN: And he said, yes, but how are you going to get the platform up in space? It's not easy to get things like that up into space.

VOSSELER: There's no problem launching those. We have the technology now to do it. And what they have is three or four hundred of these vehicle carriers and they launch these anti-ballistic missiles and they move at a distance or speed of three thousand feet per second. And they tune into sound and heat and actually hone right into those missiles. If the Soviets decide to do a preemptive first strike we can actually shoot those missiles down shortly after launch. This is a real hope for the future. If we freeze we will not even be able to continue to develop technology and we know the Soviet Union is going to continue to develop technology. If it's a freeze, we're freezing; they continue to work.

GRIFFIN: What about other ways we trade with the Soviet Union?

VOSSELER: I think they are dependent on us for a few things. This is really key. You know if we look back at it we could have collapsed that Soviet monster, because it is a monster that threatens the security and safety of the world. We could have sunk it a long time ago if we would have withdrawn our technology, our food, our grain—the things that we ship to them. There's just one little classic example of how we sabotage ourselves. It's a classic example. I am not going to mention the name of the company which provided them, with a sign off of Henry Kissinger, the instrument, a grinding machine that allowed them to MIRV[13] their missiles. It grinds the actual ball bearings down to one twenty-millionth of an inch tolerance. Now that company makes $20-25 million on the deal.

---

[13] Using a MIRV warhead, a multiple independently targetable reentry vehicle, the Soviets could use a single launched missile to strike several targets, or fewer targets redundantly. By contrast a unitary warhead is a single warhead on a single missile.

GRIFFIN: We sold them that equipment?

VOSSELER: We sold them that equipment; it's approved by our officials. OK, so what does this mean? It means that essentially the Soviets have the ability now to MIRV their missiles.

GRIFFIN: That's not really the name of the bomb?

VOSSELER: It means it allows them to shoot three independent warheads and target it on three different spots. So what we are dealing with is the fact that they have improved their accuracy of their missiles ten times. Now the United States is faced with building an MX missile with dense pack or what ever you want to call it. Let's face it, it is not that great an idea simply to defend against that. So we have actually sabotaged ourselves. We spend billions of dollars now to defend ourselves against the technology which was ours. And what they can't buy they steal. All you have to do is read the newspapers and you find out they love Silicon Valley. And you've always got a bunch of boys that are working…

GRIFFIN: They've caught them with the nature theft. Thank you Mr. Vosseler for your views. I appreciate it. Gene Vosseler, Director of Californians for a Strong America.

6. BAN THE SOVIETS COALITION

Editor's Note: Vosseler, along with several other freedom compatriots started this organization to urge defections among Soviet and Communist Eastern Bloc athletes during the 1984 Olympics in Los Angeles. As a result of their astounding media efforts, the Soviet Union and their satellite nations decided to boycott the Olympics. Attached are a couple of media interviews that were indicative of the successful media campaign.

At the time of this interview, CNN was the premiere cable news station and Crossfire was one of the most popular television talk shows. Begun in 1982 as a late-night political debate show, it moved to prime time because of its popularity.

Claiming the Victory on the Day the Soviets Announced their Olympic Boycott

Interview on CNN's *Crossfire* with hosts Tom Braden and Ron Nessen with guest Gene Vosseler, May 8, 1984

BRADEN: Welcome back to Crossfire. And welcome also to our guest Gene Vosseler speaking to us from Los Angeles. Mr. Vosseler is the head of The Ban the Soviets Coalition. You've been working to disorganize the Olympics while other people are trying to organize it. Are you happy about what happened today?

VOSSELER: Well, I don't think you can say we worked to disorganize the Olympics, we simply say that it's time for the world conscience to wake up. We are concerned about such things as national security, we are concerned about such things as human rights and the honoring of the Helsinki Accords and other documents that the Soviets are signatory to. It's very interesting that Peter Ueberroth who has made some very negative statements about our coalition of about 165 member organization groups as, "nutty, he wouldn't confer dignity on them." As if he has the power to confer or take away dignity from mainstream Americans and many individuals who actually fought against Soviet tanks in Hungary, who escaped the terror in Afghanistan and [who are] certainly not naive babes in the woods when it comes to dealing with the Soviet Union. We simply raise the banner of human rights that if the Soviets do come the right to defect will be protected.

We've raised the issue of the spy ship, the cruise ship, the so called "Love Boat," which according to Soviet defectors is in fact a spy ship with sophisticated surveillance devices.

BRADEN: Let me ask you this, Mr. Vosseler, let me bring this back to the specifics about the Olympic Games. Were you and your group going to help Soviet athletes to defect?

VOSSELER: Well, number one, you don't have to encourage Soviet athletes to defect. Obviously if they have an opportunity, some of these individuals have probably fantasized forty or fifty different ways to defect. We would definitely support their right to defect under the Helsinki accords and under UN protocol and for them not to be turned back to the Soviets.

BRADEN: Well, in their statement the Soviets called your group and similar related groups extremist organizations. Are you acting like an extremist organization in this case?

VOSSELER: No, I think basically we are very law-abiding people. We had a press conference and three of our men who spoke, one was an attorney, one was an architect, one was a physicist. These are mainstream Americans who are simply concerned about the Soviet Union.

BRADEN: ...What you are really doing is hurting American athletes.

VOSSELER: ... American athletes were hurt from the (U.S.) withdrawal of the (1980) games in Moscow. But what about the hurt of 269 individuals shot down in KAL 007, what about the hurt of genocide that is taking place right now in Afghanistan with over a million casualties and four to five million refugees. Now, what about their hurt!

BRADEN: What's your answer to the question that Mr.

Ueberroth gave that what you are really doing is hurting American athletics?

VOSSELER: Well, you know it's very interesting. American athletes were hurt from the [U.S.] withdrawal of the [1980] games in Moscow.[14] But what about the hurt of 269 individuals shot down in KAL 007, what about the hurt of genocide that is taking place right now in Afghanistan with over a million casualties and four to five million refugees. Now, what about their hurt! Mr. Ueberroth is very concerned...

NESSEN: What I've never understood is how disrupting the Olympics, or as Tom points out, ruining the opportunity of young athletes to compete, is going to solve any of these big international, foreign-affairs problems. Is this the right forum and are you going at it in a proportionate way?

VOSSELER: Well, let me respond to you, Mr. Nessen, this way. Mr. Ueberroth said we were a minor embarrassment; obviously the Soviet Union considers us a major embarrassment.

BRADEN: Do you think that you were really the cause that the Soviets pulled out or was it some larger international issue? Are they only using you as an excuse? Mr. Vosseler let me get back to that boat that you mentioned, the Soviets want to tie up a ship in Long Beach Harbor which is not very far from Los Angeles. What is really wrong with that? Do you really think that we are in danger of spying from that ship? That this vast country can't take care of some athletes on a boat in Long Beach Harbor?

---

[14] Following the December 1979 Soviet invasion of Afghanistan, President Jimmy Carter implemented sanctions against the Soviet Union including a grain embargo and the U.S. boycott of the Olympics in Moscow. Additionally, SALT II (Strategic Arms Limitation Treaty) did not get ratified.

VOSSELER: You know it's interesting that you ask that, Mr. Braden, in view of the fact that we can't take care of the technology drain from such spies as Harper and Bell recently. Obviously if you turn loose some two hundred people in each of twenty-five airport jets, that's approximately four to five thousand individuals who have access to airport jets and who have Olympic identity cards and give them free access to travel and if you have a spy ship, which according to a Soviet defector who's been on that ship, that top deck is for entertainment of those individuals who are not too particular of their company, but on the lower deck there are the most sophisticated surveillance electronic devices. And interestingly enough an official who will remain nameless and faceless who made the statement that for the U.S. to search that ship would be a nuisance.

NESSEN: What about the protests that I've heard that you people are going to hand propaganda leaflets to the Soviet athletes?

VOSSELER: Well, I'll tell you what. We were preparing a brochure printed in Russian, English, and German and this brochure would simply give information on how to defect. We were also planning a little aerial advertising; it depends on what comes over from the Eastern Bloc. We also plan to put the messages up on billboards. One of the messages that would be beautiful was, "Defect now, avoid the rush."

Exposing Soviet Human Rights Violations on ABC News, *Nightline*

May 9, 1984 with Ted Koppel and guests
Gene Vosseler, Ban the Soviets Coalition
Vladimir Posner, Chief Commentator Radio Moscow
Peter Ueberroth, President Los Angeles Olympic Organizing Committee

KOPPEL: One group of Americans known as the Ban the Soviets Coalition must feel tonight that it is has succeeded beyond its wildest expectation. The organization has been working to keep the Soviets out of the Los Angeles Olympics. Joining us now in our Los Angeles bureau is the head of the Ban the Soviets Coalition, Gene Vosseler. Mr. Vosseler, I don't know if you feel the word credit or blame is most appropriate but do you accept it?

VOSSELER: Well, we are quite pleased over the fact that the Soviets have suffered a real defeat. I think it was a victory for the cause of freedom. I think that the Soviet Union, by their actions as of late in the international community, has shown themselves to be irresponsible whether it is the shooting down of KAL 007 for which they are unrepentant and which was a catalyst for the action of our ad hoc coalition...

KOPPEL: Just let me ask you the degree to which any of the Soviet concerns are justified? You had been publicizing the notion that you would try to get Soviet defections. True?

VOSSELER: We've been very concerned about the protection of the rights of defectors as guaranteed by the Helsinki Accords to which the Soviet Union is signatory. We do know for a fact that the eleven monitors of the Helsinki Accords in Russia have all been arrested [and] many of them are in psychiatric hospitals. We are concerned very simply that human rights are protected. And we don't really need to encourage Soviet defectors, or I should say Eastern Bloc athletes, to defect. Most of them have probably fantasized thirty to fifty different ways they are going to defect.

KOPPEL: Be that as it may, you are nevertheless, encouraging. You made public the fact that you have safe houses available, that you were indeed going to have demonstrations; you were going to pass out information as to how they might defect. Was that an appropriate thing to do?

VOSSELER: I think it is very appropriate; very simply, I think it's the first time the Soviet Union has been challenged in this whole area upfront in terms of human rights. The kind of people who make up our coalition are ethnic groups, the Afghans, the Poles, Hungarians, and Czechs. And we are concerned right now that nothing has changed since 1980. The Afghan war continues with over a million casualties and over four to five million refugees. And the latest stunt from what I hear from Dr. Claude Malhuret[15] is that the Soviets are dropping little bombs in the form of toy trucks and pens and when the child picks them up, they blow up and you have children who are maimed.

Now I don't know Mr. Posner, I hear he is very glib; he is very smooth.[16] But when you cut through the rhetoric, we get down to Soviet actions. Not what they say. The Soviets are great at playing victim, and again they are placing blame on the United States. They have accused our group of being kidnappers, extremists, and terrorists and all the other things.

---

[15] Dr. Claude Malhuret, the current mayor of Vichy, France, was the president of Médecins Sans Frontières, a non-profit humanitarian aid organization that provided medical relief inside Afghanistan. Dr. Malhuret was an eyewitness to Soviet atrocities in Afghanistan and reported on them in western media. He later became Secretary of State for Human Rights in France in 1986.

And then Peter Ueberroth, on the other hand, makes the statement that our group is nutty and that he won't confer dignity on us and that he simply puts us down as a coalition to hurt athletes. We are going to get it from all sides, but on the other hand, we figure that we are being successful because we know that Ueberroth and the Olympic committee have big bucks at stake. We know that the Soviets are concerned that they do not have the kind of security and control which they had in Moscow where they simply swept up the streets before the Olympics. And any possible potential embarrassment was simple put aside for a while.

> "Mr. Vosseler, I've been waiting for you to take a breath, but you have extraordinary breath control."
>
> —Ted Koppel, Nightline host

KOPPEL: Mr. Vosseler, I've been waiting for you to take a breath, but you have extraordinary breath control. Let me just turn to Mr. Posner in Moscow for a moment. Have they won in a sense, this coalition? Has this rather small group succeeded in keeping the Soviets away? But no one has threatened your athletes?

---

[16] Vladimir Posner is an American-educated Russian journalist and propagandist who is best known in the west for appearing on television to represent and explain the views of the Soviet Union during the Cold War. During the 1980s, he was a favorite guest on *Nightline*. Years later he apologized for his role in disseminating propaganda. "As someone who spent many, many years of his life, and I think probably the best years of my life, doing something that was wrong, I say it just isn't worth it."

POSNER: Well, there have been threats, I have read about this in *UPI* and *AP* and in the *Washington Post* and as a matter of fact, interestingly enough, I have received letters from Americans from Los Angeles saying do not come to Los Angeles; we're your friends so we are telling you, don't come because your boys are going to be hurt there.

KOPPEL: Well, if you had been reading, I think it was the *Associated Press,* this evening you would see that the police chief of Los Angeles, Daryl Gates is particularly upset because he says that as far as he is concerned and indeed as far as the Israelis, who are probably more security conscious than any other government in the world, are concerned, security arrangements in Los Angeles were superb and he said no Soviet officials came to check them out.

POSNER: Well, I don't know how you can check them out, but I do think that this whole issue of security is very much at stake. And then there's a second part which you were asking me about which is the effect of this group. To us, to this country, the fact that a group like that is going to be active and it is going to have access. Of course it's not going to be in the Olympic Village, obviously, it's not going to be at the venues, but they are going to have a high profile or they would have had a high profile. It's an insult. It's an insult to our national pride. We don't see why during an Olympic game, of all things, we should be subject to this kind of political blatantly [anti-] Soviet activity.

KOPPEL: Better than no Soviets? You understand better the way things operate in the United States. The government isn't going to tell these people they don't have the right to demonstrate, you know that.

POSNER: That's true Ted, but on the other hand, I know that in the United States a city can limit demonstrations to a certain time, to a certain area, to a certain place, in such a way as to make the demonstration totally ineffective, if it's aimed at, let us say, at another group of people, in this case the Soviet athletes. It can be done. And to me the Olympic Games are bigger than any country and even than any constitution. Way back when, wars were stopped because of the Olympic Games. Now you can't even stop people from trying to indeed coerce or invite people to defect, to put political and psychological pressure on them. Maybe they would not compete as well as they would otherwise. Why should we go into it with this kind of stuff? I just don't really see the reason.

KOPPEL: Alright, Peter Ueberroth, there seems to me there is a point here that Posner has raised which you can answer very easily and that is how far away would these groups have been kept from the Soviet athletes? Just out of the Olympic Village? Or would they have been kept some specific distance? Had any agreement been reached on the distance between demonstrators and athletes?

UEBERROTH: Simply put they will be far enough away so as not to bother the athletes' performance, their attitude or be at the sight in any way. So they really won't be a part of the Olympic Games. The athletes can come from any country, play on the field to play and in fact they will and do and they will come from all over the world. And this just will not be a factor in the Los Angeles Games. They are way away from sight or vision or ears. There will be no way they interfere with the games.

KOPPEL: Vladimir, I can't imagine you saying anything different than the chairman of the Soviet Olympic Committee said today but since you always pride yourself on speaking as an individual then tell us as an individual, was there a snowball chance in hell that your team would be coming to Los Angeles this summer?

POSNER: Well, it doesn't have anything to do with what

the chairman would say only in one sense, when he was asked that question at the press conference he said absolutely that the decision is final. Now I doubt very much that you'd say that if there was a snowball chance in hell that the team would go.

KOPPEL: And what is your assessment?

POSNER: My assessment is that there will not be a Soviet team at the Olympics in Los Angeles.

KOPPEL: OK, Gentlemen, Thank you.

7. DEFENDING AMERICA—THE CASE FOR BALLISTIC MISSILE DEFENSE

Editor's Note: While working with Lt. Gen. Daniel Graham and Americans for High Frontier, and later with the group he founded, Citizens for a Strong America, Gene conducted five tours throughout the United States taking Saint Germain's message on the need to defend America to the grassroots—on college campuses, on radio and television interviews, and in print interviews. He and his wife, Wanda, were commended by Saint Germain, El Morya, and our messenger Elizabeth Clare Prophet for his excellent service promoting the defense of freedom. What follows are a lecture delivered at the Royal Teton Ranch as well as several media interviews and Gene's press kit. Gene's gift of communication enabled him to tailor his message to our spiritual community as well as the community at large in a meaningful and inspiring manner.

The Threat is Now!—Easter Class Presentation

April 4, 1996

It's good to be home again. You don't realize how much you'll miss home until you are away. As some of you are probably aware, I've been in Washington, D.C., advocating for strategic ballistic missile defense. My interest in this subject goes back fifteen years when we first battled the nuclear freeze issue in California. Later, after the Soviets shot down KAL-007, that unarmed jet, we created Ban the Soviets Coalition to keep the Soviets out of the Olympics in Los Angeles in 1984. More recently in 1987 and 1988 I worked with the late Lt. Gen. Daniel Graham, who is the father of the Strategic Defense Initiative (SDI). I lectured for him for about two years. The issue we are talking about tonight is an issue that doesn't want to be handled. Lots of times when you bring up the subject of ballistic missile defense and nuclear missiles and people's eyes glaze over and they tune you out.

Tonight I am going to be speaking about things that are going to go against the conventional wisdom of our time. Some of the things I am going to say are politically incorrect but you are going to get a straight message tonight. I want to share with you the nature of some of the current nuclear threats. We are going to get some insight into the arms control treaties that we have with Russia. We're also going to take a candid look at how the American leadership is responding to a world that is like one giant tinderbox that could explode at any moment in at least a half-dozen flashpoints around the world...

Some of you know I am heading up a group called Citizens for a Strong America. It's a grassroots organization that is involved in fighting this battle. Currently, I've been doing a lot of syndicated radio shows. We've done shows that have been broadcast on 627 radio stations in the last five weeks. When you do a syndicated show like *The Jim Bohannon Show* you have 400 stations. Or you do an *Oliver North Show* and you have 125 stations. So you have a multiplication factor coast to coast. You understand how the multiplication factor can work and how talk shows and interview shows are a great way to get the message out to the people. Remember when Congress tried to do that big raise for themselves a few years back and talk radio blasted them and they simply withdrew that little bit of featherbedding that they were involved in.

Tonight we are going to take a look at a life-and-death problem involving the survival of our nation as a free land...

There is No Peace

Prior to World War II when the so-called peace movement was very active after World War I, the West unilaterally disarmed. The Kellogg-Briand Pact[17] message was that since we won the war to end all wars, we can now relax. At that time Nazi Germany did a massive buildup, aided and abetted by many powerful economic institutions in the West. As a result of that military buildup there was one man who was the gadfly. He was the one that gave warning. His name was Winston Churchill and he urged us to look at what the Germans were

---

[17] The Kellogg-Briand Pact, also known as the Pact of Paris after the city where it was signed on August 27, 1928, was an international treaty "providing for the renunciation of war as an instrument of national policy." It failed in its purpose but was significant for later developments in international law. It was named after the American secretary of state Frank B. Kellogg and French foreign minister Aristide Briand, who drafted the pact. In its original form, the Pact of Paris was a renunciation of war between France and the US. However, Frank B. Kellogg, then U.S. Secretary of State, wanted to retain American freedom of action; Kellogg thus responded with a proposal for a multilateral pact against war open for all nations to become signatories, in hopes of diluting the French proposal into a meaningless statement of utopian idealism.

doing, not look at what they were saying. But it fell on deaf ears. It was a time of moral and military disarmament and the peace movement. When Neville Chamberlain, a mustachioed man with the bowler hat and umbrella, came back from Munich, Germany, waving this peace pact with Adolph Hitler he said, "We have peace in our time," and everyone applauded. Then England went back to sleep until the bombs started dropping on London. Winston Churchill was simply branded a warmonger. He was giving unpleasant truths to people who did not want to hear it.

The Worst Crime is to Not Tell the Truth

Churchill made a very interesting statement at that time; he said, "The worst crime is to not tell the truth to the public, to keep the people in ignorance and blindness, in darkness." This is a crime that is being committed against American people today in the under-reported issue of ballistic missile defense and the nature of the threat that this nation faces. We all know it; we've heard it many times from the pulpit. We've heard it from dictations from the masters. We are well aware of this fact. But the average American, over 60 percent of them, believe today we are defended against missiles when in reality we can't stop one.

A MAD World

Churchill's comments apply very much to the media, to the government, and particularly to the many liberals in government who are keeping the meek people in the dark about this issue. Even Henry Kissinger, the architect of the 1972 Anti-Ballistic Missile Treaty made the statement recently, "It's nuts to make a virtue of our vulnerability." Now this is a man who crafted and developed the 1972 Anti-Ballistic Missile

Treaty that keeps us to this day undefended. In a doctrine called Mutual Assured Destruction with the appropriate acronym, MAD, we agreed not to build ballistic missile defenses. Under the treaty we were allowed to build one hundred missile defenses, at one hundred missile sites. And we started work in Grand Forks, North Dakota. But then under this great feeling of magnanimity we unilaterally scrapped them. Meanwhile Russia has ringed Moscow with anti-ballistic missiles, surface-to-air missiles, 10s and 12s and 5s. They built deep, hardened shelters because they never accepted the idea of Mutual Assured Destruction for a moment and engaged in a massive military buildup. So you understand we in the West are totally undefended, meanwhile they are well defended.

Now we live in a dangerous world, that's a given. Almost everyone in this room agrees with that after the bombing of the World Trade Center.[18] Of course you can imagine what would happen if a nuclear device would have been used there. Some of you are aware that there are twenty-six nations that now possess ballistic missile capability. These include some of our most devoted enemies, North Korea, Iran, Iraq, and Libya. These missiles can be loaded with either nuclear warheads or

---

18 The 1993 World Trade Center bombing occurred on February 26, 1993, when a car bomb was detonated below Tower One of the World Trade Center in New York City. The 1,500 pound urea nitrate-hydrogen gas enhanced device was intended to knock the North Tower (Tower One) into the South Tower (Tower Two), bringing both towers down and killing thousands of people. It failed to do so, but killed six people and injured 1,042.

The attack was planned by a group of conspirators including Ramzi Yousef, Mahmud Abouhalima, Mohammad Salameh, Nidal Ayyad, Abdul Rahman Yasin, and Ahmad Ajaj. They received financing from Khaled Shaikh Mohammed, the mastermind of the 9/11 attacks, as well as Yousef's uncle. In March 1994, four men were convicted of carrying out the bombing: Abouhalima, Ajaj, Ayyad, and Salameh. The charges included conspiracy, explosive destruction of property, and interstate transportation of explosives. And in November 1997 two more were convicted: Yousef, the mastermind behind the bombings, and Eyad Ismoil, who drove the truck carrying the bomb.

chemical and biological weaponry which is the "poor man's nuclear weapon." Now the technology to launch these weapons is available on the open market.

The Threat is Now!

Now listen carefully because this is very shocking. Recently, in an agreement between President Clinton and Boris Yeltsin, our president has agreed to allow Russia to sell on the open market, to anyone who has the money, intercontinental ballistic missile launchers. That means the capability to launch missiles of intercontinental range can be purchased by anyone who can afford the price. Now it may well be that they are not able to acquire nuclear warheads but that launch capability allows them to target any city in America. We also know that the leaky security in Russia today allows plutonium to leave the country. There is concern that suitcase nuclear weapons can't be accounted for by the Russians. Even Russia slipping some of these nuclear warheads to some of their buddies like Libya or Iran or Iraq is a possibility. All of that danger is there. If they can't acquire nuclear warheads they use that chemical, biological warfare. Can you imagine warheads with anthrax hitting an American city, and in a few days destroying a population?

Any Third World state now can buy intercontinental ballistic missile launchers. And what is the national intelligence estimate from the Department of Intelligence Agency (DIA) or the CIA, who are responsible for reporting to the president and Congress the nature of the threat? They recently said there is no threat of strategic missiles for at least fifteen years. We are talking now of these nations developing their own technology. Why develop your own technology when they can buy it in the open market? You get the picture. Clinton used the national intelligence to justify his delay of deploying ballistic missile defenses for another six years from now. I am not even sure what missile defenses we are going to deploy.

According to a Congressional Technical Assessment report, these turnkey missile launchers I've been talking about can be armed with the payload from conventional warheads with radioactive material, biochemical devices, or a full-fledged nuclear warhead in three hours. That's all it takes to put a warhead on these intercontinental ballistic launchers. This makes a mockery, then, of the notion that we have fifteen years of grace time before we are threatened by ballistic missiles, thanks to President Clinton. You need to know it. That threat is now.

When I do debates on radio shows, I receive questions and statements from out there in radio land that none of those nations would be crazy enough to launch a nuclear missile against America. Well, what can you say when you have a fundamentalist [Muslim] who believes that this is the quickest way to paradise? These are people who strap dynamite on themselves and go in and blow themselves and a whole busload of people up. Or you have 242 marines killed by a guy driving a suicide truck loaded with explosives. Actually Saddam Hussein made the statement very recently that he wished he had this kind of capability. And Muammar al-Gaddafi, the Libyan President, said he desired to acquire missiles that could hit New York City. These are the kinds of people we are dealing with. They are not rational. They don't look at life realistically like we do.

> "We now have the unique situation where a Third World nation with the right amount of money can get access to missile launch capability that can hit any city in America."
>
> —Rep. Curt Weldon,
> Chairman, House National Security Subcommittee on Military Research

We Lack Political Will

Contrary to conventional wisdom, the American people and our troops overseas are vulnerable to ballistic missile attack. Thirteen years after President Reagan made his famous SDI speech, we still have not deployed ballistic missile defense. When he made that speech it was labeled "Star Wars" by Sen. Ted Kennedy. That label stuck, and so many people think of strategic defense as science fiction. So the American people sleep on. They sleep on and believe me if I tell you this; it's a sleep of death. Although we have the technology, like the Navy Aegis system which can be upgraded and Brilliant Pebbles, a space-based defense that can be deployed within a couple years, we have not made the decision to deploy. The point is we have lacked the political will to deploy.

I will give you a little bit of hope in a moment. I am going to give you the straight shot and then I am going to give you the message of hope. But I want you to get the full impact of what we are talking about tonight.

Now, President Clinton's rigid adherence in 1972 ABM

Treaty prevents the United States from deploying off-the-shelf technology that can defend us, defend America, defend our children and our children's children. Now this 1972 ABM Treaty is fatally flawed and it has been violated up one side and down the other by the Russians. Some of you remember the Krasnoyarsk[19] radar that was built. Even [the Soviets] admitted that they cheated on this thing but it's been ignored by key officials and many liberals; they simply don't even hear it.

Red China Threatens to Nuke Los Angeles

This treaty is fatally flawed because of Russian violations and the rapid proliferation of missile capability. Then you add Red China into the mix who can lob missiles into the Taiwan Straits and attempt to intimidate a free election in Taiwan, their first free election. Taiwan is poking a stick in Red China's eye with their great economic achievements. Many people with business ties to Taiwan know what's going on. And the Red Chinese leaders, Communist leaders, the perpetrators of

---

[19] The Krasnoyarsk radar site is the largest radar system of its kind, measuring some thirty stories high and two football fields wide. It is part of a vast ABM system constructed by the Soviet Union beginning in 1983. According to a report by *National Review*, "Krasnoyarsk radar site in Soviet Union violates ABM Treaty," October 9, 1987, the Soviets have eight more big radars, exactly like the one at Krasnoyarsk, either built or under construction. The nine radars form a ring around the USSR, protecting every possible approach corridor for U.S. ICBMs or submarine-launched missiles.

When construction of the Soviet radar network is completed (for the Krasnoyarsk radar, that will be in 1989 or 1990; for three new radars discovered in 1987, it will be a few years later; the others are already finished), the rest of the Soviet ABM system—the small radars and the intercepting missiles that would destroy the U.S. warheads—can be put in place "in a matter of months," according to the CIA's Mr. Robert Gates, currently our secretary of defense. This would provide a vast ABM system to protect the Soviets from a retaliatory U.S. nuclear strike, a complete violation of the 1972 ABM Treaty.

the massacre in Tiananmen Square, the ones who raped and plundered Tibet, when you take a look at how they react, they are frightened. In their fear they simply started lobbing missiles in the Taiwan Straits in an attempt to intimidate the Taiwanese people who are not intimidated for a moment. We all know that we've been doing anti-Communist decrees for at least twenty years. And we know that one time the masters said there're more lightbearers per square mile on Taiwan than any place on the planet. We know that our light is challenging the darkness at the core of Communist China.

It's no surprise to hear that a senior Chinese official told Charles Freeman, our former ambassador to China, that we would never interfere in America if Red China invaded Taiwan because we valued Los Angeles more than we valued Taiwan. Now that is not a subtle threat. That is a very direct threat. Red China has intercontinental ballistic missiles. Fortunately the arsenal is pretty small right now, but they are doing all they can to speed up their modernization. They also have ICBMs on subs. It was not an idle threat and of course we glossed over it. There was not even much of a response in the West to this threat. It got in a few papers. How many of you read about it? In this room there're about twenty of you who have even read about this threat. You would think it would be bannered in every headline and across America, "Red China threatens to nuke L.A." Great headline, right? This is some of what we are up against, how the media fuzzes over these issues and how the American people are kept in the dark.

Now we add to this mix, then, Red China's bellicosity toward Taiwan, the continuing India-Pakistan prewar state between those two nuclear powers that almost touched off a few years back in 1990-1991. Only the intervention of American diplomacy at the right time stopped that one from exploding into a nuclear confrontation. We had the terrorist flare-ups in the Middle East. While the world has become highly combustible, nuclear missiles have become an integral part of the equation everywhere.

How has President Clinton responded to this world in crisis? In addition to agreeing to allow Russia to sell intercontinental ballistic missile launchers on the open market, this president vetoed the 1996 Defense Appropriations bill, which would have mandated the deployment of nationwide ballistic missile system by the year 2003. Since the Republicans didn't have enough votes to override the veto, instead of playing it tough, what did they do? They capitulated. They allowed the President to remove the line item about deployment of ballistic missile defenses in order to get him to sign the Defense Authorization bill for $265 billion. If they remained firm in support of deployment, they could have made it a presidential election issue. This president does not believe in defending America. We believe in defending America.

Worthless Paper Treaties

The Wall Street Journal had a number of excellent editorials, one of them called "Unprotected," saying Republicans ought to keep sending back to this president defense bills called for deployment of strategic defense. Eventually, the American people are going to wake up to what's going on as he continues to veto. Clinton vetoed that bill contending that the provision to deploy ballistic missile defense would violate those sacred icons of our arms control treaties which are shot full of holes like swiss cheese. If you take a look at every arms control treaty that this nation has entered into with Russia, you will become aware that they have violated every one, whether it is the conventional weapons treaty, the Conventional Armed Forces in Europe Treaty (CFE), whether it be Intermediate Nuclear Force Treaty (INF), whether it be Strategic Arms Limitation Treaties (SALT I and SALT II), whether it be Strategic Arms

Reduction Treaties (START I and START II). And what did we do just recently? The United States Senate approved START II, another fatally flawed treaty which puts yet another obstacle in the way of getting rid of the 1982 ABM treaty which we have got to scrap before we can deploy ballistic missile defenses. And there is a mechanism for doing that. So are you beginning to get the picture? START II that was approved by the U.S. Senate, there were four men who stood strong and said, "No. We should not do this unless there is the commitment by this president to deploy." Sens. John Ashcroft of Ohio, James Inhofe was another gentleman of Oklahoma, Robert Smith from New Hampshire, and Jesse Helms of North Carolina. So do you get the picture?

Now you have a president who has thrown down the gauntlet, it's on the table. He has put his trust in arms control agreements, which have in the past proved worthless. Russia has violated fifty out of fifty-three of the treaties they have been engaged in in the past. Afghanistan had a friendship pact with the Soviets dating back to 1978. Before that there was a non-aggression pact and look what happened to Afghanistan —genocide, one million dead and another four to five million refugees. When you sign an arms control treaty with Russia it's like getting a white rose from the mafia. It's not even that comfortable. The Balkan states all had non-aggression pacts, they all got swallowed up in a deal that Moscow and Stalin made with Hitler prior to world War II—an agreement which was formalized in the Yalta by FDR, Churchill, and Stalin following the war. Do you remember that? Do you remember the expansionism of Russia since Communism took over in 1917? You have seventeen sovereign nations swallowed up by the dragon of World Communism and people still think today you can sit at a table and negotiate an arms control treaty that will be honored by a totalitarian state, which currently is committing genocide and slaughtering its own citizens in

Chechnya. If you believe that, you believe in the good tooth fairy. There's no way they are going to honor their agreements. Historically this is true.

No Moral Equivalency

I remember when I used to debate Marxist professors on the lecture circuit almost every night. They were always telling me how great the Soviet Union was and how bad we were. And they always had nothing but praise for the Soviet Union and nothing but bad things to say about us. I remember they used to argue, look the Soviet leadership is just like our leadership. We are morally equal. With recent actions I am beginning to believe it you know. But they made that idea of moral convergence and their argument is that eventually Russia and United States will get together and converge. And our former secretary of state made the statement, "our president and the president of the Soviet Union share the same dreams." And they have the same aspiration; they have the same visions. Secretary of State Cyrus Vance, one of the most naive secretary of states we have ever had. Are you getting the picture now? How can you sign an agreement with a slave state? Particularly a state right now that is reinvigorating the hard-line Communist, who won two to one the last election, with the likes of [Vladimir] Zhirinovsky[20], an ultranationalist who threatens the West with missiles. And you can't really depend on that

---

[20] According to the *Encyclopedia Britannica,* when Vladimir Zhirinovsky's Liberal Democratic Party won 22.8% of the vote in the Russian parliamentary elections in December 1993, the West gasped. It had previously not taken much notice of the man known for his boorish, bullying behavior or for his promise to create a dictatorship when elected President, and they had not listened very closely to his threats to expand the borders of Russia to include Alaska and Finland, use large fans to blow radioactive waste into the Baltic states, and reduce crime by instituting summary executions. People did not know if they should take his high-decibel nationalistic comments seriously.

because right now our president is putting all of his horses on Yeltsin who not only has a drinking problem but he has heart trouble. And this president recently negotiated with him.

The Washington Times reported something you'll find interesting. They reported that there was a classified conversation between Yeltsin and our president and it had to do with chickens and drumsticks. Arkansas produces 40 percent of the chickens in America. Dan Tyson had to be one of the greatest contributors to President Clinton. Recently Russia has embargoed our chickens. Yeltsin suggested, and this is reported wildly in the Russian press, that he and Clinton ought to support each other's re-election bid. In exchange for lifting the [chicken] embargo, President Clinton is helping Yeltsin get a $10.2 billion loan which was recently negotiated with the international monetary fund—thanks probably to the intervention of this president. We live in a very, very strange world, when yes means no and no means yes, and that's the kind of world in which we live.

So I simply ask you this. Isn't it time for America to assume its own moral leadership in the world as a free state? Isn't it time for us to take control of our own destiny rather than rely on the false promises, vagaries, and the whims of unpredictable foreign totalitarian leaders? Can we really trust a nation such as Russia to keep its word when it's creating genocide in Chechnya? In light of their past violations of all arms control agreements, isn't this foolhardy to the extreme? You'd think this was logic that should be inescapable to anyone with half a brain. For anyone that thinks at all can see this. Should we do business as usual? Should we help now and build up any nation like Red China technologically and economically with loans and credits? After all, we built the best enemy that money can buy with Russia. We built over one thousand turnkey factories. Wall Street backed the Communist and Bolshevik revolution from day one.

The China and Russia Threats

Why should we do business as usual and why should we currently allow Red China to acquire our super computers, the Cray supercomputer that gives them the capability to target and direct missiles? After all we gave Russia under a $25 million deal with a ball-bearing company with a sign-off from Kissinger and Nixon. The sale of ball bearing technology gave the Soviets the capability to grind a ball bearing down to one twenty-five millionths of a inch tolerance, making their missiles far more accurate and far more lethal. This allowed Russia, the Soviet Union, to MIRV their missiles, to create missiles with ten independent warheads that could lock into ten different targets and improve the accuracy ten times. Now that's not shooting yourself in the foot, that's shooting yourself in the head. And we did it. We, the American people, didn't do it. But our leadership did it behind the scenes as a fait accompli. Usually we don't find out these things. Usually we didn't find out for example that Deng Xiaoping, the de facto leader of China, was being toasted by Lawrence Eagleburger, who was the Deputy Secretary of State, our number two man at State and Brent Scowcroft, our National Security Adviser, were in a secret meetings with Chinese officials just one week after the Tiananmen Square massacre.

When do we regard human rights as a necessary requirement for Most Favored Nation status? Not with China. Apparently our government wants to give China MFN status so that we can resume open trade with them despite their gross human rights violations and their threats to Taiwan and the West.

I am just going to allude to an article that appeared in the Sunday *New York Times,* that the Kremlin is embracing radical states. I will just mention one of two quotes out of this. Soviet President Yeltsin has been buoyed up by a $10.2 billion loan;

> "There are certain people in this world—the power elite—who have no love of freedom, no love of light, no love of God, no love of country, no love of people, and will use the little people and manipulate them any way they can with their wars."

this makes him look pretty good. At the same time a Russian Deputy Minister went to Libya and met with Muammar al-Gaddafi with a message from Mr. Yeltsin expressing support for Libya. Remember when they shot down that Pan American plane at Lockerbie.[21] Russia is now supporting al-Gaddafi by lifting sanctions on Libya. In Russia, the hard-liners are coming back including Yevgeny Primakov, head of the KGB and dangerous. Listen to what he did. Right after Mr. Primakov was installed as a foreign minister in January, the Kremlin wrote off $8 billion in loans to Libya. Libya owned $16 billion to Russia and he wrote off $8 billion of it. Primakov also praised Iran and its terrorist policies. On Wednesday a senior Chinese nuclear official said Moscow has offered a $2 billion loan, probably out of the $10 billion they got out of the IMF (International Monetary Fund) loan. The purpose of this low-interest loan is to supply two Russian nuclear reactors to China and another nuclear power plant in Northeast China. This is a fifteen-year loan that carries a remarkably low interest

---

[21] Two hundred and seventy people were killed when Pan Am 103 was blown out of the sky over Lockerbie, Scotland, on December 21, 1988. One Libyan was convicted of murder; his case is on appeal. In 2002, the Libyan government accepted responsibility for the crime and paid $2.7 billion in compensation to U.S. families in return to a lifting of sanctions.

rate of 4 percent. The estimate for the first phase of construction is $4 billion. Now this article shows you the real face of Russia and Russian Communist leadership.

> "I will spit in your eye and you will think it's holy water."
> —Russian proverb

Everyone thinks the cold war is over; we won. Russia is wiped out; they are nothing. And when you take a look at the press that is what you read. But recently the Russian Dumas (Parliament) voted that the dissolution of the Soviet Republic a few years back is no longer valid. Now they are inviting all of these independent Eastern Bloc states to come back into the warm embrace of Mother Russia. Every one of these ten independent states is run by a Communist or an ex-Communist.

For all those people who simply have been downgrading a potential attack and ballistic missile defense, I'll give you the straight facts of what's happening in Russia. According to Secretary of Defense William Perry, Russia has 25,000 missiles of which approximately 9,000 have an intercontinental ballistic missile capability. We reduced our aging nuclear arsenal down to 8,000 and, counting of which, approximately 2,500 have intercontinental ballistic missile capability. Perry goes on to say that we are ahead of schedule in dismantling our ICBMs, and Russia is behind schedule. This is bureaucratic euphemism for they are cheating again. You have to read between the lines and take a good hard look. Now the Soviets have a three to one superiority. People say what does that mean? After all one missile is enough; one missile can do a lot of damage...

Let me just give you a few more closing things on this issue. I don't want to leave you completely hopeless. I want to leave you with some positive stuff.

We are still trusting the fatally flawed START II Treaty. Not one warhead is destroyed under START II. Of the twenty-five to thirty thousand warheads, not one warhead is destroyed; missiles are destroyed[22] but they are still allowed to continue to build and modernize.

The Pentagon, under the Clinton Administration, refused to spend $275 million already appropriated by Congress for ballistic missile defense. In an agreement with Yeltsin, our president has agreed to dumb down and reduce the effectiveness of our regional missile defenses. As a result, if you have a U.S. Navy Aegis cruiser off the coast of Japan with an upgraded upper tier system, it can actually shoot down a missile attack directed on Japan but it couldn't stop an attack directed on Seattle because of the 1972 ABM Treaty. Can you believe this? We can actually defend Japan from a nuclear attack, but we can't defend our own country because our president dumbed down our interceptor capabilities. He also delayed a deployment decision for another three years. Clinton approved technology transfer of Silicon Valley's supercomputers to China while expressing no outrage over the threat of Red China against Los Angeles. When President Clinton vetoed the fiscal year 1996 Defense Authorization bill, he made a political statement. He threw down the gauntlet; he's not interested in defending America against incoming missiles launched by accident or design from Red China, a reinvigorated Russia, or a rouge nation.

Saddam Hussein said, at the time of the [first] Persian Gulf War, his missiles couldn't reach Washington. If they could

---

[22] A missile is the device that carries the weapon system; a warhead is the front part of the missile that can contain a nuclear, chemical, or biological weapon.

reach Washington, he'd strike at our nation's capital. And of course we know Washington, D.C., is totally undefended against missiles. The national security of this nation transcends any difference between people, parties, and politics. Whether it be a political difference between liberals and conservatives, whether it be a religious difference between Jews, Roman Catholics, and even New Agers, the need for defense and security transcends these differences. United we stand, divided we fall. National security is an issue that affects everyone. The U.S. Constitution calls on the government to provide for our common defense. That's the primary purpose of the federal government.

"In a world of tyrants and would-be tyrants, freedom is still a precious, fragile commodity...Peace through strength—politically, economically, militarily, and, above all, spiritually is still the best guarantee of our four sacred freedoms."

Isn't it time for the American people to wake up from their sleep and slumber? Isn't it time for you to get involved, get informed, start informing your neighbors, and start writing those letters to your congressman? Letting them know you will no longer tolerate this idea that we no longer need to be defended against missiles. When the missiles start flying, and they will, believe me they will unless we are defended, you can always wave those worthless scraps of papers, those arms control treaties that we made with Russia [and say] "We had a deal, don't you remember we had a deal." And it won't stop a single missile. It will not stop one missile. And the American people when they know and wake up to this, they will demand defense. But now they are sleeping.

America as we know it will not exist in the twenty-first century unless we get ballistic missile defense. That's how important this issue is.

As I said before, the world is like a tinderbox. It can explode at any time. The Middle East, North Korea, South Korea, there are over one million troops on the demilitarization zone from North Korea, right there, right now. India, Pakistan—they've been at it for a long time over Kashmir. China, Taiwan—the list goes on and on. Our military resources are spread thin. We are all over the globe in Europe, South Korea, Bosnia, even Macedonia. And none of these troops can be protected against a missile attack. We ought to have learned that in the Gulf War, our greatest loss of life was from a Scud missile.

In a world of tyrants and would-be tyrants, freedom is still a precious, fragile commodity. From Christians we learn this truth, that peace is maintained only through strength. As the Bible says, when the strong man is armed, his goods are in peace. Peace through strength, politically, economically, militarily, and, above all, spiritually is still the best guarantee of our four sacred freedoms. To a sleeping America, Thomas Jefferson's words still speak today, "Eternal vigilance is the price of liberty."

Deploy Now!
Challenging the Reagan Administration[23]

Conservative Political Action Conference
Kenneth Adelman,[24] Former Director U.S. Arms Control and Disarmament Agency and Gene Vosseler, Americans for High Frontier
February 20, 1987
Omni Shoreham Hotel, Washington, D.C.
Broadcasted Live on C-SPAN II.

Editor's Note: The Conservative Political Action Conference (CPAC) is the largest annual conference of conservative activists and organizations. Frequently, presidential candidates and leaders in the U.S. Senate, House of Representatives, and political action organizations speak at this event. Past speakers include Ronald Reagan, Margaret Thatcher, George W. Bush, and others. Los Angeles Times calls CPAC "a showcase of the heart and soul of American conservatism." Gene Vosseler debates Ken Adelman in this segment that was broadcast on C-SPAN II.

---

[23] President Ronald Reagan strongly advocated ballistic missile defense, then called SDI. However, some members of Reagan's Administration, while voicing support for research, didn't support deployment. The Democrat-controlled Congress strongly opposed missile defense. Reagan, despite ongoing nuclear freeze talks with Gorbachev, always held firm in supporting ballistic missile defense and famously didn't back down when meeting with the Soviet leader in Reykjavik, Iceland in October 1986.

[24] Ken Adelman served as assistant to U.S. Secretary of Defense Donald Rumsfeld from 1975 to 1977. Adelman was U.S. Ambassador to the United Nations during the Reagan Administration. At the time of this debate, Adelman was Reagan's Director of Arms Control. Adelman was an adviser to Pres. George W. Bush and was an early proponent of the invasion of Iraq but later regretted his support. More recently, Adelman pledged to vote for Barack Obama for president. Today, Adelman is a frequent media commentator with apperances on Fox News, CNN, and NPR.

VOSSELER: I agree with so much of what you said. I even hate to raise this but I really must. Prior to World War II, supporters of appeasement were very strong. We know that Winston Churchill was considered a warmonger when he pointed out the facts to those individuals who thought they could do business with Hitler. I am reminded of Charlton Heston when he debated with Paul Newman on the nuclear freeze initiative in California, an issue in which I was very involved. On a late-night show, Charlton Heston asked Paul Newman point blank a very searching question which I think is very relevant for today. He said, "Paul, if this was 1939 would you sign a nuclear freeze agreement with Adolph Hitler?" The same kind of question applies today. If you take Soviet actions in Afghanistan, Nicaragua, the attempted assassination of the pope, the Bulgarian connection right on down the line [to] KAL 007, by God's green earth what makes us think that the Soviet Union is going to comply with a worthless scrap of paper in view of the fact that in the past they have never complied to any treaty?

The other thing is we cannot know what an SS-20 missile looks like. We've never seen one. We don't know, for example, where they are located. They say they have a certain amount of sites, where are the other sites? We can only inspect certain sites. And if we do verify that they are cheating, who is going to enforce compliance? There's no enforcement. Are you going to get the United Nations to enforce compliance? There's no way. So when you get right down to it, what do we get? Another worthless scrap of paper which takes Pershing II[25] out of Europe, which is the thing the Soviets really fear because they are accurate enough to place one down the Kremlin smokestack. That's what they are concerned about. Are you going to take that away from the European people, the one real thing the Soviets fear? You take the warheads, none of which will be destroyed, you place them on SS-24s or SS-25s and what do you get? Once our Pershing missiles are out, they are out; they are never going to go back in again. I appreciate what you say and I agree with so much of what you say I just have to challenge you in this area.

ADELMAN: Fair enough. And that's a legitimate argument. And it's well done. Let me address it. Because I've thought about it for five years now. Number one, Pershing IIs did not exist in West Germany until 1983. You cannot say the alliance was relying on them for all the time because the alliance held together quite nicely during Soviet aggression without any Pershing IIs or ground launch missiles of 1983. Point number two, I don't believe for a moment we would have gotten any deployment in Germany of the Pershing II's unless zero option had been the device used by the politicians to explain that.

---

[25] Pershing II, intermediate-range nuclear force (INF) missiles, were deployed in five European countries beginning in January 1984. According to defense expert Frank Gaffney, "That action consummated a decision taken years before by a NATO alliance determined to counter the coercive threat posed by powerful Soviet SS-20 ballistic missiles. And it was achieved despite what was, arguably, the most sophisticated, well-financed, and determined political-warfare campaign ever waged against democratic nations, mounted by the Soviet Union and its sympathizers in Western Europe." At the time of this event, the U.S. was negotiating with the Soviet Union on the elimination of the Pershings from Europe as part of INF Treaty (Intermediate-range nuclear force). On December 8, 1987, President Reagan and Soviet Premier, Mikhail Gorbachev, signed the INF Treaty in a White House ceremony, while thousands protested in weeklong demonstrations in Washington, D.C. The Pershings were removed in 1988 following the ratification of the INF Treaty. In 2008, a similar challenge confronted the United States and Russia as President Bush sought to deploy ballistic missile defense systems in Eastern Europe which would protect our allies from short-range missiles from rogue states. Russia has vehemently opposed this move..

I debated Henry Kissinger in Amsterdam a few months ago and he was making the point that, my God, these missiles are exceedingly important to stop deterrence right now, the point that you made with great eloquence a minute ago. Henry Kissinger was one of the managers of foreign policy of United States for eight years. During that time there was no mention that I had ever seen of about employing and deploying these missiles in Western Europe at that time. We thought to have an alliance able to deter Soviet aggression without them. I go back to the point of saying, if you are telling me that it's detrimental to us, we would rather not take the Pershing IIs out, not take the ground missile cruise missiles out, I agree with you. The question is, are you willing to live with 1,400 warheads for the SS 20, as opposed to 350 warheads of the Pershing II and the ground launch cruise missiles.

VOSSELER: Certainly.

ADELMAN: If you say certainly, then your argument is very consistent. That is not the argument that the Europeans have been using. Me, and I'll tell you a little peek of history here. In 1980 I talked during the transition period of Alexander Haig about the idea of maybe not going along with the dual-track decision that NATO had agreed to in 1979. I did not think it was ever wise to tie arms control to deployment. I thought it would lead to a big mess, to tell you the truth. I talked to Haig on Saturday morning about it and he came up with the argument, which is not a dumb argument, that we could not walk into office and say what the alliance agreed to, sixteen countries is immediately reversed by the new administration. That's just not a proper way to deal with the alliance. But I think once the die is cast, once you have a dual-track decision to have arms control and deploy it [missile defense] at the same time; then the best outcome you can have is the one we had with the zero option.

I think the bigger point is not what happens with 350 warheads of Pershing IIs that did not exist before 1983 in Europe. The bigger point is where does this lead? If this leads to Detente II, this leads to more economic assistance to the East, that this leads to lowering our guard, this leads to the idea that, as Cyrus Vance said, a well-meaning man but terribly naive, said, "Well, the president of the United States and the president of the Soviet Union dream the same dreams and have the same aspirations for the world," then that will be a disaster.

VOSSELER: Let me respond real quick. You can see that's exactly where it's leading. See why Congress is pushing the Department of Commerce and saying, "Look, if we get 15,000 Jews able to immigrate each year we ought to give the Soviets Most Favored Nation status." Now here's a guy who heads up the Department of Commerce. The technology hemorrhage, which is bad enough, is going to get worse.

My feeling is this that SS-20s when they were placed in Europe to target all of Europe there was no outcry from the West. But when our allies act to respond with Pershing IIs and a great expense in terms of political stuff over in Europe we placed them. And the Soviets left the bargaining table in Geneva in a huff saying, "We'll never return as long as you've got those Pershings." They came humping back for one reason, SDI, Strategic Defense. Now I could probably go along with you in terms of the INF treaty. I don't like it, period. I don't think it's going to do any good. If we deploy the shield, we put up SDI, deploy now! Not wait five, ten, fifteen years, not negotiate with the Department of State, a seven- or ten-year delay which means fifteen years by the time you actually get the weapons into deployment while the Soviets are going full tilt with their anti-ballistic system, with their anti-satellite weapon system. And where are we? We are going to be very vulnerable within the space of two or three years I think, to either Soviet blackmail or a nuclear first strike. Now that may be an unrealistic scenario, but that is how I see it.

And my gut feeling is about this INF Treaty that is really taking away a lot of effort and energy toward the crucial decision of which this president should make before he goes out of office and that is a decision to deploy now Strategic Defense.

ADELMAN: And here we are getting very close to each other and I think the terms of the INF agreement are fine. I think part of the reason that the terms of the INF agreement are fine is that they do not nick SDI one iota. I know the Soviets twice tied the INF to SDI, I know we've had meetings in the situation room about that and the president always came down on the side of those and it was not unanimous advice to him was fine just tell them, no, there's no big problem here. You know the Chinese have a wonderful expression, I've been to China twice on arms control delegations, they say, "We can't do that, that's no problem, it's not even a close call, it's no problem to us. No we can't do that so forget it. If you don't want an INF agreement we can live without it."

VOSSELER: My point is deploy now—a decision to deploy now. Because unless you make a decision to deploy, when we made a decision to deploy Poseidon, within four years we had it. What we are talking about is research, research, research ad infinitum. Research is not going to resolve, it's what is going to keep the researchers happy. But we have engineers who are going to make this system work.

ADELMAN: I believe that the legacy of this Administration should be the three-fold idea of restoring America's strength, deploying SDI, and really aiding the freedom fighters. If we can get that kind of legacy then we have served a marvelous purpose of being the last best hope on earth. Thank you.

Working the Media to Wake Up America: Radio Interview Broadcast on 400 Stations Nationwide

The Jim Bohannon Show with guest Gene Vosseler, October 22, 1996

BOHANNON: Joining us on *The Jim Bohannon Show* is Gene Vosseler, who represents a group called High Frontier. High Frontier was founded in 1981. The group is dedicated to defending America from the threat of ballistic missile attack, I guess among other things.

You were, as a group along with other people, responsible for the flurry of activity in the 1980s behind strategic defense initiative, which is commonly known as Star Wars. And for a while everybody was talking about it. There was some funding and some research but it never really happened and now some people would say, "Gene, why do we need it at all?" Aren't you fighting a war that's already been won?

VOSSELER: Well, actually the basic problem is that America is totally vulnerable against missiles today. We can't stop one launched by accident or design. And I think that the average American would prefer that we were defended, particularly since we have technology that can be deployed that can make sure that we can sleep better at night knowing that we had that security. Currently something like 60 percent of the American people believe that we are defended against missiles. And the reality is that we cannot stop one.

BOHANNON: We've never been defended against missiles?

VOSSELER: We've actually depended upon a doctrine called Mutually Assured Destruction or MAD.

BOHANNON: We use offensive capabilities.

VOSSELER: Right. And this again was holding hostage the population of America, the population of Russia to a nuclear retaliation. And of course that might have made sense in a bipolar world where both Russia and the United States had intercontinental ballistic missiles. But currently there are thirteen nations now who are members of the nuclear club. We have a proliferation of ballistic missiles with approximately twenty-six nations having them, including such third world states as Syria, Lebanon, Iran, and Iraq.

BOHANNON: Now you said we had the existing technology. We have technology right now that we could use?

VOSSELER: We could actually deploy in the space of the next two years, the Navy's Aegis system. This is according to sixteen defense experts on Team B at the Heritage Foundation. This is a shipboard system where we upgrade the Navy's current lower-tier system and upper-tier system that can take out ballistic missiles. We can deploy for a cost between two to three billion dollars, 650 interceptors on twenty-two cruisers currently and place those near the coast and give a little defense against missiles to America. This was and can be done in the next couple of years.[26]

BOHANNON: During the Gulf War we couldn't even shoot most of those Scuds out of the sky.

VOSSELER: Well the Patriot was never really designed to take out missiles. If we have to look back on that particular scene [it was] relatively effective, who knows, there's all sorts of reports, possibly from 50 to 60 percent effective.

BOHANNON: Well, 50 to 60 percent effective isn't going to protect us if the nukes are coming.

---

[26] U.S. Navy's Aegis is a sea-based ballistic missile defense system that can provide theater-wide defense against medium and long-range ballistic missiles. As of June 2006, the U.S. Navy has equipped three cruisers with anti-ballistic missile capability. The U.S. Navy is currently converting fifteen additional destroyers, to incorporate the Aegis BMD capability, which are scheduled to be completed by 2009.

VOSSELER: But you have to understand that these were dumbed down in a big battle between [Senators] Ted Kennedy and [Dan] Quayle in terms of the Patriot. Since then, the Patriot has been upgraded. And of course Israel's going to be the second nation defended against missiles after Russia. Currently Russia is surrounded by ballistic missile defenses because they never bought into the doctrine of Mutually Assured Destruction.

BOHANNON: What about the ABM Treaty?

VOSSELER: In 1970 the ABM is an anachronism. Actually it was orchestrated by Henry Kissinger who now says it's "nuts to make a virtue of our vulnerability" in the kind of multipolar world in which we live.

BOHANNON: Isn't it still in effect?

VOSSELER: Currently it's still in effect.

BOHANNON: All right you just said the Russians have an anti-ballistic missile capability.

VOSSELER: They are allowed one hundred missile sites under that particular treaty. To show our good faith we simply said we're going to leave our America naked and vulnerable to missiles, which is what we did. They never accepted it for a moment. Like I said, Russia and a hundred miles of Russian real estate [including] Moscow and the Kremlin is currently defended against ballistic missiles. Washington, D.C., right now is naked and totally vulnerable and can't stop one.

BOHANNON: Now there are obviously nuclear warheads on top of big giant missiles in silos in Russia, [but they are] no longer in Ukraine. They've been removed from Ukraine. What about other former Soviet Republics?

VOSSELER: Well basically, as you are well aware, Russia is actually pulling back all the missiles into Russia. According to Secretary of Defense Perry...

BOHANNON: Do we know that to be the fact?

VOSSELER: Well, then again, who knows ultimately? We don't know what they may have squirreled away in that big deep hole up in the southern Urals. We don't know, no one knows in our intelligence agency. The bottom line is that currently Russia has twenty-five thousand warheads left. They should be down to about eight thousand under the START I Treaty (Strategic Arms Reduction Treaty I). Currently America is down to eight thousand warheads. And of course, Secretary of Defense Perry says that [the Soviets] are behind schedule, which is, I say, a bureaucratic euphemism for they are cheating again. Because the bottom line is [the Soviets] continue to modernize their strategic forces. The SS-27 [ICBM] is an upgrade of the mobile SS-24 and 25; one warhead has one million pounds of TNT or five hundred times what landed on Hiroshima and Nagasaki.

BOHANNON: Do we have eight thousand warheads for missiles now?

VOSSELER: We have eight thousand warheads of which two thousand have ICBM capability. Russia has twenty-five thousand warheads and of course they have six thousand plus ICBM capability.

BOHANNON: Eight thousands warheads; that will still provide a bit of a deterrent. If we were struck first wouldn't we have a second-strike capability? Wouldn't we have it with eight thousand warheads?

VOSSELER: We have what you call a Triad. In other words, our offensive capabilities are based on launching [ground-based] missiles, and from our subs, and of course our bombers. Half of our subs are at port at any given time—they are gone, they are history. And it's estimated that anywhere from 85 to 90 percent of our bombers won't get off the ground and 85 to 90 percent of our missiles won't get out of the silo.

BOHANNON: Couldn't our subs wipe out a country the size of Russia? Couldn't we wipe out their defensive capability against us?

VOSSELER: No...If half of your subs are gone, a lot of your capability is already destroyed. And the retaliatory strike is not going to have a say if they launch a massive first strike. And by the way, they still practice first-strike-scenario runs on a regular basis.

BOHANNON: Well, don't we?

VOSSELER: No.

BOHANNON: We don't? We don't have war games that may be...

VOSSELER: Not in terms of [testing] missile launching capabilities, we don't.

BOHANNON: Then what do they do? I read in the newspaper they have groups of people who get together and they simulate different situations.

VOSSELER: We have war games, but again, not the kind of first-strike scenarios the Russians play...It's very important that people know that third world states can now purchase on the open market from Russia, intercontinental ballistic launchers, that thanks to...an agreement made by Yeltsin and Clinton which means that Russia can now sell to Iran, Iraq, Libya, Syria, any third world state, the capability to launch a missile that can hit any city in America. And according to the Congressional Technical Assessment report, warheads can be placed on these missiles in the space of three hours...Even if they don't acquire nuclear warheads you have the chemical and biological warheads which are simply the poor man's bomb, the poor man's payload on missiles. So the threat is not ten or fifteen years away from now. The threat is immediate and the danger is very, very real and apparent. You have Red

China recently making a threat to nuke Los Angeles. Do you remember reading about that in the *New York Times*?

BOHANNON: Well, it could be interpreted that way. Tell us what the quote was.

VOSSELER: No, this actually happened when China was attempting to intimidate a free election in Taiwan and they were allowing ballistic missiles in the Taiwan straights. A senior Chinese official told Charles Freeman, a former assistant to the secretary of defense, that if they did invade Taiwan, America would never intervene because we valued Los Angeles more than we did Taiwan. Also the [Chinese official] stated that they were willing to give up millions of lives to retain their sovereignty over Taiwan. Now China has intercontinental ballistic missile capability. They have…approximately one hundred ICBMs that can be launched from either submarine or land. And of course they are now able to secure our latest in supercomputers. The export requirements have almost all been removed. And now they have the kind of systems that will allow them to improve the targeting of any missiles they do ever launch.

BOHANNON: Gene Vosseler is our guest. He is an adviser to the group the High Frontier. He believes we need an anti-ballistic missile defense system here in the United States.

We have a caller on the line from Missoula, Montana.

BOHANNON: Hi, welcome to *The Jim Bohannan Show*, Missoula…

CALLER: irst off I wanted to ask, he said that half of the submarines are in shore all the time; so how many does that leave out at sea at one time?

VOSSELER: We may have anywhere from twelve to fourteen out there at any given time.

CALLER: And how many missiles does each one carry?

VOSSELER: Probably about sixteen.

CALLER: So I'd say that's pretty good deterrence enough to wipe out most of the Russian major cities.

VOSSELER: But there again they are not that accurate... They're not the city-busting kind either.

BOHANNON: Wait a second, there's such a thing as a nuclear warhead that is not a city-busting kind?

VOSSELER: Yes.

BOHANNON: What, neighborhood busting?

VOSSELER: Well no. You consider for example megatonage like the SS-27 and that's city busting, that's really city busting.

BOHANNON: But the atomic bomb that we ended World War II with was a dinky little bomb compared to today's bombs and that looked like a city buster.

VOSSELER: Compared to the SS-27 that's twenty-five times difference. If half of your subs are in port at one time and you get a nuclear first strike, what president in his right mind is going to order retaliation. Ronald Reagan even made the statement at one time, because basically at that point…you weigh six thousand [Soviet] ICBMs against two thousand [U.S. ICBMs] of which 89 percent can't get out of the silos after a first strike… [and] one SS-18 with ten warheads can take out not only six or eight cities, but three or four military bases at one time. So the question is, would any president in his right mind [retaliate] if a first strike ever did take place? [Imagine] reinvigorated hardliners come into power. Yeltsin is dead, all of a sudden you have [Gennady] Zyuganov[27], God forbid [Vladimir] Zhirinovsky[28], you have a coup take place; who knows? The future is very, very unpredictable.

Do we as a nation believe in defending America? Right;

Russia obviously does. Israel is going be the second nation to have missile defenses. Arrow II, they recently did a test firing, shot a missile up, four minutes later fired another missile up, one minute later metal to metal hit and within the next two years Israel will have ballistic missile defenses just like Russia.

BOHANNON: The Russians are upgrading those SS-18s aren't they?

VOSSELER: The Russians are upgrading the SS-24 and 25s, the mobiles which actually have about three warheads on them. That's the SS-27 we're talking about now. They may be a basket-case third world economy, but one thing they put their money in and it's not in their army, [it's] their strategic forces [that] they continue to upgrade. And President Clinton actually made the statement for the eighty-second time by actual count, that currently there are no Russian missiles aimed at American children.

---

[27] Gennady Zyuganov, a fierce opponent of the reforms that led to the collapse of the former Soviet Union, is currently the leader of the Communist Party of the Russian Federation. Zyuganov barely lost to Pres. Boris Yeltsin in the 1995 presidential campaign. Zyuganov ran again in 2008 against Vladimir Putin's chosen successor, Dimitry Medvedev and finished a distant second with 18 percent of the vote. Medvedev won with 78 percent While Russian missiles are no longer targeted on America, it can take approximately twenty minutes for these missiles to be retargeted. In fact, Russia has threatened to retarget these missiles when former Soviet Bloc nations jointed NATO and, more recently, when the U.S. floated plans to deploy an anti-ballistic missile system in Czechoslovakia and Poland.

[28] Vladimir Zhirinovsky, an ultra-nationalist and founder of the Liberal Democratic Party of Russia (LDPR), launched a failed coup against Mikhail Gorbachev in 1991. In 1993, the LDPR gained 22 percent of the vote and achieved broad geographic representation in the Duma, the lower house of the Russian legislature. Zhirinovsky, who has praised Hitler and Saddam Hussein, has called for Russia to take back control over independent Estonia, Latvia, and Lithuania and for the use of tactical nuclear weapons against Chechnya. Zhirinovsky ran for president of Russia in the 2008 elections and finished a distant third with slightly more than 9 percent of the vote.

BOHANNON: Well, that's probably true but it only takes a few minutes to target those people.

VOSSELER: That is true, it only takes a few minutes to retarget. So that's smoke and mirrors.

CALLER: But sir is there anything we can do to cut them in half technology wise?

VOSSELER: If we ever deploy Brilliant Pebbles[29] in space, these are a couple thousand tiny interceptors with sophisticated computer guidance systems, we can actually take out missiles in the launch space, and it takes three to five minutes for the boxcar to release the warheads. If we have those two thousand little Brilliant Pebbles, we've had the technology seven or eight years, up in space they lie inert, they are activated only in case of a launch, and their speed is at seventeen thousand miles per hour.

BOHANNON: Mr. Vosseler, how on earth can anybody make a rational decision in two to five minutes that could change the world?

VOSSELER: You have sophisticated computers; you have command and control.

BOHANNON: Computers make mistakes.

VOSSELER: Well, I'll ask you, what's the alternative?

BOHANNON: I was just trying to picture the scenario just for a minute. Thank goodness I don't ever have to worry about being president. Imagine having to make a decision in

---

[29] Brilliant Pebbles, the top anti-missile program of the Reagan and the first Bush administrations, was an attempt to deploy a four-thousand-satellite constellation in low-Earth orbit that would fire high-velocity, watermelon-sized projectiles at long-range ballistic missiles launched from anywhere in the world. Although the program was eliminated by the Clinton administration, the concept of Brilliant Pebbles remains among the most effective means of ballistic missile defense.

three minutes time.

VOSSELER: I wouldn't want to be in that position either, but I will tell you in the event of a first-strike capability without us having missile defenses we're totally vulnerable. The cost [of deployment] of missile defense…over the next ten years is two to three billion dollars. We can deploy land-based and sea-based defenses that will actually make those big ICBM missiles obsolete. And what I can't understand is why anyone, Republican, Democrat, conservative, liberal doesn't believe in using a system that is non-nuclear, that is defensive only, whose purpose is to defend America against the threat of a rogue third world state, reinvigorated Russian hardliners, or an emerging Chinese threat.

BOHANNON: Now, Mr. Vosseler, the Republican Congress has been in office now for two years, we don't know whether they are going to be able to survive as a majority past the seating of the new Congress on January 3, that's up in the air at the moment. But that Republican majority made a missile defense part of their Contract with America and while in the majority they've never really done much. What's that all about, didn't they solemnly pledge?

VOSSELER: Well, let's generalize what they did. OK, when the Defense Appropriation Act of 1996 was put before Congress, actually Congress recommended deployment of missile defenses by the year 2003 and the president vetoed that bill because he said there is no threat for ten or fifteen years. Besides [deployment was] going to interfere with our arms control agreements with the Russians. And the result of that veto they didn't have enough votes to override the president so they dropped that. But later they came back with a Defend America Act of 1996 sponsored by the Senate and by the House, SR 1635 and HR3134… The liberal Democrats shot it down and the Senate filibustered it; they couldn't even get it off the ground in order to discuss it because they were four votes short.

BOHANNON: They had fifty-six votes?

VOSSELER: Yeah, you have to have three-fifths majority [for cloture in order to end the filibuster] and they didn't have it. So currently those bills languished. But this nominee for president, Bob Dole, says that President Clinton's current policy is irresponsible and potentially catastrophic. He said in his nomination acceptance speech that if he was elected he would make the decision to deploy his first day in office. Now we have that against the current policy of President Clinton which says, "Look we're going to wait three years, three plus three, we're going research some more, then we'll make a decision to deploy, possibly we'll deploy." And that's basically the position of the two men. [They are] totally antithetical, totally opposite on where they stand on this issue.

BOHANNON: I understand that there was in fact documented a very, very, very close call as recently as January 1995. Is that correct?

VOSSELER: I can take you back to 1990.

BOHANNON: Mr. Vosseler, I have before me a copy of an article that was published September 24 in the *Washington Times*. I'd like to read just a little bit of it for you. President Clinton, by the way, on January 4, 1995, in his State of the Union address said, "This is the first State of the Union address ever delivered since the beginning of the cold war when not a single Russian missile is pointed at the children of America."

Now on the very next day of January 5, President Yeltsin received a chilling message, Russian's every message system detected a possible surprise attack from the United States. For the first time he activated his nuclear black box to place his strategic forces on alert—a move toward retargeting nuclear warheads toward America's soil. He immediately contacted the defense minister and the generals. Mr. Yeltsin told Interfax and we kept track of that missile from beginning to end. Well the surprise attack was a Norwegian meteorological rocket. Oslo had informed the Russian Foreign Ministry in advance but the notice never reached the Defense Ministry. John B. Stuart, former director of the Office of Foreign Intelligence at the Department of Energy, later sighted an authority who described Moscow's miscalculation as coming closer to a Russian nuclear launch than at any previous time during the cold war including during the Cuban Missile Crisis.

Now we hadn't heard about that before. That's pretty frightening.

VOSSELER: Yes. Well, Russia's system is now launch on warning and that could have triggered it. I am going to take you back to 1990 when another thing that was never really reported in the West. According to a Russian general cosmonaut in a report in *Pravda,* not picked up and not reported anywhere else—I caught it in a military journal, a Russian missile did get away during maintenance. Fortunately for us it misfired and crashed a short distance from the launching sight. Now, the Secretary of Defense [William] Perry says that the chances of an accidental launch are very, very remote but so was Chernobyl and so was Three Mile Island and so is a possible nuclear missile launch.

With the instability right now in Russia we are dealing with leakage of technology and technicians going to work for rogue third world states. You have breakdown, guys aren't getting paid and in many, many cases, an accidental launch could take place. We have a film called, *One Incoming,* narrated by Charlton Heston, which I have shown currently on a university tour. It's a wake-up call to America. And this film goes through a practice scenario in the sense that one gets away and we're not sure if it's a first launch or it's an accident or what. The scenario is chilling as you watch the thing unfold... And of course in that particular video the description is made of Brilliant Pebbles, what it is, and what space technology we have that will actually defend America.

BOHANNON: Mr. Vosseler, just a question to get off the subject for a moment. Would you describe yourself politically as being conservative?

VOSSELER: I would say this. I have been a blazing liberal, OK. And I would say in the last fifteen years I have changed my mind and primarily it is on the issue of defense.

BOHANNON: But basically you are a conservative.

VOSSELER: I am not going to put a label on myself because on some things I am very liberal on and on other things I am very conservative on.

BOHANNON: If you were a conservative, I was just wondering how on earth you managed to find thirty-four college campuses that would allow you to speak. Except Hillsdale College in Michigan, there's very few universities that make conservatives feel welcome.

VOSSELER: Well, you are right but in this particular tour I used to debate Marxist professors every night when I did these tours back in 1988 and '89 for Danny Graham and it was always fascinating because they are always quoting Mikhail Gorbachev[30] to me that our SDI program was technically unfeasible, unworkable, would cost a trillion dollars, and was destabilizing and I still get those arguments whenever I debate anyone on the left and a lot of times when I do PBS.

BOHANNON: You just mentioned Danny Graham; that would be the Lieutenant General of the United States Army Retired who was the director of the Defense Intelligence Agency.

VOSSELER: Right and it was the same guy who basically pushed for missile defense back in the 1980s.

BOHANNON: We have a caller on the line from Auburn, California. Hello, Welcome to *The Jim Bohannon Show*.

CALLER: Oh, thank you. I have a couple of comments. One, in regards to Russia, I think it would be more intelligent to make Russia so dependent on the United States, we wouldn't have to worry about that because right now, we don't. There's not a whole lot of incidences that have happened other than the incident up in Oslo, Norway, with the Norwegian metrological event. I know about that and I've thought about that. But I think that's about the only thing we have to worry about.

Rather than spending all this money on the defense system, why don't we just invest in Russia; that way they'll be so dependent on the United States and we won't have to worry about it.

Another thing I want to mention on is the third world getting technology. If Russia does rely on us for all this money we can influence them not to sell this information. Also these third world nations, they don't have the targeting technology, which is the GPS Global Positioning System.

BOHANNON: Anybody can get the GPS for their off-road vehicle these days, can't you?

CALLER: Yeah, but it takes a lot more to put it into a

---

[30] Mikhail Gorbachev, the last Soviet President, tried to convince President Reagan to abandon the strategic defense initiative as a requirement for normalization of relations between the superpowers. Reagan refused. Gorbachev's perestroika and glasnost reform policies, the Soviets' economic challenges, their humiliating defeat in Afghanistan, and the surge for independence from the Soviet Central Asian Republics and Eastern Europe ultimately led to the collapse of the Soviet Union. On December 25, 1991, Gorbachev resigned. The next day, the Soviet Union collapsed.

targeting system to update like that. It takes a lot. China is working on it and they are getting pretty close I know. As far as targeting, it's one of the most difficult parts, even the target of Washington hitting Texas. It's very difficult.

VOSSELER: In terms of the first part of your question… making Russia dependent on American. Russia has been dependent. We just cranked about $30 billion into it, $10.2 billion from the International Monetary Fund. We've pumped in $1.7 billion of non-Lugar money to help them dismantle their missiles. And of course when it comes to dependency, who do you suppose has built up Russia technologically, building a thousand turnkey factories, providing the technical support, loans, and assistance we've given over the years? I'll give you one example; we have given them the technology with a sign-off from [Henry] Kissinger to allow them to MIRV their missiles. And we thought it would take up to ten years.

BOHANNON: Define MIRV for our friends who may not know the terminology.

VOSSELER: That's to shoot one missile with ten warheads and hit ten different targets and improve the accuracy ten times on a sign-off of Kissinger. Now basically that allowed the Bryant Grinding Company to sell for $25 million the technology that allowed them to do that. Then we had to spend billions of dollars to defend ourselves against our own technology. That's just one example. Our supercomputers are going over to China now. This, to me, is the height of folly. If you think Red China is a beneficent nation just look at the 1.2 million Tibetans that have been killed in that invasion of that sovereign state, or where the hundreds of students were killed in Tiananmen Square.[31] You have to look at Red China as who and what they are in terms of leadership. We are not talking about the Chinese people; we're talking about their leadership.

BOHANNON: Gene Vosseler is our guest, he represents a group called High Frontier and they believe that we desperately need an anti-ballistic missile defense system here in the United States. And we have a caller on the line from Harrisburg, Pennsylvania. Hello.

CALLER: Hello, I am calling from my home in Three Mile Island, which you mentioned a little while ago. I have had many discussions with the United States Representative Robert Walker on this topic. The problem I have with this type of a system is the people who are attacking us are not necessarily going to deliver their mayhem with ballistic missiles. We have suitcase-size nuclear bombs, and they could attack us with a virus, they have a commercial nuclear power plant, each one having more than a thousand times the radiation of a nuclear bomb. If we were to spend the money necessary for that type of system there are easily other avenues available to other countries and terrorists.

BOHANNON: How would we defend ourselves against terrorists?

VOSSELER: I think this is a very good question. It's a question that is usually raised. And I would simply say on a scale of one to ten if you take a nuclear missile with ten warheads hitting ten different spots as overt an act of terrorism.

---

[31] Tiananmen Square, a large public square in Beijing, China, was the site of a massive demonstration for democratic reform initiated by Chinese students in April 1989. It was brutally and violently repressed on June 3 and 4 by Chinese troops and tanks that killed many of the demonstrators. The number of deaths ranged from 400-800, according to the CIA, and 2,600, according to the Chinese Red Cross. Following the massacre, supporters of the demonstrators were arrested, the foreign press was banned, and media coverage was strictly controlled. Two images dominate these demonstrations: the site of one Chinese demonstrator halting the approach of Chinese tanks and a replica of the Statue of Liberty that students carried while demonstrating. Despite these activities, Beijing, China was awarded the host city of the 2008 Olympics.

Now on the other hand what you say is very, very true. We know these terrorists are getting more and more imaginative. We know too that a Stinger can actually take out a commercial jet... But the bottom line is, terrorism is with us and I think we've been very weak in handling the terrorist issue. It's not a matter of more wire-tapping and more surveillance. It has to do with sending a loud, clear message to any terrorist state that if you kill one American you take on the whole United States. And that message hasn't gotten down because Warren Christopher, our secretary of state, visited Syria about twenty-six times in the last couple years and Assad is the leader of a state that sponsors terrorism. And you have to ask yourself the question if we are depending on guys like Assad to help bring about peace in the Middle East. To me that is the height of ridiculousness.

So the message I say is this; we need to stiffen up our resolve in how we deal with terrorists. We have to give them a loud, clear message. You don't find terrorists messing with Russia. You might find some homegrown stuff and some Chechen rebels getting involved, but you don't find them dealing with any of the Arab states because basically the Arab states and the radical third world states are very, very good friends of Russia. They are being wooed by Russia. A Russian loan to Libya of eight billion dollars has been waived by Soviet Foreign Minister [Yevgeny] Primakov and of course they praised Libya's anti-terrorism position. Yet, when you come right down to it, that's the state that's got these two guys we think are responsible for bombing the Pan-American flight at Lockerbie, Scotland.[32]

Look at the Russian activities right after that little love fest that Yeltsin and Clinton had in Moscow where Clinton compared Yeltsin to Abraham Lincoln. Yeltsin flew down to Red China; they signed thirteen agreements. Russia's going to build two nuclear power plants, costing $10 billion dollars. And they toasted each other. [Chinese President] Jiang Zemin blessed the genocide in Chechnya and of course Yeltsin turned around and reciprocated a blessing of the genocide of Tibet. So when you take a look at world leaders and tin-pot dictators and rogue third world states and the emerging threat and the Russian Dumas controlled by Communists, if Yeltsin is gone tomorrow the hardliners are back; suddenly we're back in the soup of the cold war again.

BOHANNON: Let's go to Utica, New York. Hello, you're on *The Jim Bohannan Show.*

CALLER: Hello. First off I'd like to ask does your organization have a newsletter mailing list? I'd like to get on it.

VOSSELER: Yeah we do, let me give you a phone number for High Frontier. I am also heading up a group called Citizens for a Strong America, a grassroots organization of a hundred chapters organized about a year ago, has one sole purpose: to get this nation defended against missile defense. One number you can get is 888-NONUKES. We'll send you a copy a little new handbook that I just recently wrote, called *Undefended: The Case for Ballistic Missile Defense.* The foreword is by Ambassador Hank Cooper from High Frontier who heads up also Team B at The Heritage Foundation. You'll get a copy of that little book. If you want to get on the Shield, the Shield is a monthly publication of High Frontier, you can call (703)

---

[32] The bombing of Pan Am Flight 103 resulted in the deaths of 270 people from twenty-one countries and contributed to the bankruptcy of Pan Am. Two Libyans, Abdelbaset Ali Mohmed Al Megrahi and Lamin Khalifah Fhimah, were accused of the 1988 PA103 bombing. Megrahi was convicted of murder on January 31, 2001, and was sentenced to life imprisonment. His co-accused, Fhimah, was acquitted. Megrahi's appeal against the conviction was rejected on March 14, 2002. One year later, the Libyan government accepted responsibility for the bombing and offered payment of $8 million to each family as compensation, a move which people felt was motivated by Libya's desire to have international sanctions removed.

671-4111. They will put you on their mailing list and you'll get up-to-date information exactly what's taking place.

BOHANNON: Let's go to Wausau, Wisconsin. Hello, welcome to *The Jim Bohannan Show.*

CALLER: Hello. My question has to do with the actual threat of global nuclear war. If we look back at history and we look at the actual true nuclear threat to this country we can address the Berlin blockade, we can look at the Cuban Missile Crisis, we can also look at Dien Bien Phu, which was a very serious potential threat. History and the media have been moving so fast together and most recently over the last ten to fifteen years. Can you give me an example, and I am talking about a real true threat to global nuclear war, similar to the three I've given you?

BOHANNON: Okay, Gene, you've been challenged.

VOSSELER: Any third world state that can buy the technology, but more than technology, [they] can buy missile launching platforms that [can] hit any city in America is obviously a threat. Talk about history, I am going to give you a lesson from history. We can go back to Carthage and Rome, but let's go back to WWII. What happened when the West was armed following WWI, where we made the world safe for democracy. That time Nazi Germany built up. The guy that warned about the buildup of the axis powers, Winston Churchill, was labeled a warmonger, a traitor and of course when Neville Chamberlain came back with his infamous Munich Peace Pact, the world all cheered, the peace movement all cheered, until the bombs started dropping on London. Fortunately we had time then to build up and defeat the axis powers, but because we were weak, because we were appeasing, because we used political expediency, the cost of being weak by the West was fifty million lives, and more than six million lives in the holocaust.

Now my position is this; a nation such as ours, a free nation which enjoys the freedom and blessing of liberty which we have, can only be maintained in the kind of world in which we live, a Communist world, a world of sharks and dictators, through strength. And I'm talking about military, economic, political, moral, and spiritual strength as well because a nation can decay from within. Arnold Toynbee once made the statement that a nation reaches a point materially and scientifically it either etherealizes, raises to another level of consciousness, or goes down. And that's the history of civilization repeat with this. Carthage is another example. Rome destroyed Carthage in [that] they didn't believe in defense, they didn't believe in military. Rich culturally, materially, every other way, they sent three hundred of their sons to appease Rome. Rome slaughtered all three hundred sons, invaded it, leveled, and wasted it to the ground. So the bottom line I am getting across through this is, learn the lessons of history. This nation is the hope of a free world with all of our problems and all of our faults. Peace is still maintained through strength.

BOHANNON: We have a caller on the line from Jersey City, New Jersey. Hello.

CALLER: Could you expand on an alternate form of defense that we did away with ballistic missiles?

VOSSELER: He wants me to expand on the various missiles, the various defenses we could deploy. Yeah, I could do that. Right now the Air Force's working on the Minuteman III, converting them, some of them, into defensive interceptors, and for again for the cost of approximately $3.5 billion, according to their estimates. They can actually deploy a missile system using Minuteman III that can handle eighteen missiles coming in. And also the Air Force is working on laser programs, a technology a little farther down the road. So there're a variety of things we can do if we get the political will to deploy. And that's really our catchphrase question right now. Do we have the will to deploy defenses and do we have the will to deploy it in time?

BOHANNON: All right, let's take another call. Carterville, Illinois. Hello.

CALLER: Hello, Mr. Vosseler. Good evening sir. Again what kind of money are we looking at again for the [Brilliant] Pebbles defense system?

VOSSELER: We are looking at actually for less than 2 percent of our currant military budget, we can actually deploy Brilliant Pebbles, we can deploy space- and land- and sea-based systems over the next ten years. Less than 2 percent of our currant military budget, that's two cents on the dollar we can give for America security.

BOHANNON: All right, now let's go through the telephone numbers again if our listeners want to contact you and discuss this issue further. And on what university campuses will we find you next, sir?

VOSSELER: You'll find me tomorrow at George Mason; I did Georgetown on Monday, George Washington University tonight.

BOHANNON: All right, thank you Gene Vosseler for taking the time to join us this afternoon. Gene Vosseler, our guest from High Frontier.

Stumping for the Defense of America in a Nationwide Lecture and Media Tour

High Frontier, August 12, 1996

NEWS RELEASE

Gene Vosseler Campaigns for Ballistic Missile Defense
Senior Advisor, High Frontier, Chairman of Citizens For a Strong America

E. Gene Vosseler, a veteran writer, lecturer, and activist in the area of ballistic missile defense is on a nationwide tour in "a renewed campaign for ballistic missile defense." His tour of 36 cities is being cosponsored by Americans for the High Frontier and Citizens For a Strong America.

Before an audience of 2,000, Mr. Vosseler was one of two speakers who addressed defending America against missiles at the Conservative Political Action Conference (CPAC) held in Washington, D.C., earlier this year. Since then, Mr. Vosseler has discussed the topic on over 1,200 radio and television stations across the country, including *The Jim Bohannon Show* (400 stations), *The Oliver North Show* (125 stations), and *The Barry Farber* Show (100 stations). During a debate on C-SPAN's *Washington Journal* in May, he expressed his total disagreement with the Clinton administration's stance on the issue. Mr. Vosseler's TV media credits also include *Nightline, Crossfire,* Merv Griffin's *Celebrity Show,* and *Good Morning America.*

Vosseler maintains that "America is increasingly vulnerable to a missile attack from a rogue nation such as North Korea, Iran, Iraq, Libya, or Syria. Also, with the disintegration of the Russian Federation, the possibility of an accidental launch, or a radical hard-line faction taking over the Russian government and using the nuclear card, is becoming a distinct possibility. Although 60 percent of Americans think that we are already protected (and they are shocked to find out we are completely vulnerable), America is incapable of shooting down one missile," said Vosseler.

Recent events have increased our vulnerability to a missile attack:

- President Clinton agreed to amend the START I Treaty (without U.S. Senate approval) to allow the Russians to sell mobile ICBM launchers to any country—including Iran, Iraq, Libya, and Cuba.

- China threatened the U.S. with a missile attack on Los Angeles if the U.S. came to the aid of Taiwan (from *New York Times*, January 24, 1966 and *Chicago Tribune*)

With recent tragic events bringing to our awareness that there are people who would not hesitate to cause mass destruction in America, it seems a logical conclusion that we should begin to seriously consider how we can defend our nation from the horror of an inter-continental ballistic missile launched at one of our cities by accident or design. Vosseler says, "We can upgrade the Navy's Aegis systems as a sea-based defense against short-range or longer-range ballistic missiles. For a little over $1 billion, deployment could begin in about three years. For a total of about $2-3 billion, 650 defensive interceptors could be deployed on 22 cruisers as early as 2001. (This will utilize the $50 billion already invested in the Navy's Aegis system)."

Note: High Frontier, under the late Lieutenant General Daniel Graham, pioneered the Strategic Defense Initiative (SDI). Citizens For a Strong America is a 100-chapter, national grassroots organization founded by Mr. Vosseler.

E. Gene Vosseler, Biography

Writer, Lecturer, Media Personality, and Authority on Strategic Defense

Gene Vosseler, a senior advisor to Americans for the High Frontier, is one of the leading voices on defense issues in America today.

A seasoned speaker with many network media credits on television shows such as *Nightline, Crossfire,* and *Merv Griffin,* Mr. Vosseler is at his best as a hard-hitting and lively debater—yet he is also warm, witty, and diplomatic. In short, he is the ideal media personality.

Currently touring the eastern half of the U.S. on a twenty-five-city speaking tour, Mr. Vosseler addresses what he believes is the most profound issue facing the American people today: the increasing vulnerability of the United States to a Soviet first strike or to nuclear blackmail.

Publicity Credits

Television: Appeared nationally on *Nightline, Merv Griffin, Crossfire, Good Morning America,* and every major station in Los Angeles; internationally, on French, British, West German, Italian, and Australian networks.

Radio: A frequent guest on numerous local, national, and international radio talk shows.

Since 1980, has lectured widely in Canada and the U.S. for the American Security Council on the nuclear freeze and related defense issues.

Participated in over 50 televised debates and university appearances throughout California in opposition to the nuclear freeze referendum, Proposition 12. Produced antifreeze television commercials with Charlton Heston and rebutted Paul Newman's pro-freeze argument on *The Merv Griffin Show.*

Major Accomplishments

1981, Founder and first President, Friends of Freedom Council, a non-profit corporation which includes over 700 writers worldwide who are concerned with human rights and freedom issues.

1982, Director, Californians for a Strong America. Led the opposition to California's Proposition 12, the bilateral nuclear freeze referendum that was barely enacted by a 52-48 percent majority.

1982, Founder Coalition for a True Peace (CTP), an organization of refugees from Communist nations that keeps the spirit of hope alive for the many in captive nations by exposing violations of human rights by Communist regimes.

1984, National Coordinator, Ban the Soviets Coalition, a group of 165 organizations. Was instrumental in bringing about the Soviet withdrawal from the 1984 Olympic Games. Gained national recognition for speaking out on behalf of the right of Soviet and Eastern Bloc athletes and attendees to defect, as defined by the 1975 Helsinki Accords. The Coalition was prepared to offer assistance and sanctuary to defectors and was denounced by the Soviet news agency Tass and by Soviet television as the prime reason for the pullout.

Frequently published opinion writer for major news dailies such as the *Los Angeles Times,* the *Los Angeles Herald Examiner,* the *Sacramento Bee,* and the *Washington Times* as well as national and international magazines. Also authored a chapter in the book, *Peace and the Management of Fear,* a Canadian publication of essays by prominent defense experts.

1. Photo of Gene Vosseler from High School Yearbook, 1944. Gene was president of high school senior class. Wanda Vosseler working at Sacramento State University.

2. Gene Vosseler played football at Midland Lutheran College in Missouri.

Record Breakers

3. Gene was considered one of the best guards in the state. In 1946, he won the Babe Petrow award given to the best student-athlete at Midland.

4. Gene with his father on ordination day at Central Theological Seminary, 1951.

5. Mark L. Prophet, messenger of the Great White Brotherhood, crossing the Altantic Ocean.

6. Mark Prophet takes a well-deserved break during a conference.

7. Portrait of Elizabeth Clare Prophet, messenger of the Great White Brotherhood affectionately referred to as Guru Ma or Mother by her devotees

8. Mother in Montana

9. Portrait of Gene Vosseler

10. Gene and Wanda Vosseler on their wedding day, September 19, 1977.

11. Portrait of Gene and Wanda.

12. Gene and Wanda at Lake Tahoe, 1994.

13. Gene and Wanda in Kwan Yin's Chapel, Royal Teton Ranch.

14. Gene talking with students after teaching at Summit University.

15. Rev. Gene Vosseler in Mark Prophet's robe.

16. Gene Vosseler officiated at numerous weddings throughout the years including the wedding of Michael and Kaylie Utter.

17. Gene with his granddaughter Charlynn and Jeffrey Hayes on her wedding day.

18. Gene and Wanda with family (from l to r) Steven Paul, Linda Kay, David Gene, Jasmine, Judith Ann and Charlynn.

19. Gene with Mother at the Ashram of the World Mother.

20. Gene with Mother following his historic July 4, 1980 Freedom Address which Mother referred to as "a talk worthy of Lanello" at the Church headquarters in Malibu, California.

21. Gene Vosseler on the Merv Griffin Show, rebutting Paul Newman's comments on the nuclear freeze issue, 1982.

22. Gene Vosseler speaking on World Freedom Day, May 22, 1982, at City Hall Los Angeles, California.

23. Gene Vosseler, spokesperson for Ban the Soviets Coalition on CNN Crossfire with Tom Braden, May 8, 1984, on the day the Soviet's announced their boycott of the Los Angeles Olympics.

24. Gene, Wanda and Henry Kriegel with Charlton Heston at CPAC (Conservative Political Action Conference), 1996.

25. Gene with members of the Republican Senatorial Inner Circle including (l to r) Strom Thurmond, John Ashcroft, Wayne Newton (entertainer), Gene Vosseler, Trent Lott (Senate Majority Leader), and Mitch McConnell.

26. Gene with Michael Utter and Henry Kriegel prior to the The Summit Lighthouse 50th Anniversary Gala in Montana, July 4, 2008.

27.Gene and Wanda enjoy a light moment at the 50th Gala.

8. EDUCATION OF THE HEART— THE SPIRITUAL FOUNDATION FOR CHILDREN AND YOUTH

What can we do to maximize spirituality in the family? Rev. E. Gene Vosseler, spiritual leader, writer, and former director of social programs for disadvantaged youth, delivered a lecture for "Festival of the Family," a gathering held several years ago in Toronto, Canada. He made a number of important points in which he emphasized the spiritual nature of the family.

Rev. Vosseler stressed the importance of understanding the nature of the soul and recognizing the role of the family in providing a spiritual foundation for children and youth.

In the first place, I believe we have to promote a true understanding of what the family is intended to be: a unique spiritual training ground for each of its members. Contrary to what today's mass media and popular culture are trying to tell us, we must restore the understanding that each family member has his or her own indispensable role to play and that each gains immeasurably in personal growth if these roles are fully realized.

The Grand Design of Destiny

To understand our role in the family, we must first understand who we are as unique human beings, unique individual souls. We must understand God's grand design for the destiny of souls and every soul's individual calling from God. The ascended masters teach that the timetables of the conception and birth of every child are directed by Almighty God and his angels. Our divine parents choose the very special moment in history for each soul to return to earth to take part in the divine plan of the decades and the centuries.

Just think how wondrously you were made, how God cared for you personally, how your own divine Father and Mother watched over your conception, your parents, your life, your purpose, your reason for being, and carefully oversaw the nurturing of your soul and body in the womb, and you were born at that precise moment in cosmic history.

Even before a child is conceived, the divine plan of a soul has been worked out in intricate detail. The grand design of God is so exact that at the moment of conception the genes in that tiny embryo are already suited to the specific soul who will inhabit it. Before conception ever takes place, a board of spiritual overseers (the Karmic Board) together with the Higher Self of the soul, determines when and where and under what circumstances the soul will embody. These circumstances are tailored to the individual's needs in order to give the soul the best opportunity to work out her karma.

The Law of the Circle

For those of you not familiar with the term karma, let me briefly explain. Karma is a Sanskrit word meaning, "act," "deed," or "work." Karma is energy/consciousness in action; it is the law of cause and effect and of retribution. The law of karma is also known as the law of the circle, which decrees that whatever we do comes full circle to our doorstep for resolution.

The law of karma is inseparable from life upon earth. It implies reincarnation, even as reincarnation implies karma. Karma contains positive and negative momentums—momentums we have set in motion by our free will, by actions, by words, by deeds, by thoughts, by feelings, and also by inaction, not speaking out when we should, not taking action but simply sitting back and being an observer, taking life as a spectator sport.

Karma is reaping what we have sown—yesterday, five minutes ago, and ten thousand years ago. Many of us do not reap in a given lifetime what we have sown in that life. We don't know if it will take a thousand or twelve thousand years for that karma to come full circle.

Every one of us who is preparing to come into life is charged with that sense of going back to pick up the dropped stitches, set our houses in order, and then give the world something of ourselves, that great creative gift, that gift of love and sweetness, of kindness or some great monument of achievement we are meant to bring forth.

And so before conception, the parents of every child—whether they are aware of it or not in their outer consciousness—have agreed at inner levels to receive that soul. And who is that soul?

The Nature of the Soul

God is a spirit and the soul is the living potential of God. The soul's demand for free will and her separation from God resulted in the descent of this potential into the lowly estate of the flesh. When the soul descends into earthly existence, she is clothed upon with the four lower bodies.

The four lower bodies are four energy fields, interpenetrating sheaths of consciousness. Each of these bodies vibrates in a different dimension. They surround the soul for her journey through time and space—they are her vehicles of expression in the material world of form.

The body you see is your physical body. Your mental body is the cognitive body, your thinking and reasoning mind. You have an emotional body that is called the astral, or desire, body. It is the body of your feelings and your desires. The etheric, the highest vibrating of the four, is the memory body. It serves as "the envelope of the soul." The etheric sheath is the gateway to our three higher bodies, which are the Higher Self, or Christ Self; our Divine Self, or I AM Presence; and the causal body…

The ascended masters teach that it is the ultimate destiny of all of us on earth to so purify ourselves, our souls, and to so accelerate in consciousness that we will become immortal, God-free beings. The first step is to learn to listen to the Christ Self, or Higher Self, which functions as our guardian angel and guide in this life… Our great example for attaining union with our Higher Self is Jesus Christ. Jesus demonstrated complete oneness with the Christ mind while still in human form. And as we follow in his footsteps we are meant to do the same.

The ultimate goal of the path taught by the ascended masters is our soul's union with our God Self, the I AM THAT I AM, in the process called the ascension… Once we are ascended, our soul becomes an immortal atom in the great body of God and there is no further need for reembodiment.

Every soul knows deep inside that the path of growing and perfecting the self is her personal mission on earth and that immortality is her goal. We also know at a soul level that in order to reunite with our Divine Presence, we must reincarnate again and again until we gain mastery over the lower aspects of self. Thus, the soul travels from lifetime to lifetime in her etheric body, or memory body, which contains the pattern of her karma as well as the details of her divine plan. And with each new incarnation we don the remaining lower bodies—mental, emotional, and physical—and embark upon a new adventure in physical form.

The Impact of Karmic Ties

What many parents do not understand is how karma operates to reunite souls who have known each other in previous embodiments.

An enlightening little book is *Life Between Life,* by Dr. Joel L Whitton and Joe Fisher. Whitton, as you may know, is a Toronto psychiatrist who has done extensive research on the mechanism of reincarnation by means of hypnotic repression. Many of his case studies show how negative karma draws souls together again and again in the same families in order to work out their old adversities and finally free themselves from those karmic ties. When raising a family, it is essential to understand that much tension between family members may originate in the outplaying of old karma. This fact shows us the need to analyze and comprehend these patterns in order to avoid creating even more negative karma.

Whitton's research also shows how karmic tests not passed compromise the individual's progress. For example, a person who committed suicide in a precious life learned how she had aborted her opportunity in that life to fulfill her karmic plan, which included a brilliant musical career. Speaking of her previous life, she said that if only she had been patient and persevering, she could have had it all.

Whitton and Fisher state that "time and time again (subjects) have asserted…that they must undergo certain experiences in order to purge imperfection and to further personal growth." One account tells of a man named Ben who in past-life regression "reexperienced a succession of male and female lives in which he participated in vicious exchange by killing those who treated him badly.

"In this life, he has been plunged once more into a repugnant situation in which he has been tempted to opt for a violent solution. Severely brutalized as a child, Ben grew to hate his father so intensely that, at the age of eighteen, he came very close to killing him… Then, listening to the promptings of an inner voice, he changed his mind…

"This decision to desist became a major turning point in Ben's life. From that moment on, his characteristic aimlessness was replaced with ambition, he grew more outgoing, and he went on to pursue a career that brought administrative responsibilities," Through past-life repression "Ben learned that he was embroiled in karmic circumstances that were designed to teach him to withstand extreme provocation without recourse to violence."

How many of you feel like you've been placed in family situations where you have had to withstand extreme provocation? There's probably nobody here that's an exception to that, including me.

Ben discovered that prior to taking embodiment he had chosen his difficult childhood "knowing he would be severely tested by a father who had figured prominently in a series of antagonistic relationships in previous incarnations… Ben was aware of a voice which said, 'If you do it right this time, things will work out all right.'" Luckily for him, he still had an ear for the voice of conscience, the voice of the Holy Christ Self. It's a saving grace when we can listen to that voice.

The voice of conscience said to him, "If you don't do it right, you will require a learning environment of even greater intensity." By acting with restraint toward his father, he "had wrestled a karmic predicament into submission. By passing his…test, he had finally extricated himself from the pattern of error in life after life."

Whitton and Fisher also point out that "group reincarnation, in which the same set of souls evolve through constantly changing relationships in different lives, recurs frequently." This corroborates the teachings from the ascended masters. They tell us that we have all been male and female, friends and lovers, teachers and students, employers and employees, parents, husbands, wives, and children to the same souls many times over in order to work out our karmic differences and to gain mastery in each of these roles and relationships.

The ascended masters teach that a newborn child is a fully developed soul, a complete and whole being, mature as we are. Our function in relation to this child is to assist the child in having the soul make the adjustment to her four lower bodies. This is our role as parents. We are acting for and on behalf of the Creator for this child, who is not ours, but God's child, and our job from the moment of conception is to assist the child to integrate with the new temple, the new four lower bodies.

One of parents' most important tasks is to be sure that children understand the hierarchy of the family—the father and the mother respectful and loving of each other and the child as a soul they love and teach. No matter how many children are in the family, each one should be valued as an individual. Each one is special in his or her own turn. And we must be very careful to give equal time and attention to each child and equal love, for does not God love them equally?

The Role of Father and Mother

As members of the family strive to become more of their Higher Self, they begin to fulfill the role that God intended them to play. Let's take a look at these roles.

The father of the household holds the presence of God as the Father and needs to be given the dignity and respect by the family and acknowledged by the mother. She needs to uphold him so that the children know that he is the one to whom everyone turns, the rock of the Christ and the Buddha.

A wife and mother supports her husband and his position insofar as he follows the path of the Universal Christ… A husband and father likewise supports the wife and mother as she too follows the promptings of the inner Christ Self. And both parents uphold their children when they are bonded to Christ.

Paul said: "Let the husband render unto the wife due benevolence; and likewise also the wife unto the husband." In this role the father is called to raise up the Christ in himself. In Jesus' words: "And I, if I be lifted up from the earth, will draw all men unto me." The father needs to be true to his calling so that the mother can defend his honor and his actions.

The mother bears a great responsibility to protect the family, to pray for each member, to assist them in gaining control over their lower nature. At the same time she sets the example of walking in the presence of God, the Mighty I AM Presence and the Christ Presence. It's simply not possible to conquer the lower nature unless the Real Self is made plain.

The Real Self needs to shine through us every day, not with fanfare but just being that sweet presence of the mother or that firm presence of the father, depending on which role each of the parents is expressing at the moment, for, of course, both can be sweet or firm.

Regardless of whether the mother has an outside job or not, it is absolutely essential that she tend the Mother flame on behalf of the entire family. Keeping this flame in prayer and invocation, in holiness and a closeness to God makes her the listening one. Mother Mary, the blessed mother of Christ, was always listening and she listened to God and kept this inner guidance in her heart. Listening to God in this way, the mother can give strong direction to her family.

The light of the Divine Mother that the mother raises up in her meditation on God is the foundation of the parenting process. Every mother is a world mother in her own household. Through her invocations to God, the souls entrusted to her care are strengthened and uplifted.

Your Children Will Wear Your Psychology

Parents, of course, need to demonstrate harmony and love in the home. When they share a mutual commitment to God and his Christ and this is reflected in their interaction with each other and their children, each child develops a profound devotion to the parents and the parents become a pane of glass through which the child can see and love God. The child is a reflection of the levels of attainment of the parent. When it comes to the parent's self-indulgence or what the parent allows himself to get away with, the child will follow the patterns of the parent's emotions and desires.

Most of us let ourselves get away with something now and then. We think we can get away, at times, with ignoring or disobeying God's laws. As long as we're good most of the time and do everything else right, we think we can cut corners a little here and a little there. Whereas we may be able to keep ourselves in control by skipping around the edges of the law, our example may be multiplied without restraint in our children... If you do something once in their eyes, they may make it a habit and decide, "If daddy or mommy does this, it's okay."

Children tie into their parents' emotional bodies and the pattern of karma that is communicated through the parents' subconscious. And the parents transmit their unspoken self to the child.

We've all seen a father and mother duck waddling along with their baby ducks all in a row behind them. They waddle the same way. They quack the same way. And like little mirrors, the ducklings will incorporate the same emotional strengths or weaknesses as papa and mama duck.

Your children will put on your psychology and they will wear it. They imitate everything you are—how you walk and laugh, smile or frown, your speech patterns, your likes and dislikes, what you eat or don't, your tastes in entertainment, sports, politics, et cetera, et cetera. And so the greatest gift you can give to God is to understand parenting, parenthood, and parental responsibility.

If you follow a path of discipline and set standards of sacrifice, surrender, selflessness, and service, your children will take for granted that this is the way life is.

So what parents find in their offspring is many times what they have not challenged in themselves. For example, if you have a habit of losing your temper, you may see this habit manifesting in your children.

On the other hand, children have their own unique karma

for which they are solely responsible. Parents can only do their best and set an example of excellence for children to do their best.

Even if you do not have excellence in every area, you can make very clear in many, many ways every day of your life that mediocrity itself is a sin, that laziness is a sin, that there is not room for self-indulgence that allows us not to give the best of ourselves to every job we undertake. This level of excellence is the level for which a child should be praised.

The Need for Discipline in the Household

Let's look now at the need for discipline in the household. Some parents think that whenever anything goes wrong it's the parents' fault, that when children misbehave the parents should not become angry or punish them but should try to show more love. To me what that is doing is rewarding anger with love, misbehavior with love.

Now, there is an unconditional love for a lifestream for a person in his evolution toward God. But there is not unconditional love when it comes to behavior. We don't unconditionally love someone who is a perpetual alcoholic and who is destroying everyone in the family, including himself. We may love the soul that is there. We do not love the behavior and we do not love the person when he is engaged in that behavior.

The important thing to remember about discipline is that the child will develop devotion to the Father-Mother God in direct proportion to what his parents give him as love and wisdom and the discipline that he is yearning for.

When we give children an understanding of why something has to be a certain way and not simply exact blind obedience, we find that children, without exception, are little philosophers; they can reason and they can understand if we give them the logic as to why something is important to do or not do.

What are the reasons? Is it for their health or their safety, for the principle of trust, for the principle of obedience? There are many, many reasons why we ask children to do things. We are not obliged to tell them, but it does help. It does help them to be obedient.

And remember, we are all trying to avoid that intimate confrontation that demands the spanking. We try to lead the child so that he will never have to get to that point and we will never have to get to that point. But we don't shirk it and avoid it when the time comes.

If we bring up our children properly, they will become devotees who love the Father-Mother God all of their lives and who can accept themselves as dearly beloved sons or daughters of God.

So you can see yourself in this loving relationship where you are teaching the child and the child is actually your disciple—disciple meaning "the disciplined one." The child is really the disciple of God, but for now the child sees you and so you are the child's teacher...

Television, the Pseudo-Teacher

Before we talk about parents as teachers, let's take a look at the subject of television—the great pseudo-teacher... Television presents a distorted picture of society. That's the conclusion of the book *Watching America: What Television Tells Us about Our Lives,* by Robert and Linda Lichter, of the Center for Media and Public Affairs, and professor Stanley Rothman.

A review of the book reports, "According to *Watching*

America, millions of TV viewers nightly are visiting a nation where sexual infidelity is the norm, where citizens are murdered at a rate 1,400 times higher than actuality, where the rich commit most of the crimes, where businessmen almost always are bad guys, where only liberal politicians operate in the public interest...and where religion is a silly superstition."

So what can we do about this situation? If you have children, the first thing you must do is to get control of the television in your house. If you can't monitor the TV set twenty-four hours a day, you can buy and install a lockbox that blocks the flow of electricity to the TV.

Marie Winn, author of *The Plug-In Drug: Television, Children, and the Family,* comments on the dangers of using video as a baby sitter: "It interferes with socialization, the long and tedious process that teaches children the rules of acceptable behavior." She says that when parents use video to solve child-rearing problems, their opportunities to teach their children the daily lessons of life are diminished. They could end up with kids they can't control and who can't control themselves.

The Role of Parent as Teacher

A primary role of parents is to be a teacher. Your child wants to relate to you as teacher. From the moment the child is born he cannot wait for you to teach him. That is what is on every baby's mind the moment he is born. He doesn't just want you to cuddle him and love him and coo to him. He wants you to sit down and have a formal lesson to teach him. He also wants you to teach him the boundaries of cosmic law. He wants you to teach him about the world we live in, the world he has come to by your grace.

You can talk to your baby about everything, about your favorite subject. If you're an engineer, sit down and have a discussion with him about what you're doing at work and be animated, and he will smile back and get all excited because that baby is totally in touch with his adult being and his Inner Self. He is absolutely delighted that you know this and that you're talking to him about adult subjects. You can go on and on about anything that is on your mind—just don't tell your baby your problems.

So if you want to make your child feel loved, it is just as important to talk to him and teach him as it is to touch him and hold him. And as your child grows, you will of course want to continue this interactive process.

It is up to you to surround your child with constructive choices. He may be an adult within, but he is a child now and he's coming into integration with his four lower bodies and his Holy Christ Self. You do not leave him to his own devices at a young age to choose right and wrong. It's your job as a parent to help him learn to discriminate.

Surrounding your child with constructive choices is the foundation of the Montessori method. You preselect the environment of your child because the child must first learn to discriminate by your example between good, better, and best. You give the child the tools and the equipment that allow him to unfold the petals of the mind and heart and to develop spirit, soul, and body. In these early years you don't expose him to things that you don't want him to choose. For example, you may not want him to listen to heavy metal or rock music or spend hours playing video games.

The Value of Community

As we ponder the value of the nuclear family, we realize how important it is to raise our children in such a way that they are ready to become constructive, creative members of society. In order to be able to do so and to hold the fortress against the onslaughts of a civilization that appears to be rapidly breaking down, I believe that parents who are fighting for traditional values can be greatly supported by affiliation with like-minded individuals—in other words, by community, where values and beliefs are shared for the sake of mutual reinforcement.

We all know that our values and beliefs are important to us. They become a way of life as we internalize them and live them. We are drawn to others of like mind and heart because we can share our thoughts, feelings, and ideals. Community in this sense is essential for sound physical, mental, emotional, and spiritual growth.

Throughout history, communities have been recognized as strong social units, especially those with shared religious beliefs or convictions. We can think of historic communities, such as the Essenes or the early Christians, who banded together in the face of great persecution. We know of the Hindu ashram and the Buddhist sangha. In more recent times, the communities of the Hutterites, as you know, are well known here in Canada. In the United States we think of Quakers, Mormons, Amish, and many other groups. History has shown us that such groups are strong and often better able to withstand outside pressures for undesirable change than isolated individuals or families.

Prepare Young People to Make a Difference

Whatever way of living we choose, I think we all agree that caring for children and supporting them with strong family ties must be our major concern. We simply have to prepare our young people for the harsh realities of modern civilization. We have to equip them with the tools with which they can make a difference to today's challenging society.

We can't define our children's future. They will have to make their own choices. But we can provide a firm foundation of positive values, which they can fall back on in times of trouble.

Our children are a God-given gift to us—but his gift is not for keeps. We must reciprocate and return that gift to God—with increase. Our children must be given back to God as mature individuals who are ready to embark on a path of spiritual self-discovery and service unto God and their fellow men. This is the great challenge that lies before us, and all of us, whether we are parents or not, should consider how we can assist and guide the next generation.

I'd like to close with the words of Elizabeth Clare Prophet: "Remember, the servant is not greater than his Lord. You, the parent, are the servant of the Holy Christ Self of your child. You are also the servant of his soul. But you are role-playing in the role of teacher and of parent and authority figure. You never forget who that child really is."

The above is a chapter written by Gene Vosseler published in *A Spiritual Approach to Parenting; Secrets of Raising the 21st Century Child,* by Marilyn Barrick, Summit University Press, 2004.

The spiritual concepts in Rev. Vosseler's presentation are based on the teachings of Mark L Prophet and Elizabeth Clare Prophet and augmented by his many years of experience in youth and family ministry.

9. TAOISM: CHUANG TZU, WORLD PHILOSOPHER AT PLAY

A Summit University Lecture by Gene Vosseler, Summer Session 1995, August 4, 1995, Royal Teton Ranch, Corwin Springs, Montana

Editor's Note: As an instructor with Mother at Summit University, Gene delivered four lectures on Taoism—all of which are deeply compelling and provocative. What follows is Gene's lecture on Chuang Tzu, his favorite Taoist master. In this lecture Gene quotes extensively from the book, The Complete Works of Chuang Tzu by Burton Watson, published by Columbia University Press who has granted us kind permission to use these excerpts.

Good morning everyone. My attire this morning with my sandals is not a reversion to Berkeley days. It happens to be my big sore toe. As my Buddhist master would say, the most profound piece of wisdom he ever gave me that I'll never forget, "When your big toe hurts, your whole world is your big toe!" I definitely can attest to that. Fortunately it is not fractured or broken. It is just badly bruised, so I am being comfortable here today. There is no way I was going to try and get into those tight shoes.

Before we take up our third lecture on the subject of Taoism entitled, "Chuang Tzu, World Philosopher at Play," which is the title of our lecture today, I would like to share three or four illustrative vignettes of the third Taoist luminary that we've been studying and that is the great Lao-Tzu. One of the great stories on self-mastery that he told is the story contained in this little vignette.

Lao-Tzu was demonstrating his archery to Pol Hun Wojen. (Don't worry about the names, right? I can't pronounce them and you can't spell them, so we're all equal.) He drew the bow to the full. Now you get this picture, you get the visualization; he is demonstrating archery. He drew the bow to the full and placed the bowl of water on his left forearm. After he released the arrow, he fitted a second arrow to the string, released it, and fitted a third while the first was still in flight. Now this is a little bit of a hyperbole, but the whole time he was like a statue. By the way, the bowl of water did not jiggle. "This is the shooting in which you shoot," said Pol Hun Wojen. "It is not the shooting in which you do not shoot."

Now, that is a paradox or seemingly an absurd statement, right? If I climb a high mountain with you and tread a perilous cliff overlooking an abyss a thousand feet deep, will you be able to shoot? Now that's a little bit different situation, right? You're up there in this high mountain pass and there's an abyss a thousand feet? Pol Hun Wojen did climb a high mountain, and he tread a perilous cliff overlooking an abyss a thousand feet deep and he's walking backwards. Now imagine this abyss a thousand feet deep and he's walking backwards. He walked backward until half of his foot hung over the edge. Then he asked Lao-Tzu to come forward. Lao-Tzu was lying flat on his face, sweat is streaming down to his heels, and Pol Hun Wojen said, "The highest man peers at the blue sky above him, measures the yellow spring below him; tossed and hurled to the eight corners, his spirit and his breathing do not change. Now you tremble and would like to shut your eyes. Isn't there danger within you?"

That's quite a story. It's very illustrative of a great, profound truth of life. We carry within us the seeds of our own defeat. If you have fear lurking down there somewhere deep in you and you get put into a position where suddenly that trigger hits that spot of fear and it comes to the surface, who knows how you'll react to a situation?

How many of you have been in a situation where you've experienced a sudden trigger event that precipitated something in your consciousness you didn't even know was there? Virtually all of you. I think it's true. So part of our self-mastery that we gain is "go for that self-mastery in everything."

Here's another one on self-mastery: The King Shien of Chu had a slave called Yang Yang. (These names, aren't they something?) He was very skillful in rearing wild beasts and birds. He collected them and fed them in his garden and yard, and never failed to tame even creatures as savage as tigers and wolves, eagles and ospreys. Male and female herded together without fearing to couple and breed in his presence. Different species lived side by side and never pounced or bit each other. The king was concerned that the secrets of his art should not die with him, and he ordered Mao Chiu Yan to become his apprentice.

Yang Yang told Mao Chian Yan, "I am a vile slave. What have I to teach you? But I am afraid his majesty will say that I am keeping secrets from you. So let me say a few words about my method of rearing tigers. Generally speaking, it is the nature of everything with vigor in its blood (a tiger certainly has vigor in its blood, to be pleased when you let it have its way and angry when you thwart it). But you must not suppose that joy and anger come at random. When they are offended it is always because we thwart them." Try thwarting your cat. You get a real reaction, right? When that cat of mine is sitting in my favorite chair and leaving cat hair all over the chair, and

I lift it up and dump it, she squawks, and really lets me know she doesn't like it a bit.

"The man who feeds tigers does not dare to give them a live animal because they will get into a rage killing it. He does not dare to give them a whole animal because they will get into a rage tearing it apart. He keeps watch for the times when they are full or hungry, and penetrates the motives of their anger. Although tigers are a different species from man, when they fawn on the man who rears them it's because he lets them get their way. And likewise when they kill him it is because he thwarts them. That being so, how would I dare to make them angry by thwarting them? But I do not please them by giving them their way, either. For when joy passes its climax we're bound to revert to anger. And when anger passes its climax we always revert to joy, because in both cases we're off balance. Since in my heart I neither give them their way nor thwart them, the birds and the animals regard me as one of themselves. It is not only reasonable that when they roam in my garden they do not remember their tall forests and wild marshes. When they sleep in my yard they never wish to be deep in the mountains and hidden away in the valleys."

A rather humorous vignette from Lao-Tzu: Yen Hui asks Confucius a question. "Once I crossed a deep lake of Shan Shen. And the ferryman handled the boat like a god. I asked whether one can be taught to handle a boat? 'Yes,' he told me, 'anyone who can swim may be taught it. A good swimmer picks it up quickly. As for a diver, he can handle a boat even if he has never seen one before.' I questioned him further but that was all he had to say. May I ask Confucius what he meant?"

I've been playing with you on the surface for a long time. But we've never penetrated to the substance. Have you really found the way? Anyone who can swim may be taught it because he takes to the water lightly. A good swimmer picks it up quickly because he forgets the water altogether. As for a diver he can handle a boat without ever having seen one before because to him the depths seem like dry land. And a boat turning over seems no worse than a car slipping backwards. Though ten thousand ways of slipping and overturning spread out before him they cannot enter the doors of his mind. He is relaxed wherever he goes. Gamble for tiles and you play skillfully; for the clasp of your belt you lose confidence; for gold and you get flustered. You have not lost your skill but if you hold yourself back you give weight to something outside of you, and whoever does that is inwardly clumsy. You've heard the statement, "No one has any power over you except what you given them." This is definitely illustrative of that particular point.

The last modern-day parable from Lao-Tzu is a humorous anecdote on forgetfulness. Some of us may have a little problem with this subject of forgetfulness. I do from time to time.

In middle age, What Soo of Liang Lee in Soong lost his memory. He would even receive a present in the morning and forget it by evening, give a present in the evening and forget it by the morning. In the street he would forget to walk, at home he would forget to sit down. Today he would not remember yesterday, and tomorrow he would not remember today. His family were very troubled about it, and they invited a diviner to tell his fortune but without success. They invited a shaman to perform an auspicious rite but it made no difference. They invited a doctor to treat him but it did no good.

There was a Confucian of Liu who, acting as his own go-between, claimed that he could cure it. And What Soo, the wife, and children offered half their property in return for his skill. The Confucian told them, "This is clearly not a disease which can be divined by hexagrams and omens or charmed away by auspicious prayers or treated by medicines in the needle. I should try reforming his mind, changing his thoughts; there is a good chance that he will recover." Then the Confucian tried stripping What Soo, and he looked for his clothes; tried starving him, and he looked for food; tried shutting him up in the dark, and he looked for a light. The Confucian was delighted and told the man's sons, "The sickness is curable. All of my arts have been passed down secretly through the generations and they are not disclosed to outsiders. I shall send out his attendants and stay alone with him in his room for seven days."

They agreed. No one knew what methods the Confucian used but the sickness of many years was completely dispelled in a single morning. When What Soo woke up he was very angry. He dismissed his wife, punished his sons, chased away the Confucian with a spear. The authorities of Soong arrested him, and wanted to know the reason. "Formerly when I forgot," said What Soo, "I was boundless. I did not notice whether heaven and earth existed or not. Now suddenly I remember. And all the disasters and recoveries, gains and losses, joys and sorrows, loves and hates, of twenty or thirty years past, rise up in a thousand tangled threads. I fear that all the disasters and recoveries, gains and losses, joys and sorrows, loves and hates to come will confound my heart just as much as it did before. Shall I ever again find a moment of forgetfulness?"

You have a man who was in bliss because he was ignorant or forgetful of his past. *Ignorance is bliss* as they say, right? He didn't remember all of his past slights and hurts and pains. He was just bopping along through life, living and enjoying life, not worrying about the past, and not worrying about the future either. Again, this is one of those little stories with a point.

One more story I can't resist. It's about normal and abnormal. You've heard a lot said today about what is normal behavior. Normal behavior in one society is considered abnormal behavior in another culture. Normal behavior in one family, which could include yelling at the top of your lungs at everyone in the house, is considered abnormal by another family, but very normal in some families.

"Mr. Pang of Chien had a son, and was clever as a child but suffered from abnormality when he grew up. When he heard singing, he thought it was weeping; when he saw white, he thought it was black; fragrant smells he thought noisome; sweet tastes he thought bitter; and wrong actions he thought right. Whatever came into his mind—heaven and earth, the four cardinal points, water and fire, heat and cold—he always turned upside down.

"A certain Mr. Yang told his father, 'The gentlemen of Liu have many arts and skills. Perhaps they can cure him. Why not inquire among them?' The father set out for Liu, and he passed through Chien and he came across Lao-Tzu. He took the opportunity to tell Lao-Tzu about his son's symptoms. 'How do you know that your son is abnormal?' said Lao-Tzu." Nowadays, everybody in the world is deluded about right and wrong, confused about benefit and harm. Because so many people share this sickness no one even perceives that it's sickness. If you're all blind and operating in a state of density, and everyone's in the same space, who knows the difference? If the consciousness of America is operating at a very dense, low vibrational level, and almost everyone's into it, anyone who's not into it is considered weird, strange, and odd, right? No one perceives that it's sickness. "'Besides, one man's abnormality is not enough to overturn his family, one family to overturn the neighborhood, one neighborhood to overturn the state, one state to overturn the world. If the whole world were abnormal how could abnormality overturn it? Suppose the minds of everyone in the world were like your son's, then, on the contrary, it's you who would be abnormal.'" Right?

That's the point we're making. Joy and sorrow, music and beauty, smells and taste, right and wrong, who can straighten them out? One man's medicine is another man's poison. This is what you have—problems when you get the rigid moralist, who's got the answers for everything, operates like this. Anyone who doesn't operate like that is considered abnormal—strange, irreligious, unspiritual, you name it. Can you make the application?

This is what a religious fundamentalist, who is basically very moralistic in their attitude toward anyone else, would define us, as totally being servants of the devil.

Lao-Tzu says to this man. "I am not even sure these words of mine are not abnormal, let alone those gentlemen of Liu who are the most abnormal of all." You're going down there to be cured by these guys, you know, going to people who are abnormal to be cured of abnormality? Like the blind leading the blind. You better go straight home instead of wasting your money. Good advice, right?

Well, I just wanted you to get the flavor of Lao-Tzu, a great teacher and Taoist master.

Now for Chuang Tzu, my favorite. A professor of Chinese at Oxford University provides a snapshot of Chuang Tzu, the brilliant and insightful writer of Taoist teachings. He wrote, "Socrates had his Plato, Confucius his Mencius, Buddha his Gosha, and our Lord his apostle Paul, so Lao-Tzu has his Chuang Tzu. Mencius and Chuang Tzu, who were contemporaries, are the two most brilliant writers of antiquity—perhaps of all Chinese history—and Chuang Tzu, though so little read, in imaginative power the greater of the two. There is a depth of sincerity wedded to a paradoxical plainness, a spirit of humor allied to an incisiveness of argument which in both of them reminds one of Plato's dialogues." Now that's a pretty beautiful analysis of Chuang Tzu. This is one man's view of him and I've got to tell you that I agree with him totally.

"Just as the pages of Mencius are less laconic than those of his master, so it is with Chuang Tzu. The well nigh incomprehensible terseness and abstruseness of Lao-Tzu are amplified in the pages of his disciple with a wealth of interesting and amusing incidents which adds to their fascination."

In other words, when you read Lao-Tzu he takes you in pretty deep places in terms of abstract thought. While it's very, very challenging, it's less challenging than the imagination that you find in Chuang Tzu. Chuang Tzu makes different kinds of demands on you. He appeals to your imagination. His work has that flavor of being unfinished in the sense that in order to really get what he's driving at you've got to finish it yourself.

I am going to deal with that later because you can't read Chuang Tzu with cognitive, literal, and logical thinking. You don't read him that way because he speaks in metaphors. He speaks in ways that challenge you to tap in to your own intuition and your own imagination. We need that in life today. So much of life is logical, analytical, linear, commonsense, and one dimensional that sometimes we get totally bored with what passes for true wisdom.

We know very little about him. What it says is that he actually worked in a lacquer garden. We don't know if this is a specific location or it means lacquer-tree groves. The location of even where he was born in Meng is uncertain, though probably in present-day Honan, south of the Yellow River.

We think that he lived at the same time as King Hui of Wei, which would make him a contemporary of Mencius, a principle interpreter of Confucianism. Chuang Tzu wrote a work in 100,000 words, much of it in the nature of a fable. Since King Hui lived in 370 to 319 BC, Chuang Tzu probably lived somewhere in the 300s BC.[33]

Now, "whoever [he] was, the writings attributed to him bear the stamp of a brilliant and original mind." It is a very original mind.[34] It's a mind that as you turn corners with him you find unexpected surprises. "Instead of speculating on the possible source of where this mind came from, let's just look at his ideas themselves."[35]

The basic reason I love Chuang Tzu the most is that he had a great love of freedom. That is his philosophy summed up in one word. The central theme of Chuang Tzu is freedom. Everything he writes explodes the forces of anti-freedom. Whether it be in politics, in the state; whether it be in religion; whether it be in relationships, on the art of governing; whether it be in warfare—every analysis primarily supports "freedom" —freedom of the individual soul to pursue his path and his destiny, freedom to get rid of the conventional ideas that so often hamstring people, that start getting laid on you when you are a small baby, right on up through the years.

Before long you've got person and people and the masses that never have an original idea. Everyone is conditioned by their environment, their training, their teachers, and their ministers. As a result they have conventional values, conventional attitudes, and conventional morality. Underlying all is what I call "slow death"—slow and stultifying death of the soul, slow death of the spirit, slow death of that dynamic force that keeps men driving for greater spiritual awareness and attainment.

Most people are trapped in little boxes; "ticky, tacky

---

[33] Burton Watson, *The Complete Works of Chuang Tzu* (New York: Columbia University Press, 1968), p. 1.

[34] Ibid, p. 3.

[35] Ibid, p. 3.

houses." Remember that song of the sixties when they all looked the same? In fact, you don't want to be different because to be different is to be considered strange or unusual. Now, think what would happen if the great souls and the great lights in history, science, religion, or any aspect of life didn't want to be different. We'd have less than half of the inventions and innovation we enjoy today. We'd be living in a totally different world. So the central theme is freedom—that it nurtures creativity, innovation, and advancement.

Usually it's interesting, when you think we live in a world that oft times appears to be dominated by chaos, confusion, suffering, and absurdity, most people come with an answer. They say, "Well, look we're going to reform the society. We're going to give you the great, new society, the welfare state, and take care of you from the cradle to the grave. We're going to reform society, and you're all going to have, what?—a chicken in every pot, a car in every garage," that kind of philosophy, right? Most people are willing to settle for fringe benefits and a free beer. Right? Security. Security, then, is the life.

Can one have security in this life on this planetary body? What's secure about life? One day you open up your eyes and the next day you don't open them. Right? So life's secure? One day you have a nice, fat bank account and the next day you're broke. The stock market bottomed out. You're secure? One day you get in your car, a nice, new Cadillac, and you're driving down the road, all of a sudden some drunk plows into you and messes up your nice, new Cadillac and messes you up physically. You're secure!? So what security is there?

What do you go for? You go for freedom, spiritual freedom; freedom of the soul, freedom to be who you are. You tune into your own inner being. You walk your own road. You're true to your "lights." You understand that no one—and I mean no one, absolutely no one—has the word for you. There are guideposts along the way; pointers that you can turn to, the so-called expedient means that Gautama talks about and which the Taoist masters talk about. Expedient means are simply pointers. Can anyone have a spiritual experience for you, I ask you? No way! Can anyone give you, ultimately, the Truth? You have to get it from yourself, from your True Self, from your Christ Self, from your Higher Self, from that which is Real, from the Tao! Once you understand that, why be a prisoner to any man's thoughts, or any man's philosophy of life. You can't, can you, and be true to yourself?

Everyone walks their own path and everyone has to find their own way. When you do find a path with very clear signposts articulated and marked for you, you can step on to it. You can walk a path of initiation with the ascended masters, and they'll give you tests and will guide you where you need to go. They won't give it to you. They won't give it to you because they can't. They might like to but then that would deny you of your victory.

On the other hand, there is the idea that we're going to reform the individual. We have this morality that fits all of life. Bam, get into it. We're going to wham you over the head if you don't accept it and if don't get into it, you're going to hell! Now, that's how people are controlled. That's why I say that orthodox religion, for the most part, has been based on tyranny and mystery. Tyranny in that you're forced to believe in the miracle of a vanished event. That's the mystery and unless you believe in the mystery of the vanished event, you're not going to heaven. According to church dogma, the early church fathers, the Roman Catholic church, the Protestant church, Judaism—and all of orthodoxy that teaches the same basic message—you aren't going to make it. Well, I tell you what, that's a pretty good racket because you can program enough guilt and fear into a man and give him absolution and charge him a fairly good price to get it!

Yes, I am saying rigid orthodoxy... basically keeps you in a box, so the individual isn't really free to explore. If you are in a very tight Lutheran church and you're taking catechetical instruction at the age of twelve, and you ask the minister a question, the minister says, "Well, you have to take it on faith. It's a mystery. You got to believe it." If you don't believe it, you're bad. Orthodoxy is a prison. Orthodoxy, whether it be in the world of politics or in the world of government or whether in science, considers those who are innovative and those who disagree or digress from orthodoxy a sinner. Orthodox science is as fundamental as you can get. Every great scientist that has come up with a really great discovery has been considered a real nut or a heretic or a fruitcake, you know? You name it.

Where do the great advances come? They come when the individuals walk the path and are true to themselves and true to their inner being. They're not hampered by the hypocrisies and the social mores of the time. They are not limited by conventional wisdom, which, as I have indicated, is often stupidity. It's a lonely walk and you're very fortunate to find souls on that lonely walk too, who are seekers of truth, and who are open and growing. The only thing that's constant in this world is change. Think about it for a moment. You're not the same person you were when you walked into this room fifteen minutes ago. That's how fast we change. You're not going to be the same people, hopefully, after this lecture as you were before you came here today.

Chuang Tzu is a prophet of freedom. That's why I love him. Most people say you reform the world, you reform others, you reform yourself. You know what Chuang Tzu says? "Free yourself from the world!" That's his way to do it. "Free yourself from the world."[36]

---

[36] Ibid, p. 3.

I remember one time I had a dream, and I was in a prison. I knew freedom was up here on a hill and I wondered, "How do I get out of this prison house that I am in, this trap, and up to the freedom of the hill, up onto the mountain top?" I began to realize that I was a prisoner of the dogma of orthodox religion, I was a prisoner of a dysfunctional home, I was a prisoner of the mores and values, many of them which I don't agree with that [were] handed down to me by my parents, and I realized I was a prisoner of what other people thought. All these different things keep us confined in prison!

Chuang Tzu says, "Free yourself from the world! Free yourself from the world."

"What does he mean by this? Section 23 tells the story of a man, Nan-jung Chu, who went to visit the Taoist sage Lao-Tzu in the hope that he could find some solution for all of his worries." Talk about trapped; he was the prisoner of his worries and his fears. "When he appeared, Lao-Tzu promptly inquired, 'Why did you come with all this crowd of people?' The man whirled around in astonishment looking for someone standing behind him. Needless to say, there was no one there. The 'crowd of people' that he came with was the baggage of his old ideas, the conventional concepts of right and wrong, good and bad, life and death and he lugged them about wherever he went!"[37]

Now, that's what you call being a prisoner of your own consciousness, right? You create your world—you do. By every choice, thought, word, and deed you create your world. You create your consciousness. If your consciousness is of fear, you've created it. The "inner child work" is designed to get back to some of the underlying causes of these fears and resolve them.

---

[37] Ibid, p. 3.

Every new insight comes on the death of an old idea. Have you realized that? Every new insight, every new bit of understanding you get about life or any part of life, usually comes upon the death of an old attitude, the death of an old life. Some people are so afraid to let an attitude die that they don't grow. They may be eighty, ninety, or one hundred years of age and they haven't had a new thought in eighty or ninety years because they're not willing to grow, they're not willing to be open to change, they're not willing to confront the so-called status quo. They've hit that comfort zone: "It's nice. I've got 'three squares' a day. I've got a roof over my head. I've got a nice vehicle. I've got a nice marriage. I've got a good job. Why don't I just simply vegetate and die eventually; I'll have a fairly good life!" How many people live like that? Probably 90 percent of the people who live, live on that level! Or the other philosophy is a libertine philosophy summed up simply as, "Drink and be merry, for tomorrow we die."

Understand Chuang Tzu: "Free yourself from the world." Get rid of the luggage and baggage of old ideas. That's what you do when you go to Summit University. You're challenged every time you turn around. If you came in like I did, a flaming liberal in 1977. I had all of the basic liberal conditioning—not that I was a liberal, raised a liberal. My parents were very conservative, ultra-conservative. When I went through my period of rebellion, I was right there with the liberal worldview of life.

I don't look at the things with a liberal or conservative worldview, I look for truth wherever I can find it. Occasionally I even find it in liberal circles—rarely but sometimes. I look at conservative circles and I see a lot of things I don't agree with. There's a lot of rigidity of consciousness, particularly in the area of spiritual growth and religious freedom. Who are attracted to our church? Spiritually, the liberals are attracted. Conservatives and right-wingers are not particularly attracted to our spiritual path. Occasionally you will find conservatives.

How many in this room were conservatives when you found the Path? You're pretty conservative? Well, that just goes to show "for every law there is an exception." Right?

How many of you were liberals, more or less, in terms of life when you came in to these teachings? The majority of you were liberals. When a person's ready for truth it doesn't make any difference whether you're a liberal or a conservative or anything.

What am I saying? "You can't be the prisoner of any idea." I just threw out an idea; the liberals are attracted to us spiritually and conservatives aren't. We saw right away, that doesn't fully hold. Right? So Gene Vosseler doesn't have the ultimate word for you on the subject of liberals and conservatives and our spiritual path? Amazing! Amazing! Right? Learn to question, learn to challenge, learn to think, and learn to think for yourself. Conventional wisdom is usually not wisdom at all.

"It is the baggage of conventional values that man must first discard before he can be free."[38] Isn't that true? Think about it for a moment. Didn't you have to get rid of a lot of baggage before you came to this path?

If you come out of a traditional Roman Catholic background or the traditional Lutheran background, you not only had to deal with your parents and your family and your friends, you had to get rid of a lot of baggage. You had to rid yourself of the idea of living one life, the concept of original sin, venal sin, mortal sin, and all of the distinctions that doctors of theology have worked up over the years to keep you in chains. You get rid of the baggage of conventional values or ideas. You've got to get rid of the shackles of orthodoxy before you can be free.

---

[38] Ibid., p. 4.

"Chuang Tzu saw the human sufferings that Confucius, Mo Tzu, and Mencius saw. He saw the man-made ills of war, poverty, and injustice. He saw the natural ills of disease and death. But he believed that these were ills only because man recognized them as such."[39]

Think of the apostle Paul who once made this statement, which is a Taoist statement, "I've learned in whatsoever state I am in to be content." Money—content; no money—content; sick—content; healthy—content. Think about it for a moment. Whatever your state of consciousness, whatever is happening in your world, the true master is content. When you stop and think about that, that's mastery. We are all a slave to the concept that suffering is bad, wrong, and no good or that having money is good. If you're not attached to either suffering or to pleasure, money or no money—you're being freed from the world. Do you get that point? It is a very, very important point.

"If man would forsake his habit of labeling things good or bad, desirable or undesirable, then the man-made ills, which are the product of man's value-ridden actions, would disappear and the natural ills that would remain would no longer be seen as negative or as ills, but as an inevitable part of the course of life."[40] That's what I mean about going with the flow. You go with the flow and the rhythm of your life. You accept what comes to you from the external world as part of life: death, loss of a loved one—part of life.

How do we know death is a bad state? Is death a bad state? A lot of people think it is a bad state. It may be a bad state if you're not in a good space in consciousness when you go through death. That's not good, right? We know what happens to the soul that goes to the other side. Death for many people

---

[39] Ibid., p. 4.
[40] Ibid., p. 4.

is simply an entryway into the kingdom of light. Many people get up into that kingdom of light, and when it's time for them to come back and reembody they don't want to return! Why go back into this veil of tears when it's really great up in the etheric retreats sailing around with the angels. It's a great space of beautiful consciousness where souls I am with are my kin brothers and sisters, studying and growing and learning together. What a great space to be! You look at death is an illusion. Why? Death is not real. Is life real? Let me ask that question, an interesting question. It is a dream about the butterfly, right?

"In Chuang Tzu's eyes, man is the author of his own suffering and bondage." Like I said, you create your world, I create my world, I create my heaven, I create my hell by my actions, by my thoughts, by my works, and by my deeds. I've been busy creating it since time immemorial, since I first took embodiment, as have you. "Man is the author of his own suffering and bondage, and all of his fears spring from the web of values created by himself alone. Chuang Tzu sums up this whole diseased, fear-struck condition of mankind in the macabre metaphor of the leper woman who, 'when she gives birth to the child in the deep of the night, she rushes to fetch a torch and examine it, trembling with terror lest it look like herself'.

"But how is one to persuade the leper woman that disease and ugliness are mere labels that have no real validity?"[41] Well, now that's a challenge to your conscious mind. Some say, "Well, yeah, I am a little bit ugly and, boy, I sure know the difference!" Right? Disease and ugliness are mere labels that have no real validity. "It is no easy task, and for this reason the philosophy of Chuang Tzu, like most mystical philosophies, has seldom been fully understood and embraced in its pure form

---

[41] Ibid., p 4

by" no more than a small number of people, the aristocratic, spiritual elite, a small group of people who are ready for this kind of teaching. "Most of the philosophies of ancient China are addressed to the political or intellectual elite; Chuang Tzu's is addressed to the spiritual elite."[42]

Now, this is a tough job. He's tackling the mass consciousness of the planet, of his age, and of his time. He is also taking on the conventional wisdom and values of his age. He is going head-to-head with the prevailing political, scientific, and spiritual philosophy of his time, and he hits it! You can imagine how he is received. Many people simply dismiss him out of hand just as they have tried to dismiss us. They say, "Oh, that crazy screwball. Oh those weird cultists up there in Paradise Valley. They believe in all sorts of strange things like reincarnation, you know?" You're in the same boat, friends, as Chuang Tzu in terms of the condemnation of the world.

Chuang Tzu used many, many devices to try to wake up people, (sort of like Soren Kierkegaard[43]—Kierkegaard was a gadfly, too. I like Kierkegaard; he's been cursed as the founder of modern existentialism, but read Kierkegaard and you'll get a lot of truth out of him, too). Chuang Tzu tells us that your values and conventional values are meaningless. "One device he uses is a non-sequitur, a non sequitur or nonsensical remark."[44] It sounds stupid when you hear it, but it jolts the mind, to help awaken you. When you hear a non-sequitur you

---

[42] Ibid., pp. 4-5

[43] According to the *Stanford Encyclopedia of Philosophy,* Søren Aabye Kierkegaard was a profound and prolific nineteenth century writer in the Danish "golden age" of intellectual and artistic activity. Kierkegaard's work crossed the boundaries of philosophy, theology, psychology, literary criticism, devotional literature, and fiction. He brought this potent mixture of discourses to bear as social critique in order to renew Christian faith within the Danish Church and Christendom.

[44] Watson, *The Complete Works of Chuang Tzu,* p. 5.

think to yourself, "What, what, that sounds really strange!" "It jolts the mind into an awareness of a truth outside the pale of ordinary logic." Most people's thoughts fit very neatly and nicely, logically into an analytical system of thought that I imagine they've worked and built over lifetimes. As I've said before, you can have a system of thought but not a system of existence. When you introduce free will, you can explode any system of thought. It's like Zen—it's the same kind of approach.

The other device he uses is what I call a pseudo-logical discussion, or debate. It starts out sounding very reasonable, very rational. Then, all of a sudden, you're getting into what sounds like inane gibberish. And you're saying, "What! My God, what's happening?" You know? But he does that.[45]

These two devices are found in their purest form in the writings of Chuang Tzu. What you have is the fiercest, the most dazzling assaults ever upon man's conventional system of values, his concepts of time, of space, causality, and reality.[46] He hits it all and spares nothing.

Finally, he uses the deadliest of weapons against all that is pompous, staid, and so-called holy. What does he do it with? Humor. Actually, most Chinese philosophers use humor very sparingly. But Chuang Tzu makes it his core. It's his style. He's learned the truth that you can actually explode more pomposity and harangues with "a laugh than you can in ten pages of harangue, right? You can get right to the point with a keen barb of humor. He's very good in the use of irony, and you've got to handle irony very carefully and sparingly because it can be very hurtful as well.[47]

---

[45] Ibid., p. 5.
[46] Ibid., p. 5.
[47] Ibid., p. 5.

To Chuang Tzu, "poverty is no less desirable than [wealth], to recognize death [no] less desirable than life."[48] Chuang Tzu doesn't withdraw. He doesn't hide from life or go up in the hills somewhere and meditate. He remains within society but he doesn't act out of the motives that drive most people, which are the desires of safety, [security,] wealth, fame, and success.[49]

Isn't that what the world is all about? Aren't those the temptations that Jesus defeated? Popularity, power, and pleasure—all of these things were the temptations that Jesus defeated.

"He maintains a state that is referred to as *wu wei*—inaction. This is not forced quietude but it is a course of action that doesn't have a purposeful motive" behind it. There is no energy, "I am doing this for this purpose, for my gain or my striving or my popularity." [Instead] "all human actions become spontaneous."[50]

This is a great state to arrive at—spontaneity, right? How much of life is spontaneous today? How many people act spontaneously out of the center of their being without having to stop to think about everything they say before they say it? Spontaneity is a lost art. You get attached to things, to ideas, to desires, and to what you want out of situations that it's hard to be spontaneous.

"But like all mystics, Chuang Tzu insists that language is, in the end, grievously inadequate to describe the true Way." In other words, you can't even describe the true Way or the wonderful freedom of the man who has realized his identity with the Tao in mere words. Once you realize your identity with the Tao how do you describe it? You don't. You experience it." Again and again, he cautions, [I am only] giving a rough, a

---

[48] Ibid., p. 5.
[49] Ibid., p. 6.
[50] Ibid., p. 6

reckless description of these things. Then you get "a passage of usually very poetic, very paradoxical" in terms of language, "that conveys very little [if anything about] the essential thing [he is talking about, or about] the state of being." But, again, it's little pinpoints of light along the way. "These mystical passages, with their wild and whirling words, don't need to puzzle the reader if you recognize them for what they are."[51]

You can't subject Chuang Tzu's thought to rational, analytical, logical thinking. Now I know this is going to upset some of you. Some of you are used to moving and operating on the analytical level almost 95 percent of the time because that's the way you've been trained. You can't subject his thought to rational, systematic analysis. As you read and reread his words and when you cease to logically think about what he is saying, you develop the intuitive sense of the mind—what is moving behind the words and the world in which it moves.

Chuang Tzu is the founder of this great school. I think he is greater in many ways than the insights of Lao-Tzu.

Actually Taoism, from time to time, did receive support from the political powers that be, but basically they liked the Confucian model a bit better. Most politicians in this day would like the Confucian model. It is a little more reliable, a little more commonsense, a little more predictable, a little more linear. You don't need to look at Taoism and Confucianism as opposing schools of thought; they're complementary. Confucianism deals with more the political, ethical, practical, and commonsense things; and the other, the Tao that is propounded by Chuang Tzu, deals with mystical philosophy and the mystical elements in life, the things that give us the deepest satisfaction and joy in living.[52]

Influencing Taoism was the gradual spread of Buddhism. And of course, Chuang Tzu was also influenced to a certain

[52] Ibid., p. 13

extent by Buddhism. He lived in a time when the age of skepticism when the political system was crumbling. It was an age of ferment, similar to today—the dawning Age of Aquarius. There is an intellectual, spiritual ferment occurring today. People are much more open to the kind of teachings that are being propounded now than they were two hundred years ago when dogma ruled supreme. You're aware that in times of upheaval and change, this is the time when people are open [to] mystical visions and more and more people are there to receive them.

Chuang Tzu, the book, is comprised of fifty-two sections. The first section includes chapters one to seven called the "inner chapters." This is the heart and guts of Chuang Tzu's writing. Scholars agree that these inner chapters are Chuang Tzu's work (as opposed to writings done by others in his name.) Then you have fifteen sections called the "outer chapters." The last eleven sections are called "miscellaneous chapters."[53]

"It is generally agreed that the seven 'inner chapters' constitute the heart of Chuang Tzu. They contain all of his important ideas. [They]'re written in brilliant, distinctive—though difficult—style. [They]'re probably the earliest in date, although we can't really prove that assumption." We know that he has "a superbly keen, original mind. [We know that there are possibly] interpolations," later editorial comments of others as well.

"In order to pry men loose from their conventional concepts of goodness and beauty, Chuang Tzu deliberately glorifies everything that to ordinary eyes appear sordid, base or bizarre —ex-criminals who have suffered mutilating punishments, men who are horribly ugly or deformed, creatures of grotesque shape or size.[55]

[53] Ibid., p.13
[54] Ibid., p. 14
[55] Ibid., p. 18

"There's one passage, very famous, in his description where master Tung-kuo asks Chuang Tzu, 'This thing called the Way—where does it exist?'

"Chuang Tzu says, 'There is no place it doesn't exist!'

"'Come,' said Master Tung-kuo, 'You must be more specific.'

"'It's in the ant.'

"'As low a thing as that?'

"'It's in the panic grass.'

"'But that' lower still!'

"'It's in the tiles and shards.'

"'How can it be so low?'

"'It's in ordure.'

"[If in] Chuang Tzu's language, ugly [sometimes] stands for beautiful, or something beyond both beauty and ugly, and bad stands for good, or something beyond it, then what do beautiful and good stand for?" Again, he challenges your thinking. "In other words, since Chuang Tzu deliberately turns the value of words upside down, how are we going to ever know for certain if he's sincerely praising something? [You don't.] This is the most serious problem that one encounters in interpretation of Taoist writings, [and] the writings of Zen Buddhism."[56]

Can you make logical sense out of Zen Buddhism? If there's anybody in this room that can make it, I'd love to hear it. There's no logical sense in Zen Buddhism. It explodes your mind. It gets you out of your normal ruts of thinking and it puts you in a different space, and it's in this different space where you encounter the Tao.

[56] Ibid., pp.18-19

"In any given passage, is the writer, regardless of what word he uses, describing a state of affairs that is in his eyes commendable or uncommendable? Depending upon how you answer that question, the interpretation of that entire passage will differ radically."[57]

Now, this is more or less a good introductory background. Much of what I've shared, except for the ad-libbing, is from Burton Watson and his book, *The Complete Works of Chuang Tzu*. He writes a very good book.

Let's turn to answer your question, "What are the teachings of Chuang Tzu?" In the first chapter we get an exposure of the uselessness of mere sense knowledge. If you have a lot of sense knowledge—a lot of people consider that very wise—he says that's uselessness. He also says that time and space is relative. We know that now from modern physics that that's true. The doctrine of relativity, which is as commonplace in Greek as it is in modern philosophy, is the basis, both in ancient and modern times, of two opposite conclusions. Either, it's argued that all sense knowledge is relative, and sense is the only organ of knowledge, therefore, real knowledge is impossible; or else [it's argued] the relativity of sense knowledge is meant to draw a sharp contrast between sense and reason—to turn away from the outward in order to listen to the inner voice. The one alternative is skepticism; the other is idealism. In Greek thought you have the former represented by the Sophists;[58] the latter by the Paracletist.

There is no doubt which side Chuang Tzu comes down on. He exposes fallacious and superficial thinking. First it looks like the destruction of knowledge because he simply lays it flat like Socrates, who was called a Sophist because of his

---

[57] Ibid., p.19

[58] The greatest contribution of Sophists, fifth century BC Greek philosophers, was their application of rational analysis to the world.

destructive criticism and his restless challenging of popular views. But Chuang Tzu has nothing of the skeptic in him. In the second chapter entitled "The identity of Contraries," which discusses the idea of opposites, he embraces and maintains with Pericles[59] that all things are one!

"For Taoism, Confucianism also, is essentially monastic." It's unitary in its thinking. "All is embraced in the obliterating unity of Tao. The wise man passing the realm of the infinite finds rest therein. The uninitiated, guided by the criteria of their own mind, see only the contradictions, the manifoldness, and the differences. The sage sees the many disappearing into the one." When we reach that point in life when we no longer look at life dualistically but look at it organically and holistically, we will have made a major step in our consciousness. "The sage sees all as one." If you see yourself as one with your brother, are you going to start kicking your brother around? No, you're going to treat your brother differently.

Subjective and objective, positive and negative, here and there, somewhere and nowhere, all of this blends in what we could call the unity of life.

"Tao, although it's possessed of feeling and power of expression, is passive or effortless and formless. It can be transmitted yet not received, apprehended yet not seen. Its root is in itself; it is self-existent, having continued of old before heaven and before earth existed." (Before heaven and earth existed, the Tao!) "It is Tao which makes the spirit Spirit, and which makes God a Spirit. It produced heaven and it produced earth. It was above the Tai Chi, the primordial mass out of which the universe was formed—" (out of the opposites, the idea of heaven

---

[59] Pericles (ca. 495–429 BC) was the leading statesman of Athens for some forty years, during her Golden Age, a period where Athens reached her highest point of power and splendor. Pericles, whose name in Greek means *"surrounded by glory"* was an able general, a distinguished orator, statesman, and leader.

and earth) "—yet it may not be deemed high. It was below the Tai Chi yet it may not be deemed deep. It was before the production of heaven and earth and yet may not be deemed of long duration. It's older than the highest antiquity yet may not be so considered. It's independent of the relations of time and space.

"What there was before the universe was Tao. Tao makes things what they are but is not itself a thing. Nothing can produce Tao yet everything has Tao within it. And it continues to produce it without end. In places, Tao seems to be confused with Ti En—heaven, as in the following instance:" (listen to this, see another bit of Taoist philosophy) "The feet of man on the earth tread but on a small space. But going on to where he has not trod before, he traverses a great distance easily. Man's knowledge is but small; but going on to what he does not already know, he comes to know what is meant by heaven. He knows it as the great unity, the great mystery, the great illuminator, the great framer, the great infinite, the great truth, the great determiner. This makes knowledge complete. As the great unity he comprehends it, as the great mystery he unfolds it, as the great illuminator he contemplates it, as the great framer it is to him the cause of all, as the great infinite all is to him its embodiment, as the great truth he examines it, as the determiner he holds it fast. Thus heaven is to him all." Heaven is all.

'Accordance with it is the brightest intelligence. Mystery has in it this pivot: such being the case the explanation of it as if it were no explanation, the knowledge of it is as if it were no knowledge, at first he does not know it but afterwards he comes to know it. In his enquiries he must not set himself to any limits and yet he cannot be without a limit; now ascending, now descending, then slipping from the grass, the Tao is yet a reality; unchanged now as in antiquity and always without defect may it not be also called that which is always capable of the greatest display and expansion.

"Why should we not inquire into it? Why should we not be perplexed about it? With what does not perplex? Let us explain about perplexed until we cease to be perplexed. So we have arrived at that great freedom of all perplexity." Sound like gibberish? Yeah! Sounds like gibberish. Blowing our minds, right?

"The question of a first cause which is raised and discussed in the following manner:" (everyone talks about a first cause: which came first, the chicken or the egg, right?) "Ti Chen said Chou She, or little wit, taught the idea of chance. Ti Chen taught causation. In the speculations of these two schools, on which side did the right lie? 'The cock crows,' replied Ti Tung Chow, 'and the dog barks. So much we know. But the wisest of us cannot say why one crows and the other barks. Nor guess why they crow and bark at all.'" Who can explain it? Can anyone in the room explain that one? No.

"Let me explain. The infinitely small is incomprehensible, the infinitely great is immeasurable. Chance and causation are limited to the condition—consequently both are wrong. Causation involves a real existence; chance implies an absolute absence of any principle. To have a name and the embodiment thereof, this is to have material existence. To have no name and no embodiment, of this one can speak and think but the more one speaks the farther off one gets."

Isn't that true? With all of the cobweb spinning of the philosophers and the intellectuals about life, the more they spin the farther off they get from the Tao, the more they get into their ego and the more they get into the abstract world of Never Never Land, a "Disneyland." You understand why metaphysical and philosophical speculations may be a nice mind-bending experience; it may be a nice mind-teasing experience. It may tickle the intellectual curiosity bone but it has no real value or no real validity. If you tap into the Tao you tap into the ultimate wisdom of who you are, what life is all about and you go with the flow. From that time on, when the realization of the Tao comes, you're free—you're free from the binding limitations of what the world, or anyone, would impose on you.

This is what the Masters want for each one of us. They want us to have the ultimate freedom to be who we are: the living manifestation of our I AM Presence, the Christ Reality, the Tao which is in us and which creates all of life, to become those co-creators with God. Causation and chance are simply limited to material existence. They have no bearing upon the infinite. Were language adequate it would take a day, fully, to set forth the Tao. Not being adequate, we could talk all day and only explain material existence; in other words, we could talk about what we see with the sense world. You can't convey it by words or by silence. In that state which is neither speech nor silence, its transcendental nature may be apprehended.

Well, that's enough for the heavy stuff. Here's an interesting point. "Can you possess Tao? As you possess a 'thing,' no. Chung asked his tutor Chang, 'Can one get Tao so as to have it for one's own?' 'Your very body,' said Chung, 'is not your own. How should Tao be?' 'If my body is not my own,' said Chung, 'pray whose is it?'" A logical question, right?

"'It is the bodily form entrusted to you by heaven and earth for the universe. Your life is not your own." We know that, don't we? "It's a blended harmony entrusted to you by heaven and earth. Your nature, constituted as it is, is not yours to hold. It is entrusted to you by heaven and earth to act in accordance with it. Your posterity are not your own. It is entrusted to you by heaven and earth. You move, but do you know how? You are at rest but you know not why. You taste but you don't know the cause. These are the operations of the laws of heaven and earth. How then could you get Tao as to have it for your own? You can't possess it.'

"Chuang Tzu frequently amuses himself by showing up Confucius at a disadvantage, often representing him as in ignorance, seeking enlightenment from Lao-Tzu or some other Taoist worthy. Here's one of several fictitious interviews in which Confucius is depicted as seeking wisdom from Lao-Tzu.

"'Today you're at leisure,' says Confucius. 'Pray tell me about perfect Tao.' The answer by Lao-Tzu, 'Purge your heart by fasting and discipline. Wash your soul as white as snow. Discard your knowledge. Tao is abstruse and difficult of discussion. Man passes through sublunary life as a white horse passes a crack—here one moment, gone the next. Neither are there any not equally subject to the ingress and the egress of mortality. One modification brings life, then another in its death. Living creatures cry out, human beings sorrow. The bull sheath is slipped off, the clothes bag is dropped.'" How's that for a description of this human body, the "clothes bag?"

"'The clothes bag is dropped and, in the confusion, the soul wings its flight and the body follows on the great journey home. The reality of the formless, the unreality of that which has form, this is known to all. What is ultimately real? That which looks out from behind your eyes or your eyes? Those who are on the road to attainment care not for these things, but the people at large discuss them. Attainment implies non-discussion; discussion implies non-attainment.'" Folks, we're all in the same right?

"'Manifested Tao has no objective value, and silence is better than argument. It can't be translated into speech, better then say nothing at all. This is called the great attainment.'" With these words I will shut up. No, I am going to continue. Shucks, right?

"Tung Prow Su asks Chuang Tzu, 'What do you call Tao; where is it? Where is Tao, hmmm?' 'There is nowhere where it is not,' replies Chuang Tzu."

Here's an interesting statement about how one master taught another master. Chuang Tzu depicts the manner in which an old Tao-imbued man taught another man, Who Li Ing Ee, to enter Tao. The characters are fictitious. The novice is presented as a man of great ability and high character. The old Taoist is represented as of great age, yet he has the complexion of a child, which he attributes to the influence of Tao. For the Taoist believes it is possible to avoid both old age and death. "Who Li Ing Ee had the abilities of a sage," says the old Taoist, "but not the Tao, while I had the Tao but not his abilities. I wish, however, to teach him, if peradventure he might become a veritable sage. Accordingly, I proceeded to do so by degrees. After three days he was able to banish from his mind all worldly matters." That's quite an accomplishment—in three days to banish all worldly matters!

"This accomplished, I continued my intercourse with him in the same way. In seven days he was able to banish from his mind all thought of men and things. This accomplished, my instruction continued. After seven days he was able to account his life as foreign to himself. This accomplished, his mind was afterwards clear as a morning. And after this he was able to see his own individuality. That individuality apprehended, he was able to banish all thought of past and present, the idea of time. Freed from this, he was able to penetrate to the truth that there's no difference between life and death; how the destruction of life is not dying and the birth of another life is not living. The Tao is a thing which accompanies all other things that meet them, which is present when they are overthrown and when they attain their completion. Its name is tranquility amid all disturbances, meaning that such disturbances lead it to perfection." It's a lot of meat for thought in that one.

"Like Lao-Tzu, Chuang Tzu taught that man had fallen from a primitive state of innocence, and he could only regain his lost condition by discarding his so-called wisdom and artificial civilization. In Chapter 9 he raises a protest against the artificiality of civilization and government, and asserts the superiority of primitive naturalness—illustrating his view by showing how much happier the horse is in its native condition; how much, even, the potter destroys the character of the clay; the carpenter the tree by his interference with its original nature. Po Lo drove horses from their native wilds, branded and clipped them, pared their hooves, haltered and shackled them, kept them confined in stables, and a third of them died. Then he kept them hungry and thirsty, trotted, galloped, groomed, and trimmed them with the misery of bit and bridle in the front, and the fear of the whip behind, and more than half of them died.

"In like manner trees and even clay suffer at the hands of interfering skill. Those who govern the empire make the same mistake, for the people have certain heaven-sent instincts, and interference with these is the cause of human nature." (Now, that's an interesting thought!). "In the days when natural instincts prevailed, men moved quietly and gazed steadily. At that time there were no roads over mountains, boats or bridges over water. All things were produced each for its own proper sphere. Birds and beasts multiplied, trees and shrubs grew up, and the former might be led by the hand, and you could climb up a peep into a raven's nest. For then man dwelt with birds and beast and all creation was one." (Sounds like Maitreya's Mystery School before the fall.) "There were no distinctions between good men and bad men."[60]

What is a good man and what is a bad man? People will

---

[60] Watson, *The Complete Works of Chuang Tzu*, pp. 105-106.

say the bad man does bad things. What does that convey, a good man and a bad man? A lot of it is perception and a person's sense of values. We know that certain things are contrary to life, certain things are enemies of life.

The world has views of what is a good man. The conventional worldview of good man is a man who goes to church and pays his taxes and treats everyone well, but he may beat his wife in private. Yet he's still considered a good man in some circles. That's probably too extreme of an example.

Have you ever thought of doing business with an extreme pietist? An extreme pietist is a man who wears his religion on his sleeve. Like the Pharisee, he'd pray in public and he'd make a great display of how religious he is, and he does all things right from an outward viewpoint, but his heart is dirty. You'd never want to do business with him because he'd screw you every time. The conventional idea of what constitutes goodness and what constitutes badness is what Chuang Tzu explodes and gets you to look at a little bit differently.

"When sages appear, tripping people over with charity and [unintelligible] duty to one's neighbor, Tao found its way into the world. And when there was gushing over religious music and fussing over ceremony, the empire became divided against itself." (He's going to give you some very straight messages here.) "Had the natural integrity of things been left unharmed, who could have made sacrificial vessels? Had the natural jade been left unbroken, who could have made libation cups? If Tao had not been abandoned who could have introduced charity and duty to one's neighbor?"

In Maitreya's Mystery School it was natural. We were all living with the Tao, in the full understanding and the full awareness of the Tao. So all these things come as a result of man's fall in consciousness.

Had Tao not been abandoned, who could have introduced

charity and duty to one's neighbor? Where man's natural instinct is good, what need would there be for religious music and ceremonies? Usually I find that the greater the ceremony, the greater the ritual, the greater the love of ritual, the farther there's a departure from Truth. Not always, but you might want to think about that a little bit. Ritual is beautiful and it has a natural place in the order and scheme of things. But when ritual is elevated to the point where ritual and sacrifice—just like the Old Testament prophets used to lampoon against—became the all-important thing and did not affect conduct for everyday life, then it becomes a crutch, it becomes an obstacle to man's relationship to God.

"Destruction of the natural integrity of things in order to produce articles of various kinds, that's the fault of the artisan. Annihilation of Tao in order to practice charity and duty to one's neighbor, that is the error of the sage. Horses live on dry land, eat grass, drink water; when pleased, they rub their necks together. When angry they kick up their heels at each other. Thus far only do their natural dispositions carry them. For put a bridle and bit, a plate of metal on their foreheads, and they learn to cast vicious looks, turn their head to bite, to resist, to get the bit out of their mouth or bridle into it. And thus their natures become depraved.

"In like manner, the people are innocent until sages came to worry them with ceremonies and music in order to rectify them, and dangle charity and duty to one's neighbor before them in order to satisfy their hearts. Then people begin to stomp and leap about in their love of knowledge and their struggle with each other, and their desire for gain. That was the error of the sages. In that golden age of innocence, the golden age of innocence the people were upright and correct." Isn't that true? Everyone walked in full awareness of their Mighty I AM Presence and their Christ Self without knowing that they were righteous. They wouldn't stop to think that they were righteous, if that's [unintelligible] of your natural awareness of who you are. "They loved one another without knowing that to do so is benevolence. They were honest and light-hearted without knowing it was loyalty. They fulfilled their engagements without knowing that to do so was good faith. In their simple doing, they employed the services of one another without thinking that they were conferring or receiving any gift."

What's he talking about here? He's talking about a golden age when people lived in full awareness of the Tao! So you understand all these different concepts we have, we wouldn't need them if we were living in a golden age, would we? Would we need the Ten Commandments? In the golden age we wouldn't need the Ten Commandments. Why, everyone would naturally obey them because they're living in the full identity of the Tao. When you're living in the full identity of the Tao do you need to have rules of right and wrong? Do you have to have regulations and all of the different things that bind life together today? Usually you find the more rules, the more regulations, the more laws, the more corrupt the society. "Well, let's have a law for this; let's have a law for that." It's usually the powers that be that use it to exploit the little people.

He said that command of the armies is the lowest virtue. Rewards and punishments are the lowest form of education. Ceremonies and laws are the lowest form of government. Music and fine clothes are the lowest form of happiness. Wailing and mourning are the lowest form of grief. And these five should follow the movements of the mind.

"Perfect politeness is not artificial. Perfect duty to one's neighbor is not a matter of calculation. Perfect wisdom takes no thought. Perfect charity recognizes no ties. Perfect trust requires no pledges. Therefore, discard the stimuli of purpose." [For example,] "I'll give you if you give me," quid pro quo; "I gave you this, why didn't you return this to me? I sent you a Christmas card. How come you forgot me? I remembered your birthday, you never remember mine!" Purpose. Motivation. Get at the cause of it.

"Free the mind from disturbances and get rid of entanglements to virtue." Can you get tangled up with virtue? "Oh God, I am so busy being virtuous today! I am going to think how virtuous I am going to be today. I am going to do this, I am going to do that and at the end of the day I am going to pat myself on the back and say, 'Look how virtuous I was, look at all the things I did that were virtuous today!'" Who wants to think about it? You simply flow with the inner being, flow with the Tao, flow with your God Reality. You give to those in need and don't even think about it.

The old Taoist is represented as instructing Confucius. He did have a lot of fun with the Confucians. Then again, why? Confucians had a very stable, ethical, commonsense system approach to life. As a result, he would simply lampoon it or stick needles into their balloon. Of course, the case is fictitious but one can compare other Confucian books with the Tao Chuang Tzu. There are many features that are described as Taoistic in both systems. You can't just simply say Confucianism had no elements of Taoism—it had a lot of freedom in it, too.

Chapter 31 tells [of an] old fisherman who is supposed to be giving instruction to Confucius. Imagine, Confucius, the master, is being instructed by this old fisherman. The fisherman actually rebukes Confucius for running after the shadows of external rites and forms, when happiness can only be found in the substance of the Tao.

"Tell me, has anyone ever found happiness in an external rite?" Well, you may want to think about that for a moment. You may find a moment of illumination. Listen to this illustration that [the fisherman] tells. "There was a man who so afraid of his shadow, so disliked his own footsteps that he determined to run away from them. But the oftener he raised his feet the more footsteps he made. And though he ran very hard his shadow never left him. From this he inferred that he went too slowly. And he ran as hard as he could without resting, the consequence being that his strength broke down and he died. He was not aware that by going into the shade he would have gotten rid of his shadow, and that by keeping still he would have put the end to his footsteps, fool that he was.

"Now you, Confucius, occupy yourself with the details of charity and duty to one's neighbor. You examine the distinction of like and unlike, the changes of motion and rest," (which is dualistic thinking) "'the benefits of giving and receiving, the emotions of love and hate, the restraint of joy and anger. And yet you cannot avoid the calamities you speak of.'" (Again he's exploding dualistic thought.) Later he adds, "'Ceremonial is the invention of man. Our original purity is given to us by heaven. It is as it is." (A great phrase in Buddhism; I like it. Such as it is.) Good point. Good argument.

Now, the point is this. Chuang Tzu is not so much condemning ritual, he's just making a joke at one level. In real terms, that level's very valuable.

We're going to take a moment and have a dialogue here. Please step up and use the mike.

Student: The point I hear you making is that ritual or ceremony is necessary and important at various stages. If we don't have some order in our lives, we need rules. We haven't got it within ourselves. The first thing we do is put it into a discipline of order. If you're talking about any society, the first thing Confucius did in recognizing the chaos of the society was to give it order, this is the first step from the known to the unknown.

The next stage after that is the Taoist, which is "being." But we can't just jump from chaos to Tao unless we are completely illuminated, which is a gradual process.

Therefore, Confucius is quite legitimate in giving us rituals and giving us the order so that we may begin to conceive that there is some order in our lives. Then we can realize the limitations of that level in order to move to the next level, which is that there is no need for order. You need to go through it.

What Chuang Tzu seems to be doing is attack order and ritual; I think there is probably virtue in the order. Then when you get past order and ritual you get into the Tao which is when there's no need for order because it is inbred within oneself, and one knows it anyway.

Gene: OK, now let me respond. You have to remember Chuang Tzu is attacking the wide spectrum of everything that is considered conventional values. Like any gadfly, like a Kierkegaard, he will sometimes overstate his point. From a logical standpoint, that is why he has been dismissed by most people as a far-out mystic. But his message isn't essentially for the masses. His message is for the spiritually elite.

Student: —for the spiritually elite, that's fine.

Gene: That's what he said. The message of Taoism as taught by this master is not going to appeal to the everyday, commonsense, routine kind of mass consciousness. It appeals to those people who are open, searching, and growing. They can see the trappings of ritual.

Now, ceremony and ritual can be beautiful in itself; but it can also be a trap. This is what the prophets conveyed.

Student: —extreme becomes a trap so that anything becomes a trap.

Gene: What we're saying is that Chuang Tzu's message is, "Look, ceremonies are made by man."

Student: You have not concern whether made by man or by initiation?

Gene: Well, who's man? God is in man, right? We could debate this. What I am getting across is something very important here. Chuang Tzu explodes the logical and analytical way of thinking of. At this particular point he can be dismissed as being irrational, right?

Student: Yeah, but that's fine if he's pretty select with his audience. My understanding of him is that he is trying to communicate with everybody, and I kept thinking that he's tearing down ritual.

Gene: How many people read Chuang Tzu?

Student: I have no idea—

Gene: Chuang Tzu will not appeal to anyone who's in the mass consciousness.

Student: By the time you want to read Chuang Tzu, you probably agree anyway.

Gene: That's right. You don't need to be told to read him so it's not a problem.

Student: There is no problem. Absolutely not!

Gene: Very Tao, you see.

Student: And what we're saying, it's all between the words rather than the words.

Gene: Yeah, yeah.

Student: —is what it is really.

Gene: hat he's saying is that words don't really mean anything, anyhow.

Student: They don't?

Gene: Yeah. The experience means a lot; well, what is the experience?

Student: The more you listen, the more you realize they don't mean anything!

Gene: What is Chuang Tzu? In all of what we're dealing with right here, Chuang Tzu is simply exposing our natural, intuitive way of thinking and our linear way of thinking. OK, thank you.

I want to make sure we cover some of these last points. We'll go back to ceremonials and the invention of man! Our original purity was given to us by heaven." Would you agree our original purity was given to us by heaven? We all agree with that.

"It is as it is and cannot be changed." Wow, that original purity can't be changed! "Wherefore the true sage models himself upon heaven, holds out his original purity, and it seems he is independent of human exigencies. Fools, however, reverse this. They can't model themselves upon heaven and have to fall back on man. They do not hold to the original purity and esteem. Consequently they are ever suffering the vicissitudes of mortality, never reaching the goal. Alas you were, sir, early steeped in deceit and are late in hearing the great doctrine.

"What, then is Tao? There is a celestial or divine Tao and there is a human Tao. In action, effortless with honor, that's the Tao of heaven. Action, effort, striving with consequent embarrassment—that is human Tao. Of this, so celestial Tao means lordship, human Tao means bondage, the condition of a servant or a slave. How far removed are the celestial Tao and the human Tao from each other? Let us clearly delineate what they are."

This is another very interesting little story. "There was a ruler of the southern sea called Shu, meaning heedless. The ruler of the northern sea was called Hu, or hasty. The ruler of central zone was called Hun Tung, chaos, not yet formed or formless. Heedless and Hasty often met on Hun Tung's territory and always were well treated by him. And so they decided they were going to repay his kindness.

"They said all men have seven orifices for seeing, hearing, eating, and breathing. Hun Tung, alone, has none. Why, he's formless. We will bore some for him. So every day they bored one hole but on the seventh day Hun Tung died." Get that one?

In the following remarkable saying about Tao, he seems to be described as a creator, preserver, and destroyer—like the work of the Holy Spirit. He goes on to speak of the confidence of a man who knows and trusts in Tao, differentiating his divine joy from all others as the highest.

"My master, my master, thou dost, thou doest or he does break in pieces all things. Dost not account it cruelty. Thou sprinklest favor in all generations without accounting of beneficence. Thou are older than the highest antiquity, and accountest it not age. Thou coverest and containeth the Universe, shaping all of its forms, and counteth it not for skill. This is the joy of heaven. Therefore, it has been said, He who knows the joy of heaven during his life proceeds it accord with heaven, and his death is a transformation.

"The perfect man, i.e., the man who's reached the highest development, is Spirit. The wide waters might boil and he would not feel hot; the great rivers might freeze and he would not be cold. Hurling thunderbolts might split the mountains, and storms sweep the ocean without making him afraid. In such case he, or such a one, would chariot himself above the wind, driving the sun and the moon, and roam beyond his earthly sphere where death and life do not affect him. How much less consideration as good and evil.

"Concerning the illusion of death he asks himself the following question, 'If so, what do they do? What maintain, what flee from, what cleave to? What resort to, what avoid, what love and what hate?'" We have the incident when Chuang Tzu's wife died, and he says, "Here she lies face upwards, asleep in the great chamber of the Universe, and were I to go about wailing and weeping for her it would be as if I did not put myself in line with my lot. Therefore, I refrain."

Now I'd like to read a beautiful little poem on the subject of death from "The Burial of Moses" by Cecil Frances Alexander.

> And had he not high honor?
> The hillside for his pall;
> To lie in state while angels wait
> With stars, for tapers tall;
> And the dark rock pines, like tossing plumes
> Over his bier to wave;
> And God's own Hand in that lonely land
> To lay him in the grave.

The disciples were very afraid of Chuang Tzu being buried. They were afraid that he'd be simply food for crows or kites. And when Chuang Tzu replied, "Above I shall be food for crows and kites, below I shall be food for moles, crickets and ants. To rob one is to feed the other. Why this partiality?" In other words, feed them both.

You come on to this attitude toward death that is a beautiful attitude. He really sees through the illusion of death, which is one of the greatest illusions of life. As long as we think death is real, we're a slave of death. We're a slave of the fear of death because it's the unknown.

The following is taken from "Tintern Abbey," a poem by William Wordsworth:

And I felt a presence which disturbs me
With the joy of elevated thoughts.
A sense sublime of something far more deeply interfused,
Whose dwelling is the light
Of setting suns and the round ocean
And the living air and the blue sky.
And in the mind of man a motion of spirit
That impels all thinking beings,
All objects of all thought,
Rolls through all things.
That blessed mood, in which the burden of the mystery,
In which the heavy and weary weight
Of all this unintelligible world is lightened.
That serene and blessed mood in which the affections
Generally lead us on
Until the breath of this corporeal frame
And even the motion of our human blood,
Almost suspended we are laid asleep in body
And become a living soul.
While with the eye made quiet
By the power of harmony and the deep power of joy,
We see into the life of things.

Now listen to Chuang Tzu on the subject of death:

All are but parts of one stupendous whole, whose body nature is nature of the soul. A change through all, and yet in all the same, great in the earth as in the ethereal frame; warmed in the sun, refreshes in the breeze, glows in the stars and blossoms in the trees; lives through all life, extends through all extent, spread undivided, operates unspent; breathes in our soul and forms our mortal part; as full, as perfect, in a hair as heart. To it no high, no low, no great, no small. It fills, it bounds, connects and equals all.

Now, I'd like to come to the section I've really been waiting to give you. These are some of the teachings that relate to me in the deeper levels of how you reach Chuang Tzu. Some of his names are great: Uncle Lackolim and Uncle Lingait (which he spells g-a-i-t).

I'd like to turn to Professor Kuan Ming Moo. He gave us the title of our lecture today: "Chuang Tzu, World Philosopher at Play." His analysis of Chuang Tzu is very provocative, very stimulating, and in my opinion very insightful. His basic premise is that Chuang Tzu is an unfinished piece of work, and that everyone must imaginatively finish it for himself. People misunderstand this book when they first read it, when they read it as literal. They take it as literal reading.

"All of the misreadings of Chuang Tzu reflect two misunderstandings: First, they are the result of grasping the ideal of happy meandering without meandering in the midst of life's problems. Second, they're the result of grasping the message literally with a casual disregard for the life situation and the creative initiative of the reader."

That's the creative initiative of the reader. You ask yourself when you read something—how does it hit you? If it hits you right, you relate to it. If it doesn't hit you right, at least it challenges you to think. All of a sudden you're wrestling with something that maybe you wouldn't have wrestled with before.

These two points are two sides of the same coin (cognitively). By this we mean an intellectual mentality that takes ready-made statements as packages of ideas. This is how most of life and reading is handled. In this way you receive the message passively. Just open your mouth, swallow, and the author tosses it down your throat just like a mother bird feeds her little baby bird. This is how most people learn, most people think in the way they relate to life—passively.

It's an intellectual exercise. You sit, you're fed, and this is how... our students like to do in class in our educational system. You're fed the teacher's word and you're supposed to regurgitate back what the teacher says. If you regurgitate it well enough and accurately enough you get an A. This is called learning? This is called thinking? No way! But it's the modern educational system. At one level, it's a test, right?

If you try to read him passively and intellectually you're going to get griped. You're probably going to close your book and say, "Is this some kind of nut?" you know. "What's he got to teach me?" If you're in that space, you're right, he doesn't have anything to teach you because you're not open to it.

If you read it intellectually, that's irrelevant to life. You say, "He's irresponsible." That's a mystical abandonment of the self, of the world. If you have a literalistic viewpoint, you find this expressing itself in religious Taoism, which is orthodox Taoism, which is to read everything literally like all orthodoxies.

If you creatively participate as a reader and allow yourself, your mind and your imagination to roam, you find yourself going to some very beautiful and interesting places. You find yourself challenging assumptions, old ways of thinking and old values that you've outgrown. This old thinking is still hanging on because they're habit, and the bits have been grooved pretty deeply in the habit patterns of your consciousness.

If all you want to do is stop growing, just stop thinking, stop being open and stop learning. Stop seeking. Then, you'll become ossified just like the rocks out there that are simply geologically, we could say, dead, in a way. Inorganic.

There are two remedies for missing Chuang Tzu. I am going to give you the remedies. First, the rosy side of the ideal must be integrated with the other excitingly risky side of living through the activities of life. You're all living human beings. Chuang Tzu delineates the drama of such integration, and the book demands that its reading continue in the paradoxes of our own lives. In other words, if this doesn't speak to you where you live, forget it, put it aside, wait until you're ready for it.

The second, which is related to the first, we must realize that Chuang Tzu's style of writing is not literalistic but metaphorical and evocative. What is something that's evocative? It is something that evokes a response! It's evocative. If I stand up here and say something that shocks you, it'll evoke a response. "The sun is really going to rise in the west tomorrow, friends." The message evokes a response. Either you'll think the guy's either nuts and he flipped his wig. So you understand the evocative.

He evokes a response! There is nothing more deadly or dull than something that does not evoke a response! The worse kind of sermon you can ever preach is one that doesn't evoke a response! This is, "Ho hum, when will he ever finish? When will she ever finish?" You shake your watch, thinking it must have stopped. It's deadly dull, boring sermon.

Chuang Tzu is evocative; he stimulates you! Great! What is great writing but stimulating! What is great teaching but stimulating! You have to be stimulated; you have to be awakened, quickened. Isn't that what the Masters have said. "Wake up!" Sometimes they even shout it. "Wake up out there, everyone!" That's what they say, right?

It accomplishes two purposes. It gives you the message to wake up spiritually and to wake up physically.

Next week we're going to have a very interesting lecture on

the subject of the alchemy of Taoism, which is very similar in many ways to Saint Germain. Alchemy is very evocative and very metaphorical. It's metaphorical in direction, he often doesn't state everything directly and unambiguously but he states it with silence or irrelevancies.

Sometimes Chuang Tzu invokes a desire to create something significant in ourselves. That's inspiration, right? All of a sudden you get a burning desire to write a poem, or deal with a situation or a relationship.

Chuang Tzu. "The great man and his teaching is like the shadow following form, the echo following sound. He dwells in the echoless, moves in the directionless, wanders in the beginninglessness. Being selfless, how can he look upon possession as possession? He who affixes his eyes upon possession was a gentleman of ancient times. He who affixes his eyes on nothingness is a true friend of heaven and earth."

What can you possess? Is there anything you can possess? You come into the world naked; you leave it the same way. Why do we get hung up on possessions? It's in this evocative manner that he lets us meander in and through the tough problems of life.

Be at home with him. So much of Chuang Tzu's project of happy meandering embraces a rugged actuality of our lives. This is not escapism. It deals directly with reality and with life. For this purpose he uses several literary devices. He likes to poke fun, act as a gadfly, challenge the established and the counterproductive measures against evil.

The more you lampoon, speak and harp about evil, the more evil grows. The more you tell people how worthless, lousy, and sinful they are, the more lousy, worthless, and sinful they become! They buy the trip! You are what you believe and what you think and what you feel about yourself. You create your world.

The tenth chapter is about moral cultivation against immorality, governmental sanctions against social ills. Chuang Tzu puts his finger in the undreamed of areas of life where true answers to our problems can be found. He points to the drunkard who falls off the running and doesn't get hurt. He has an idea of Confucius' world peace. He talks about the world of men.

Irony is more effective than a direct attack on self-defeating moralism. I love irony. I think it's very good to use it. I am going to give you an example of irony. This is a poem I once wrote when I left the Lutheran church. It's called "From Sheep-Slave to Man-Christ." This is a picture, again, of orthodox religion from a Chuang Tzu point of view:

> With eloquent words and fine gestures,
> The divinely anointed declaims
> In phrases of sweet, flowing honey
> Binding men's souls in silk chains.
>
> The priest-king today is more subtle
> Then blustering Church lords of yore
> In exploiting the credulous convert
> And milking the gullible poor.
>
> Sheep-slaves bleat for a shepherd
> A beguiling, flattering priest
> One who will whisper sweet nothings
> While keeping their wool neatly fleeced.
>
> "Don't think—don't question too freely
> Accept things just as they are
> For God has made me your teacher
> Don't carry reflection too far."

The sheep-slaves lapse into silence
In blind acceptance of fate.
The priest-king entrenches
more firmly
And strengthens his growing estate.

And what is true of religion
Is true of commerce and state,
The tyrant rules by convincing
Each man of his sheep-slave fate.

"Freedom's too precious to squander
On the child-like masses of men.
It is better that we bear it for them."
A theme from the Inquisitor Grand.

"The laws we make are for your sake,
As leader above you—we're free.
We have no need to obey rules
Our destiny above you to be."

But freedom's urge is inherent
Though blinded, fettered, and bound
Slave-sheep eventually rise up
To cast tyrant down to the ground.

And then in history's strange pattern
A great mockery of life is repeated
The sheep can't handle their freedom
A new shepherd is sorely entreated.

O God, will man ever grow up?
Will he ever have courage to be
Mature in spontaneous freedom
Fulfilling his life's destiny?

> The drama of life is a journey
> Beginning and ending in God
> Who needs our creative endeavors
> Before we can rest neath the sod.
>
> God in His infinite patience
> Is waiting for man's liberation
> In body-soul's union achieving
> The fusion of life's integration
>
> God, like man, desires union
> In freedom exalting his tryst,
> But true life is only for equals
> God waits for the advent of man-Christ.

That poem tells you about a state of consciousness which we find today in orthodox religion. I wanted to share it with you because it came from looking back at my own experience, at what I was as a Lutheran minister, what I was propagating as a Lutheran minister, and seeing the full dimensions of it.

The message of Chuang Tzu is no message because it has no items of information to convey, for instance, in how to follow one's self or what one's nature is. (We'd all like the answer to the ultimate riddles of life.) Instead it acts on the ideals we hold dear, and the attacks are so uncompromising, unconventional, so irritatingly obtrusive and challenging that people tend to laugh them out of their attention. (It's like the last poem. How would that be received in orthodox religion? I'd be hung by my toes!)

Chuang Tzu is no system builder. He simply comforts the afflicted and afflicts the comfortable. I think this is a part of life, too, isn't it? If you're hooked on consistency, forget it. He's not too consistent. At times he's almost incoherent; at times he almost babbles. But all of it has a purpose. He's a philosopher at play, a philosopher in the sense of highest use of that word.

There is talk about Chuang Tzu's tail dragging in the mud of the world. Chuang Tzu is thus a universal thinker and the importance of this fresh and quietly radical revolution goes far beyond the confines of this culture or any culture. The life vigor of his words is also ever challenging us to let go of our self-renewing existence. He's a world philosopher in the true sense.

To sum up, according to the traditional picture, he's a good-for-nothing, he invents many sophisticated excuses to pamper himself, he's a vagabond who shuts himself off from a decadent world in which he has failed. This is the typical analysis of Cuang Tzu by a lot of Western commentators. All of these you find, yet Chuang Tzu is simply riding the clouds.

The image indicates that the challenge of Chuang Tzu, both with society and to our understanding, is of no mere passing, parochial interest. He addresses himself to the universal problem of humanity. As such, his method of indirection and evocation is in line with his worthy purpose: to call us out of social platitudes back to ourselves, and thereby into raw touch with the world. (It's a great statement, right there.)

In the realm of life, there is no authority to consult, and no need to check on the accuracy of information simply because each individual must live his life as best he can. What is needed in his life is not authoritative advice but warning against taking platitude to be oneself. We do not need norms and information, but we need evocative metaphors to provoke authenticity! To be Real!

The best thing I can say about anyone is, "He's real. She's real." I am not dealing with a phoney image or hypocrisy. Such inspiration cannot be mechanically conveyed or moralistically initiated. For conveyance and imitation are other-centered activities, not self-responsible spontaneity. Everyone must start living his own life from scratch, all by himself. If virtue cannot be taught, it is because virtue is synonymous with being oneself, being one's True Self. This cannot be taught. It can only be lived by being indirectly evoked and inspired, sometimes against your inclinations. (Someone inspires you with the Truth and, God, everything in you is resisting, but you know it's true, and you want it!)

For he who fails Chuang Tzus aspiration, fails himself. Chuang Tzu's call is to self-responsibility. It's as fresh and poignant a challenge as when it was first proposed. It's as quietly as universal and crucial as one's own life pulse. He is the world philosopher who addresses himself to the universal root issue: ife itself.

Chuang Tzu would tell all those who want to approach him historically, "Go away! Let me drag my tail in the mud." In the mud of the mundane we see his tail, but his challenge is as universal as it is radical. Chuang Tzu wants us to go away from him so we can come back home to ourselves, dragging our tails with him.

He doesn't discriminate among readers. Anyone who's interested in life can profitably read him. He speaks to human individuals as human individuals. He is [as] provocatively nonchalant as he is happily spontaneous in dragging the tail of life.

I'd like to close this lecture with a little poem called "Love's Quest."

> Life without love is a desert
> Sterile and barren and bleak,
> We all need love in fulfilling
> The oneness we desperately seek.

Each soul cries out for expression
For unlived life is a crime,
Only when hearts beat in rhythm
Is there joy and rapture sublime.

The secret of love can't be hidden
It sings a song through the eyes,
Though lips may stammer and stutter
Love shines like the sun in the skies.

Eyes may be restless and yearning
Crying out with an eloquent plea,
For response in the deeps of a lover
As the tide embraces the sea.

Love is life's core and center—
Without it the rich man is poor,
While the beggar who finds joy in loving
With the wings of an angel does soar.

Courage is the mother of true love
To be really yourself is the test
And few there be who pass muster
In a life that is fully expressed.

My dimensions are high as the heavens
With depths as deep as the sea,
And only the woman who feels this
Will rest in my arms comfortably.

One must be constantly growing
In life that is lived out on earth,
Our goal is to share in creation
To give our old world a new birth.

To create is an act of the Spirit
Fed by a life-giving stream,
And nurtured with life's glowing embers
Fulfilling our lost inner dream.

The creator stands shoulders above men
In freedom exerting his powers
In living life true to his feeling
His genius takes root and flowers.

Only the creator is a free man
Spontaneous and fresh in his thrust,
Transcending his fears about sinning
His own inner being must trust.

The saint is ensnared in his own web
Though pious he struggles with sin,
He never becomes a full—free man
His strength is all bottled within.

This is my song to the world, love,
Tell no man what he should be
Let each man discover his freedom
And live out his own destiny.

For life on this earth's a shadow
A flickering moment in time
And many on earth never know love
In their life—no reason or rhyme.

Marriage is not made in heaven
But in life lived out here on earth,
True love is known only by equals
In communion bestowing new birth.

That's our message today on Chuang Tzu. I hope you have come to know him, to get a new appreciation for him, and to maybe develop a lifelong experience in working with him.

10. DEFENDING THE CHURCH

Editor's Note: Gene strove to be a staunch defender and promoter of the Messenger and of the Church. He frequently appeared before the media and served as Church spokesman.

The following was a paid advertisement from Church Universal and Triumphant. It served as a rebuttal to a series of attacks on the church published by The Thousand Oaks Chronicle in April 1980. The paid advertisement became necessary for the church to defend itself because the newspaper refused to allow a letter to the editor or a guest editorial in response.

America In Deadly Peril, Advertisement, *Thousand Oaks Chronicle*

Press Attacks on Church Universal and Triumphant Symptomatic of Anti-God Conspiracy to Discredit Religion, Undermine Unity, and Destroy Free Society

The Thousand Oaks News Chronicle front-page coverage of Church Universal and Triumphant, "Church Universal boasts of Easter gas supply," appearing April 4, 1980, is biased, inaccurate, and misleading.

Readers of the *News Chronicle* must be getting a little tired of reporter Bob Pool's obsessive and seemingly endless series of "exposé" articles probing the day-to-day activities of Church Universal and Triumphant. Quite frankly, his mosquito-like attacks are a bit wearisome to us as well.

The *Chronicle* journalistic inquisition into the beliefs and the minute daily affairs of the Church has dragged on over months. This jaded series has promoted gossip to the level of news features and proclaimed the most wildly spectacular rumors to be gospel truth.

Press Preoccupied with Trivia

In his recent sally against Church Universal and Triumphant, Bob Pool writes from a fretful "Chicken Little" perspective. In his own version of "the sky is falling," he reports that in the church's Easter poster, members were invited to fill up "at our own Shell station." Not having the concern for trivia which seems to preoccupy Mr. Pool, we did not find it necessary to put on our Easter poster the following explanation: "The gas station is owned by the Shell Oil Company. The station is leased by Lanello Reserves Inc, a profit-making corporation associated with our church, which pays taxes as does any other such corporation. The church itself only leases three lube bays for upkeep of our vehicles. Not only are our members, but the general public invited to fuel up at the station which is open regularly for everyone."

This entire process is no big mystery, since many churches are associated with business corporations that help support their religious mission. And the above explanation was available to Mr. Pool if he had been interested in facts.

Furthermore, the poster did not instruct parents to pressure young people to come to our Easter conference, as implied by Mr. Pool. The church was inviting families to share the joy of Easter together, but knowing that teenagers need to be free to make certain choices, our poster included the request to parents to leave that decision up to the young people themselves. By a twist in context, Bob Pool has managed to convey the opposite of what was actually expressed in the invitation.

Moreover, by using such loaded phrases as "Francis sidestepped a question," "Francis admitted," and "boasts the poster," reporter Pool attempts to prejudice the minds of his readers. Mr. Pool continually insults the intelligence of his readers by his continued ridicule of respected individuals and his drummed-up version of seeming calamity.

We take comfort, however, in the fact that many of our friends and neighbors have told us that the general readership is on to Mr. Pool's "much ado about nothing" approach to news coverage. He has indeed proved to all of us that he has mastered the art of the trivial and the elevation of the insignificant.

Now as to the article, "Church's camping out, county says," April 16, Mr. Pool has indeed produced an excellent picture of our parking lot—however, the lot is not a "campground." People come to our conferences from all over the country and in all kinds of conveyances, but they are not authorized to stay in their vehicles on the grounds of Camelot or to camp out here. When we referred in our conference flier to "nearby campgrounds" as potential accommodations for our visitors, we meant public campgrounds—not church property. The church does not own or operate any campground facilities. Of course, our conferees are permitted to park at Camelot while attending activities.

Reporter Perfects "Big Lie" Technique

It is unfortunate that Bob Pool cannot seem to refrain from printing gossip and rumors, such as "brainwashing goes on within the church," and "officials try to coerce members into turning over land and other property to the church"—which were his parting shots in the April 16 article. By repeating such false charges, which he attributes to anonymous sources, Mr. Pool defames Church Universal and Triumphant while he cleverly evades responsibility for his malicious actions and avoids the possibility of a potential libel suit.

Most people are aware of the established fact that if a big lie is told often enough, people will finally begin to accept it as truth. The technique was developed and widely employed by Goebbels' propaganda machine in Hitler's Third Reich for the planned destruction of the Jewish people as "an inferior race." And this notorious strategy has been used for the character assassination of many an individual. Today, Bob Pool is using the same deadly method to discredit Church Universal and Triumphant.

Church Members Defend Their Faith

As to the other front-page article, "Church letter writing was orchestrated documents reveal" appearing in the *Chronicle* on February 29, 1980, a few facts:

Mr. Pool accused church officials of mounting an organized letter-writing campaign against the *Chronicle*. He impugned the integrity of Vice President Edward Francis, mocked the church and the ascended masters, and ridiculed the use of the science of the spoken Word in decrees. He profaned all that which is sacred and holy to us.

Bob Pool also took issue with the way the church conveys prayer requests to its members and gave an old-fashioned telephone prayer hotline the rather cumbersome title of a "national telephonic communication system." His claim that the church's prayer line was used to generate a flood of mail upon the *News Chronicle* is absolutely false.

The article charged that the church had "orchestrated a campaign" of letters to the editor when, in fact, members voluntarily wrote in defense of their faith, their leader, and their church, which were being maligned in the *Chronicle* series. Church headquarters did nothing more than inform its members of the *News Chronicle'* discrediting articles, along with sending copies of the four-part series to its teaching centers across the United States.

The message to the centers was devoted almost exclusively to future articles of two other papers, the *Los Angeles Times* and the *Valley News,* which were being written at the time. Church members were invited to share their personal experience and perspective with reporters from those newspapers to provide them with necessary background material. The very brief mention of the *Thousand Oaks News Chronicle* in the communication was incidental at most. There certainly was no mention whatsoever of any letter campaign, organized or otherwise, to be directed toward the *Chronicle.*

On a separate occasion, members were invited to write to any paper printing incorrect or derogatory articles about the church. However, this is a far cry from "orchestration" charged by the *Chronicle.* No demands were made of our people. No sample letters were sent out. No review or censoring of letters was employed. Church members were simply afforded the opportunity to witness and to share their feelings about their faith.

Attack on Church Official Unfounded

Therefore, we view the attack on the integrity of Edward L. Francis, vice president of Church Universal and Triumphant, as totally unjust and unfounded. We know him to be a man of impeccable character, and his honesty is without question. He is totally devoted to the service of God and his church. Furthermore, the letter quoted by Bob Pool went out to only one hundred of our centers. Had the church really orchestrated a letter-writing campaign, appealing to our entire membership and friends, the newspaper could easily have had the ten thousand replies that Mr. Francis indicated.

Chronicle's "Blackout" Abuses Free Press

Does the *News Chronicle* think that it should be immune from rebuttal after launching an unwarranted attack against a responsible church?

Apparently so, for on February 5, 1980, they declared a new editorial policy: no more letters from Church Universal and Triumphant or its members would be printed.

It is interesting to note that while the *News Chronicle* was claiming that the church was conducting a letter-writing campaign, the shoe was really on the other foot. To date, the *News Chronicle* has published a bulky total of sixteen articles and editorials and thirteen news photos. Furthermore, four of these articles were front-page attacks mounted after the editorial "blackout" policy for Church Universal and Triumphant. The church's only recourse since that time has been to purchase space for its defense. This is an abuse of the free press and we are certain that the injustice is apparent to all.

Church Practices Reflect Historic Tradition

As for Bob Pool's mockery of the ascended masters and the science of the spoken Word, he has only revealed his ignorance of religion. The ascended masters are referred to in scripture as the "saints robed in white," and the science of the spoken Word (use of decrees) goes back to the "Command ye me!" of Isaiah, as well as to the Old Testament Psalms which have been used for centuries as responsive readings and liturgical chants.

Joshua used the power of shouted fiats to bring down the walls of Jericho. Jesus employed what were essentially decrees in his public ministry when he taught the Lord's Prayer in spoken form to his disciples, gave his "I AM" affirmations, and denounced the false gurus of his day, the "scribes, Pharisees, and hypocrites," with a series of imprecatory "woes."

Roman Catholics have recited the Hail Mary for hundreds of years, and the music of their Gregorian chants continues to inspire and uplift the hearts of true believers everywhere. Lutherans have formal liturgies, repeat their creeds, chant Psalms, and sing the Magnificat in their worship services. And, of course, there is the chanting of the Sh'ma in the Jewish Synagogue. These great religious traditions have learned to rely on God's promise as it is recorded in Job 22:28: "Thou shalt also decree a thing, and it shall be established unto thee: and the light shall shine upon thy ways"

Thus, we see that prayers, decrees, and chants have been used for centuries to invoke the dynamism of the Holy Spirit to the plane of practicality through the hearts of devotees of God. Church Universal and Triumphant stands in the same historical tradition of the use of these sacred prayer forms.

The "Reverse the Tide" decree ridiculed by Bob is used to counteract negative energy. An obvious example of such energy on a large scale is when Khomeini and thousands of Iranians were shouting death chants to America. When this occurred, church members, as part of their world service, prayed for the enlightenment of those who were ignorantly sending forth such hatred (which we consider synonymous with witchcraft) and gave their "Reverse the Tide" decree to return that energy to its source in accordance with God's will.

A not-so-obvious example is when the combination of mass hatred and the tyranny of World Communism are directed through a myopic press as a seemingly unrelated attack upon a church. Case in point: the press attacks on Church Universal and Triumphant. In such circumstances, we also pray and ask God to return the energy, qualifying the decree by asking for only the will of God to be done. Incidentally, Bob Pool's assertion that it would take twelve hours to do the "Reverse the Tide" decree 144 times is ludicrous. Only the main body of the decree is repeated and it can be done easily in thirty minutes.

Assault on Church Symptom of Deeper Malaise

Mr. Pool used rumor, slander, and misrepresentation in his effort to discredit Church Universal and Triumphant. He relied heavily for his information on the false witness of disgruntled ex-members who have their own axes to grind. Thoughtful people must ponder—why such an attack on a church? What are the motives of Bob Pool and editor Marvin

Sosna? Is it possible that the assault on Church Universal and Triumphant is symptomatic of a deeper malaise and challenge confronting our nation in general and religion in particular? We believe that the answer is yes.

Freedom under Attack: Does America Still Have the Will to Resist?

We love America. We believe in the one true God, revere all life as holy, value the proper education of our youth, and uphold our sacred freedom of religion as a pivotal point of retaining a free society.

As Americans, we need to be aware that there is an organized world attack against freedom today—including the four sacred freedoms of religion, speech, press, and assembly. We believe that the press has a vital stake in this battle and should share religion's concern; for only a free society can provide the guarantee that the press, as well as religion, will not become puppets of a controlling government. Yet, wittingly or unwittingly, the press is falling for the strategy of those who would undermine a free America through the age-old tactic of divide and conquer.

Those who would have world power use the press to pit the institutions or segments of a free society against each other—class against class, race against race, religion against religion—creating the necessary chaos and confusion for takeover while they pose as the "problem solvers" and "saviors." Unfortunately, their "solutions" always result in more governmental regulations and loss of individual freedom.

This is part of the process by which the enemies of freedom destroy free nations from within. It is happening in America today. And we ask the crucial question, do the American people, including the press, have the vision, the understanding, and the will to defend the four sacred freedoms that will insure our survival as a free nation?

It is important that people view the *Chronicle* attacks on Church Universal and Triumphant, as well as attacks on other religious groups, in the perspective of this larger picture. For the assault on a small church is symptomatic of the all-out attack on God and religion being waged by the anti-God forces operating in America today. We pray that all Americans will see through this strategy and refuse to fall for the attempt to isolate, divide, and conquer us as a free people.

Divide and Conquer: The Power Elite's Strategy for World Takeover

Who are those who would benefit from these divide-and-conquer tactics? To answer this question, we must take a look at the big-moneyed interests who control the government, economy, education, and much of organized religion. These individuals are known as the power elite, and they manipulate and mold the people and society primarily through the press and other media, which are directly linked to these interests through large holding companies. This elitist band systematically seizes and consolidates power in every country and in every political system. They stir up confusion and conflict, shape public opinion through managed news, destroy or reduce to impotence organized religion, demoralize and propagandize the youth, subvert the educational system, manipulate the economy, and co-opt the political leadership, thus corrupting the governmental process.

These power brokers use their tactics as control mechanisms for carrying out their overall strategy for world takeover. In order to achieve this goal, they must control the people through stripping them of their inherent wisdom and essential dignity. This whole destructive process is intended to produce a slave morality and a robot mentality.

God-Fearing Patriots Cannot be Controlled

However, the man of principle who loves God and freedom cannot be so controlled. To the power elite, he is the enemy who is hated and must be neutralized or destroyed.

Aleksandr Solzhenitsyn, who spans the political and economic systems of East and West, is an example of such a God-fearing patriot who is intolerable to the would-be world controllers. He is anathema in the governmental power centers in both Russia and America today. Mr. Solzhenitsyn and every apostle of freedom constitute a threat to the power elite in their plan for global domination.

World Communism and Monopoly Capitalism Work Hand in Hand

To circumvent the lovers of freedom, the conspirators mask their effort through manipulating two seemingly contradictory political-economic systems. Thus World Communism and monopoly capitalism, which appear from an ideological viewpoint to be diametrically opposed, do in actuality work hand in hand. The leaders behind the two systems are really bent on the same goal, world control. But the cooperation is at an unseen level. Those pulling the strings behind the scenes know exactly what is going on, while the people are like proverbial ostriches with their heads in the sand, completely oblivious to the impending danger. Elizabeth Clare Prophet calls this entire strategy for takeover by the power elite the "international capitalist/Communist conspiracy."

Key to World Tyranny: Crush a Man's Faith and You Destroy his Freedom

How do the conspirators propose to take over America? The key is they have to destroy man's faith in God. The individual who has a living faith possesses strength of character, moral fiber, and enduring values. He is not vulnerable to manipulation, nor is he swayed by corrupting influences. The world tyrants know that the man of God, his church, and his religious community must be made impotent or crushed.

In Russia or in nations marked for conquest, the tactic is to discredit religion and equate it with insanity. The power elite working through World Communism attack the spiritual foundations of a targeted society through their process of brainwashing called "mental healing." By skillful use of psychological and physical stimuli they either alter loyalties or destroy minds, giving the tyrants absolute control. The individuals who practice this deadly art of mind control are called "psycho politicians."

Lavrenti Beria, former head of the Soviet KGB, in a lecture to American students at Lenin University in the early 1930s, made some chilling comments in relation to the destruction of religion in America:

> *To achieve these goals the psycho politician must crush every homegrown variety of mental healing in America. Actual teachings of [William] James, Eddy [Christian Science] and Pentecostal Bible faith healers amongst your misguided people must be swept aside. They must be discredited, defamed, arrested, stamped upon even by their own government until there is no credit in them and only Communist-oriented "healing" remains.*

This demonic program, designed to destroy religion, is taking place before our very eyes. The discrediting of faith healers in America, referred to by Beria, has been going on for years and is accelerating today.

Mary Baker Eddy, the founder of Christian Science, has been and is still attacked by fundamentalists as a false prophet and founder of a "cult." Evangelist and faith healer Aimee Simple McPherson, who founded the Four-Square Gospel Church here in Los Angeles, was maligned and suffered character assassination at the hands of a sensationalist press. Pentecostal groups are dismissed as emotionally unstable "Holy Rollers." Faith healer Oral Roberts has been recently ridiculed and lampooned on the Donahue television show and *60 Minutes*. Obviously those who have worked publicly with a healing ministry have been attacked by the media with the intent to discredit [those associated with faith healing].

Religious organizations marked for oblivion are maligned and defamed, and the integrity of their leadership is called into question. Leaders are labeled by direct charge or implication as liars who are power mad, money hungry, or mentally unbalanced. Their followers are alleged to be brainwashed. Unfortunately, the ferocity of this kind of attack by local and national media on Church Universal and Triumphant may have the effect of discrediting one of the few churches that is actively exposing the impending danger to freedom of religion in America today.

Media Used to Induce Public Hysteria

Furthermore, by labeling nontraditional groups as "bizarre cults" and linking them with Jonestown, the press has generated fear and paranoia in the American people. Jonestown, a Marxist front group parading as a religious community, was an example of collective insanity. Through guilt by association, the power elite working through the media would stamp the same label, "insane," on unorthodox religion. This is only the initial step in discrediting and ultimately labeling all religion as a form of insanity, thus fulfilling the original Communist strategy for takeover.

Unfortunately, mainline, traditional churches do not seem to see what is happening and all too often applaud attacks on religious groups that they view as doctrinally unsound or as possible competitors. They will cheer on a biased press, not realizing that they are supporting the forces that will ultimately lead to their own destruction. Furthermore, when members of an unorthodox church rise up to defend their faith and to challenge the oppressors of religious freedom, they are denounced.

The "New Morality": The Power Elite's Attack on Youth

Along with the destruction of religion another major tactic of the power elite is the demoralization of youth. How will this be accomplished? In Kenneth Goff's book, *Brainwashing*, taken from the *Communist Manual of Instructions of Psychopolitical Warfare*, [which is] used by the Communist Party in America for the training of Communist cadre, the process is spelled out.

> *By making readily available drugs of various kinds, by giving the teen-ager alcohol, by praising his wildness, by stimulating them with sex literature…the psycho political operator can create the necessary attitude of chaos, idleness and worthlessness…Creating a greed for drugs, sexual misbehavior and uncontrolled freedom and presenting this to them as a benefit of Communism will with ease bring about our alignment.*

This description is a frighteningly accurate reflection of what has been called in America, the "new morality." In our schools, over one million children are taking prescription amphetamines and other psychostimulant drugs (Schrag &

Divody, *The Myth of the Hyperactive Child*), and over 50 percent of the high school students use marijuana (The Strategy Council on Drug Abuse, 1979). Teenage alcoholism is on the increase, and the rock culture glorifies drugs, easy sex, and rebellion against authority. While achievement scores decline, sex education reportedly appears in 70 percent of our schools. Teenage pregnancy and venereal disease are skyrocketing, while sexual assault and violence in many of our schools foster a climate of chaos and fear for student and teacher alike.

Abortion: The Denial of Life

Closely allied with the demoralization of youth is the abortion of the unborn child. Last year, America led the world in the destruction of life in the womb with more than 1.3 million reported abortions, one out of three by teenage mothers (projected from 1977 poll, Alan Guttmacher Institute).

We view abortion as legalized murder of the holy innocents and its acceptance and practice as a conditioned insensitivity and loss of basic reverence for life. The new morality of "casual sex," "casual responsibility," and "casual abortion" is but the outward expression of the brainwashing of not only our young people but [the shift of] our entire culture to anti-God and anti-life values and practices. We are only one step away from the justification of euthanasia, so-called "mercy killing," and the genetic engineering of robot life through the test tube.

Power Elite Brainwashes America

It is becoming obvious to thoughtful people that the power elite are imposing their tyranny through the mental conditioning of an entire culture. The elitist controllers use the media to inculcate their system of values and to condition a passive acceptance of their power and supremacy. They program the average American to crave sex, alcohol, drugs, money, entertainment, and success at the same time that they are robbing him of his spiritual heritage and sense of self-worth.

Underlying all of this destructive manipulation is hatred of God, of self, and of one's fellow man. When such hatred is directed toward an individual, he feels the actual impact of that energy. He may feel burdened, suffer psychological problems, or even become physically ill as a consequence of such an "energy hex." Furthermore, hatred, such as we see in the tearing down of a nation, is essentially synonymous with black magic or witchcraft practiced on a massive scale. And it has its impact. As Beria could have predicted, mental illness is increasing at an alarming rate, violent crime is rampant in our cities, and in one year, 4,805 demoralized youth took their own lives (U.S. Public Health Service, *Vital Statistics in the U.S.*, Vol. II, 1977). By intent and design, the power elite have created a death-oriented culture in America.

Anti-God Manipulators Enthrone Man as God

Through this death culture these despots are attacking the very roots of our heritage as a nation under God. And at the same time that they are demoralizing a nation and stripping from the people their values and heritage, these anti-God manipulators offer their own "solution"—the enthroning of man as God. The deification of man is clearly expressed in the sterile intellectualism of the scientific humanist, the mechanistic techniques of the behavioral psychologist, and the militant atheism of the Satanist. The beliefs and practices of these ungodly philosophies make them natural allies and tools of the power elite.

Thus, God is no longer welcome in our schools. But a humanistic progressive education, which discourages moral guidance by the teacher and stresses a value system based on situational ethics, is very much in vogue. The pleasure principle is supreme. Johnny may not be able to read, write, or add, but if he is "well-adjusted," everything is just fine. Moreover, you can be certain that he knows all that there is to know about sex—courtesy of his sex education classes.

Man More than a Lump of Clay

The progressive education disciples of John Dewey and the behavioral modification followers of B. F. Skinner are part and parcel of the humanist philosophy of the denial of God and the elevation of man. In *Walden Two*, Skinner speaks of experts who "shape behavior as a sculptor shapes a lump of clay." And Professor James V. McConnell, head of the Mental Health Research Institute at the University of Michigan reportedly states:

> *The day has come when we can combine sensory deprivation with the use of drugs, hypnosis, and the astute manipulation of reward and punishment to gain almost absolute control over an Individual's behavior...We want to reshape our society drastically...So that all of us will be trained from birth to want to do what society wants us to do. Today's behavioral psychologists are the architects and the engineers who are shaping the Brave New World of Tomorrow (Walter H. Bowart, Operation Mind Control).*

Humanism: A Philosophy of Atheism

These social engineers who would be the omnipotent manipulators of their fellow man find reinforcement in the atheistic philosophy of humanism. *The Humanist Manifesto II* states:

> *As in 1933, Humanists still believe that traditional theism, especially faith in a prayer-hearing God, assumed to love and care for persons, to hear and understand their prayers and to be able to do something about them, is an unproven and outmoded faith. (Claire Chambers, The SIECUS Circle: A Humanist Revolution)*

Satanist leader Anton LaVey adheres to the same beliefs as the humanist. The Satanist realizes that man, and the action and reaction of the universal, is responsible for everything, and doesn't mislead himself into thinking someone cares… The Satanist knows that praying does absolutely no good (Anton LaVey, *The Satanic Bible*). *The Satanic Bible* also says, "man, the animal, is the godhead to the Satanist."

1984 is Just around the Corner

Actually, the behaviorist, the humanist, and the Satanist are all birds of a feather and are allied with World Communism in their denial of the reality of God, the modification of human behavior, and the glorification of man as the master of all life. The end result of this amalgamation of anti-God forces is the destruction of our freedom and the introduction of mechanized man. 1984 may be closer than we think.

Elizabeth Clare Prophet's Message of Liberation

In total contrast to the anti-God manipulators, Elizabeth Clare Prophet calls people to claim their identities as sons and daughters of God. She preaches the gospel of Jesus Christ, salvation and freedom in His name, and the dignity and sacredness of all life. It is her passion for freedom and love for America that impels her to take the message of the Coming Revolution in Higher Consciousness to the world—the message of the discovery of the True Self, the Christ within, as the key to unlocking the power of the Holy Spirit for the healing of the nations.

In the tradition of the great prophets, she preaches God's truth and challenges the evils of our times, specifically exposing the conspiracy of the power elite. She is a fearless social commentator. She presents the hard facts and offers solutions that can turn the tide of political aggression, moral decay, and religious calcification.

Elizabeth Clare Prophet is a dynamic spiritual leader who combines the rare faculties of objective realism and penetrating religious insight. She reads clearly the handwriting on the wall. She is concerned about the signs of disintegration in our society and views with great concern its downward spiral and potential destruction.

In her recent book *Prophecy for the 1980s,* delivered originally as a lecture on January 1, 1980, at Camelot, she graphically outlines the critical problems facing America as a nation and a people in the next decade. In a tight-knit, carefully developed analysis of the world scene, she exposes a litany of problems—inept and corrupt leadership, inflation and monetary chaos, contrived energy crises, rising crime and drug use, mechanization education, racism and poverty, manipulation by the media, and the seeming indifference and powerlessness of the American people.

A Prophet's Call to Action

Hers however is not a doomsday message of total despair. She sounds the rallying cry for the children of God to rise up and meet the threat of totalitarianism and the other challenges of our day. She calls the American people to return to God and to bring God-solutions to bear where human solutions have failed. Her basic message is love. For it is love and only love that gives man the courage to act.

Healing through the Power of the Holy Spirit

In addition to her preaching, teaching, and writing of the Word, Elizabeth Clare Prophet lovingly ministers to those afflicted in mind, body, and spirit. We have seen people healed of cancer, heart disease, and physical injury through prayer and fasting and the power of the Holy Spirit working through her. We have witnessed miraculous recoveries of people who were emotionally devastated as the result of being trapped in the illusory world of drugs or alcohol addiction. We have rejoiced in the opening of the eyes of the spiritually blind. Today these people are whole. God has touched their lives and they now have purpose and meaning to their existence.

The authors of this article have been moved to share what we have personally experienced and observed and we write from a professional background and our own service in the healing arts. One of us is a marriage, child, and family counselor who was also for fifteen years an active minister with the Lutheran Church in America. The other is a clinical psychologist in private practice, a psychotherapist who for ten years taught graduate students in psychology at the University of Colorado.

In our years of close association with Elizabeth Clare Prophet, we have come to know her as a sensitive and loving person, a fearless proclaimer of truth—one who is totally dedicated to God and selfless service to His children. We are blessed with the joyous opportunity of working with this great prophet-teacher whom God is using mightily to bring forth a healing ministry that truly loves life free.

Wake Up, America, While There is Yet Time

It grieves us to see the calloused insensitivity of a cynical press attacking and besmirching the character of one whom we hold in highest esteem. Since Bob Pool and Marvin Sosna have never come face to face with Elizabeth Clare Prophet, we can only wonder at the motives for their continued attacks. It is obvious that their reporting reflects little respect for God and scant regard for truth.

We regret that some of the media find it expedient to vilify a courageous and revered religious leader who challenges the combined forces of world evil that are corrupting our government, weakening our economy, infiltrating our educational system, and undermining the heritage of freedom in our country. Elizabeth Clare Prophet's voice urges in prophetic warning, "Wake up America, before it is too late!"

An opposing and foreboding voice out of the past is that of Manuilski, a strategist of the Communist revolution, who said:

> *War to the hilt between Communism and capitalism is unavoidable. Today, of course, we are not strong enough to attack. Our time will come in twenty or thirty years. The bourgeoisie will have to be put to sleep, so we will begin by launching the most spectacular peace movement on record. There will be electrifying overtures and unheard of concessions. The capitalist countries, stupid and decadent, will rejoice to cooperate in their own destruction. They will leap*

at another chance to be friends. As soon as their guard is down, we shall smash them with our clenched fist. (Excerpt from The Wurmbrand Letters by Richard Wurmbrand.)

Détente: The Betrayal of America and the Sleep of Death

We are seeing this prophecy fulfilled in our time. This lulling-to-sleep process has been facilitated by political compromise in the guise of "peace missions" and so-called culture exchange programs. Further, the policy of appeasement known as "détente" has encouraged a false sense of security resulting in SALT I and SALT II, which have led to the unilateral disarmament of America and the placing of our nation in a position of extreme peril and military vulnerability. The Panama Canal giveaway and the betrayal of Taiwan have made our allies doubt the strength and purpose of our will and whether our commitment to freedom is genuine and real.

Our nation has provided the Soviet Union with over one thousand turnkey factories, millions of tons of wheat, billions of dollars in aid and small interest loans, and 90 percent of their present military technology (Antony Sutton, *National Suicide*)—all this to a godless state that has promised to "bury us."

False Prophet's Cry, "Peace, Peace, When There is No Peace"

Unfortunately, organized religion has not challenged the political cowardice and compromise in our government that has produced this state of affairs. The prophetic voice is silent. The ministers preach, "Peace, peace, when there is no peace" (Jeremiah 6:14).

Will we in America be like the churches in many conquered nations who simply rolled over and played dead because their faith had already been compromised into a secularized, civil religion?

Rev. Richard Wurmbrand, underground church leader and prisoner for eleven years in Soviet concentration camps, gives an eyewitness account of the Communist takeover in Romania:

> *In Romania, when the Communists took over, they convened a congress of all Christian bodies in their parliament building. Four thousand priests, pastors, and ministers gathered to pay homage to their conquerors and to elect Joseph Stalin as honorary president. Almost without exception, the bishops and pastors declared that Christianity and Communism were fundamentally the same and could coexist. Deputy Bishop Rapp of the Romanian Lutheran Church began to teach in the theological seminary that God had given three revelations: one through Moses, one through Jesus, and the third through Stalin, the last superseding the one before. (From Tortured for Christ by Richard Wurmbrand.)*

Anti-God Forces are the Real Enemy

Will America follow the same cowardly course of action when facing the combined forces of anti-God that stalk the world today? The battle with evil is fought on many levels. Whether it is the imprisoning of hundreds of thousands of Christians behind the iron curtain or the attack in America on a religious group that is considered unorthodox, the enemy is the same.

Believers in God Must Unite to Defend Freedom

Americans must be willing to defend their freedom on every level. People must know that when a religious leader or a church is unfairly attacked, it is a threat to the freedom of all. Every believer in God should rise up in righteous indignation and stand as one against that invasion of religious liberty. All churches that adhere to the Ten Commandments, the golden rule, and the Sermon on the Mount have the common tie of the Judeo-Christian heritage. We should not permit ourselves to be pitted against one another; this is undermining our unity, our religious institutions, and the very foundations of our free society.

As Americans, we are a people with a rich and diverse heritage—a blending of different traditions with mutual tolerance and respect for each other. Whether it is as a nation or a small community, we share a national pride, a sense of dignity, a devotion to God, and a feeling of brotherhood with one another. We are genuinely caring toward other peoples and nations.

Camelot, a Community of Love in the Holy Spirit

Church Universal and Triumphant's community of the Holy Spirit, Camelot, is based on that kind of caring and on the love of God which is the dynamic force sustaining us. We hold that flame of love in our hearts for America and for all who will receive it, friends and neighbors alike. All who wish to share this love are welcome into fellowship with us.

Forces of Anti-Love Would Destroy the Child of God

It is obvious that there are those who have no desire for that love or to hear about it from those who would gladly testify to it. By their words, actions, and press attacks, it is clear to the members of our church that these individuals represent the collective consciousness of anti-love that is abroad in the world today. Whether that consciousness is expressed in the hatred basic to World Communism and witchcraft, or manifests as abortion, drug abuse, crime, or dishonest press reporting, its motive and intent is the same: to destroy the integrity and identity of the individual who is in truth a child of God.

Sound the Alarm: The Future is in Our Hands

And so, the alarm must be sounded. The battle lines are drawn between the forces of light and darkness, Christ and anti-Christ, love and anti-love. The destiny of America and the future of our children are at stake, and we must let nothing that is peripheral distract us from the crucial issues facing us as a nation.

It will take a people committed to God, alert and united in the cause of freedom, who are strong spiritually, economically, politically, and militarily to stem the tide of tyranny and to ensure that the flame of freedom will continue to burn in the hearts of free men everywhere.

God is our victory!
CHURCH UNIVERSAL AND TRIUMPHANT
Marilyn C. Barrick, Ph.D.
Clinical Psychologist

Rev. E. Gene Vosseler
Chairman, Department of Theology

Twentieth-Century Witch Hunt, Advertisement, *Los Angeles Herald Examiner*

Media attacks on church fan fires of fear, ignorance, and religious bigotry

During the week of January 27 to February 1, 1985, Church Universal and Triumphant experienced a coordinated, vicious media assault by Channel 2 News (KCBS) and the *Los Angeles Herald Examiner*. The attacks were a strange mixture of fact and fantasy—a dramatic appeal to the lowest common denominator of fear, ignorance, and religious bigotry.

Church Universal and Triumphant has existed as an organization for over twenty-five years, although our teachings are as old as life itself. We have been headquartered in the Los Angeles area for nine years. Our publications are well-known and are carried in major bookstores. Our worldwide membership reflects a true cross section of life—ethnically, culturally, and economically.

We love God, our families, and our country. We believe in and practice the American way of life. And we champion the inalienable rights of all others in this nation to "life, liberty, and the pursuit of happiness." We are puzzled and hurt, then, by the media attacks on one we love as our leader and teacher, Elizabeth Clare Prophet, and on our religious community.

We have pondered the question: to what do we owe this sudden burst of media attention?

Why did Channel 2 spend thirty-seven minutes of prime news time in a blatant attempt to discredit our faith and all that we believe and stand for?

Why in the very same week did the *Los Angeles Herald Examiner* devote six front-page articles, over ten pages and five thousand lines of type, to heap calumny and contempt on our church and its leaders?

And who are these "experts" and key witnesses relied upon by the media in holding its mock trial and executing judgment on us?

It appears that certain disgruntled ex-members, in concert with Channel 2 and the *Los Angeles Herald Examiner,* have deliberately planned and orchestrated a joint campaign to destroy the church, impugn the integrity of its leaders, and publicly question the sanity and judgment of its members. Why, in all the volume of material attacking our faith, was no attempt ever made to cross-examine or question the veracity of these witnesses in the spirit of true "investigative reporting"?

Both Channel 2 and the *Herald Examiner* built their case against us by relying solely on the self-serving testimony of no more than a handful of those who have an important stake in gaining this negative media attention—[as they have] multimillion-dollar lawsuits against the church coming to trial in the near future. Money is the motive and their character is well-known to us. In almost every case, they were asked to leave for serious infractions of moral or ethical standards.

But it would be stooping to their own level, and the media's, to reveal these details in a public forum. Suffice it to say that for many who fail to realize their dreams in life, a suitable scapegoat must be found.

A lawsuit making outlandish claims and using attorneys who don't need to be paid, but who collect their fees as a percentage of what they are able to "recover," is the method. For these [people], the prospect of monetary settlement and the enjoyment of public notoriety is a far better alternative than self-accountability. And what shorter route could there be to monetary settlement than negative media publicity?

If the media were doing a report on the Roman Catholic

Church, would they base their presentation primarily on the testimony of ex-Catholics who obviously were hostile to their former church? We think not.

Or in the case of ex-spouses, would one expect a completely objective report on their former experiences of marriage? Not likely in cases where the marriage dissolved in disappointment, bitterness, or a lawsuit.

These biased, misleading attacks upon our church provide a clear illustration of why people no longer trust the media for accurate or fair reporting. The current rash of libel cases involving CBS and General Westmoreland, and *Time* magazine and Ariel Sharon, are other cases in point—the media cannot be held responsible for its slander, as any other citizen would be.

The Kingmakers

To the disgrace of their profession, many in control of key organs of the news media consider themselves to be the "kingmakers," and breakers, in modern society.

Is an ambitious quest for fame and glory (maybe an Emmy or a Pulitzer Prize) the reason that investigative "experts" at channel 2 and the *Herald Examiner* violated the major canons of their profession, i.e., fairness, respect for truth, balance, and objectivity? In tone, tenor, and content, we know that their sensationalized reporting on us was an example of yellow journalism at its worst. But how is the reader to know?

Consider the tactics employed:

- Rumormongering, false witness, and character assassination in reporting unsubstantiated allegations and charges by those with highly questionable, but easily discernible motives to make us look bad—efforts more in keeping with a scandal sheet or a tabloid than a reputable newspaper or television station.

- Media treatment of our religious beliefs was sarcastic, shallow, and disrespectful, with prime attention given to alleged "brainwashing" of members through "chanting" and the use of affirmations—a charge unsubstantiated by any concrete evidence whatsoever. The fact is that both mantra and chant have an ancient, rich, and honorable tradition in the religions of both East and West.

- Channel 2 News worked on their story for almost two months and surreptitiously used "hidden cameras" to gain entry into our chapel, but only notified us of the story and gave us the opportunity to comment a few days before it was scheduled to run. We were finally informed of their plans to film our Montana ranch/retreat at 11:00 a.m. on Sunday morning when everyone was in church—after they had already spent several days scouring the area for negative comment from anyone willing to give it.

- The invasion of privacy by Channel 2 to secure pictures of our services by use of a "hidden camera" was totally unnecessary. They could easily have obtained a half hour video of one of our weekly services in the Chapel of the Holy Grail, "The Everlasting Gospel," that go out to cable TV stations all over the country—without having to violate the rights of our church and its members in the process. When we photograph our services we always obtain the permission of those in attendance first.

- But of course, this would lack the dramatic impact of Channel 2's covert effort to photograph "forbidden fruit" by using a hidden camera. This amateur ploy is, however, certainly in keeping with the practices of the news media that have increasingly lost the respect of the American people.

- Rabbi Steven Robbins was given prime space to speak of our "potential for violence" and to associate us with "Jonestown" and "Rajneesh." Again, no evidence of facts—just personal opinion. (To our knowledge, Robbins has never even attended one of our church's services or set foot on our property.) His "expert testimony" was obviously a deliberate incitement to religious prejudice and guilt by association. But can he actually point to even a single instance of a violent act by our group or by any of our members? Obviously not, or it would have been reported.

Yes, some member of the media, and those who are allied with them, truly believe they wield tremendous power—that they are indeed the "kingmakers" in society. But in this case the media didn't make us to begin with. We aren't married to them. And they won't be able to break us either.

Amusing Contradictions

We were amused by the *Herald Examiner* and Channel 2 reports, which on one hand labeled and stereotyped church members as brainwashed and manipulated zombies who give away all their money and homes to the church, and in the next breath described us as "middle-class" professionals driving our "Mercedes" and "BMWs" into Camelot, our 218-acre campus in the Santa Monica Mountains. Sound like an implausible contradiction?

The media characterization of our members is highly imaginative, tantalizing, and somewhat amusing—but totally untrue.

Since the media is obviously more interested in titillating than informing, it follows quite naturally that they would employ highly destructive adjectives and emotionally charged pejorative such as "bizarre cult," "grimly efficient money-raising organization," "true believers," and "Rajneesh-style takeover"—ad infinitum, ad nauseam. Very readable, but totally untrue.

This kind of inflammatory reporting may sell newspapers, put television ratings up a point or two, advance a career, or even qualify for a Pulitzer or an Emmy—but it does nothing for the good of society or to truly inform the public.

One hundred and fifty years ago certain elements of our society—fanned by the media—shot a few Mormons and hounded them from pillar to post. Most of them survived, but in the process the country was disgraced.

Before that, and before our Constitutional protections were secured, it was the witch hunts in Salem driven by rumors and false testimony. Many of the accused didn't survive.

It is now apparent that this media hatchet job was carried out by those forces in journalism that are distinctly secular and antireligious in nature. They treat with disdain what others hold to be true and beautiful. They trample on that which is sacred and holy.

Media Blitz Backfired

To all those who value religious freedom and recognize an attack on religion when they see it, and to those who respect truth and fair play, we must tell you that the media attacks on our church and its leader have backfired.

Our switchboard has been lit up with calls of interest and support from people wanting to know more about the teachings of the masters and the path of soul liberation that we follow.

Because true religion is a matter of the heart, pictures shown in the newspaper and on TV of our leaders, members, and the saints revered by us have sharply contrasted the charade of factual reporting and convinced many [people] of the untruths of the whole presentation.

So, while we must challenge and expose the shoddy journalistic practices of Channel 2 and the *Herald Examiner* in their callous disregard of the truth, we also wish to give them credit for exposing themselves and those who have testified against us.

People who are in touch with their hearts can always discern truth in the midst of error. As Abraham Lincoln once said, "You may fool all the people some of the time; you can even fool some of the people all the time; but you can't fool all of the people all the time."

The media has refused to give us free space to respond to their untrue claims. And it would take much more than the space in this $5,220 ad (paid for by the voluntary contributions of members and friends of our church) to answer the full range of charges leveled against us. (We will be submitting to Editor Mary Anne Dolan a list of over two hundred factual errors and inaccuracies found in the eleven articles, and we believe a retraction is in order.) But we would like to focus for a moment on the larger picture that has somehow escaped the reporters.

For those of us who are members of Church Universal and Triumphant, one of our greatest joys is a loving community of the Holy Spirit and a living legacy of wisdom from the saints and sages of East and West.

Ours is a practical path of discipleship under Jesus Christ and the saints in heaven. Thousands worldwide have found fulfillment in studying the lost arts of healing for the regeneration of the whole man—body, mind, and soul. Through the teachings of Saint Germain and other masters, they have gained a greater understanding of karma and reincarnation as it relates to individual psychology and have learned how to use the fire of God's Holy Spirit—the violet flame—for the resolution of personal and planetary conditions.

Our Montessori International School for kindergarten through grade 12 draws out the innate creativity of our children and builds in them a strong educational foundation in preparation for lives as productive citizens in a free society.

We are not trying to shield them from the world—we are trying to prepare them for it. That's why our graduating seniors get accepted to colleges like USC, UCLA, the University of Chicago, and Northwestern.

Summit University, our college of religion, culture, and science, is a twelve-week retreat experience that accelerates a student into new and higher levels of spiritual awareness. Even though the media doesn't approve of it, many are yearning for this kind of teaching and fellowship.

In addition to our activities at Camelot, our 30,000-acre Royal Teton Ranch—a self-sufficient spiritual community-in-the-making next to Yellowstone Park in Montana—offers multiple opportunities for apprenticeship in all aspects of organic farming, ranching, construction, and other community services.

Members of our Order of the Good Samaritan are taught an extensive Red Cross Multimedia First Aid Course and CPR as well as other skills that help us to be ministering servants to people in need wherever we find them on the road of life.

We are not moved by these unfair media assaults, though they tried to discredit the tremendous good that is being done. The faith and solidarity of our members worldwide has only been strengthened. For we, as all Christians, know the teaching of our Lord and Master Jesus, who said, "Love your enemies, bless them that curse you, do good to them that hate you, and pray for them which despitefully use you, and persecute you."

We are committed to truth, justice, and our four sacred American freedoms—freedom of the press, of religion, of speech, and of assembly. We believe that our nation has a divine mission to hold high the torch of freedom and to pass that flame to all who will receive it around the world.

We, the undersigned, stand in strong, united support of Church Universal and Triumphant and the teachings, ministry, and leadership of the late Mark L. Prophet, Elizabeth Clare Prophet, and her husband and co-director of the movement, Edward L. Francis. We willingly and joyfully place our names on the line in defense of truth and religious liberty and all who worship God as their conscience dictates. Can editors and reporters of the Los Angeles Herald Examiner and Channel 2 News say that they have truly championed the cause of justice and the responsible use of a free press?

To you who really want to know who we are and what we are all about, we extend a cordial initiation to attend our 10:30 a.m. Sunday services and our 7:00 p.m. Wednesday night healing services with prayers for the sick by Elizabeth Clare Prophet.

Our Easter conference will be April 3–7 at Camelot. Free registration is offered for first-time conference attendees who present this ad. Our Easter Sunrise Service on the meadow, children's Easter egg hunt, buffet breakfast, and 10:30 a.m. service are open to all.

Come and hear Elizabeth Clare Prophet, tour our campus community, and judge for yourself.

Full-page ad taken out in the *Los Angles Herald Examiner,* April 1985.
Due to limited space, 360 contributors were not listed

January 26, 1996

Editor
Livingston Enterprise
401 South Main Street
Livingston, Montana 59047

Dear Editor,

I would like to set the record straight and put to rest any speculation that might be fueled and fanned by your front-page article of January 24 on my resignation from the staff and board of directors of Church Universal and Triumphant.

You quote extensively the opinions of ex-member Peter Arnone, a self-styled expert and harsh critic of our church. Mr. Arnone can hardly be considered an objective, unbiased authority. He is obviously disgruntled with his own ax to grind.

In fact, to seek his opinion on our church would be like asking Protestant Reformation leader Martin Luther, who unceremoniously left the Roman Catholic Church, what he thought about the Pope.

In my opinion, a newspaper has certain fundamental obligations to its readers if it wants to be considered a credible source. Reporting must be factual, balanced, unbiased, and objective in its news stories. Opinion should be reserved for the editorial page.

Unfortunately your story of January 24 fails these basic criteria and flunks all four tests. The story was not factual. It was not balanced. It was not objective and unbiased, and it reflected opinion, whatever one thinks of it, that should have been reserved for the editorial page.

I know that these views may be considered old-fashioned since advocacy journalism is all the rage these days. Truth is often slanted and manipulated to reflect the newspaper owner's point of view. However, thoughtful Americans, who are staunch believers in a free press, reject this approach as being unjust and a perversion of what a free press should be and stand for.

This is the context of what I would like to share with your readers.

While I am flattered by Mr. Arnone's praise, when he described my departure as a "big loss," he exaggerated.

Most people realize that no one in any organization is indispensable. Our church has any number of members and qualified staff who can step up and fill my shoes—and probably do a better job than I have done.

For the record, almost all factual information received by the *Enterprise* from Mr. Arnone is incorrect. I have been in the church for eighteen, not twenty years, but during that time I left staff periodically to pursue outside interest. The time I was off staff pursuing my own interests totals five years (no one lamented my departure as such a "big loss" then). In addition, not only did I not play a "key role," I was hardly involved in the church's move to Park County. In fact, shortly after arriving in Montana I again took a leave of absence for two years to pursue personal interests.

I have served on the church's board of directors for eight years. It has been a great honor, privilege, and joy to serve with Elizabeth Clare Prophet, Edward Francis and other members of the board. My wife, Wanda, and I plan to continue to be very active in our beloved church and community.

Wanda and I are very happy with our spiritual community and its leadership. Before finding Church Universal and

Triumphant I was an ordained Lutheran minister for seventeen years, with parishes in South America and Hawaii, and briefly a Unitarian minister. I can truthfully say I found the answers to my spiritual quest in the teachings of the Ascended Masters as given by Elizabeth Clare Prophet.

I think that it's wonderful that we live in a free country where we are able to worship God as conscience and our inner life dictates. If we honor the basic principles of freedom of religion, speech, association, and the press, we will treat all men with the dignity and respect they deserve. However, when newspapers deliberately twist and distort information handed down to the public, they undermine the basis of their own existence and do violence to the basic, fundamental tenets of what constitutes a fair and responsible press.

Respectfully yours,

CHURCH UNIVERSAL AND TRIUMPHANT
Rev. E. Gene Vosseler

Mission Amethyst Jewel: Stumping for St. Germain in the British Isles and Africa

Church Universal and Triumphant

April 1, 1981

Dear friends of freedom,

It is with feelings of deep joy and great satisfaction that I share with you some exciting new plans of the Great White Brotherhood concerning Mission Amethyst Jewel.

El Morya's latest mighty thrust for a purpose in the saving of a planet will take a dedicated team of chelas around the world on a whirlwind eight-nation stumping tour. This spring Saint Germain is going stumping again in the hearts of his chelas, and he's planning to visit Ireland, Scotland, England, South Africa, Zimbabwe (Rhodesia), the Philippines, Australia, and New Zealand. I am writing to you because this crucial mission requires your loving prayers and wholehearted support if we are to succeed.

Archangel Gabriel says Mission Amethyst Jewel is the Darjeeling Council's solution to world problems. It is based upon the principle of the violet flame that burns within the heart of the chela. Each chela is a jewel. And as chelas place themselves together to form atoms, the atoms expand to form molecules that expand to form study groups and teaching centers—thus Mission Amethyst Jewel crystallizes.

Stumping from city to city and nation to nation with the message of the Coming Revolution in Higher Consciousness is Saint Germain's strategy for drawing together his chelas to form these centers of light in every nation. It is these groups which will stay the hand of darkness across the nations of the world. This is the plan of action in which each of you plays an indispensable role.

We come to you in the name and flame of the ascended masters—but not empty-handed. Our beloved messenger and the hosts of light have prepared a rich spiritual feast for you and your friends to digest and enjoy, and then put to work in the ongoing battle with darkness. In addition, I'm really looking forward to sitting down with you and talking about the 80s and what's happening with your families, communities, and nations. And of course there will be the joy of reunion with old friends made on the last stumping tour through the British Isles.

The dynamic stump message will be supplemented by two new, exciting two-day seminars—"Controlling the Human Aura through the Science of the Spoken Word" and "The Class of the Archangels." These seminars will feature absorbing lectures, inspirational meditations, dictations from the ascended masters, and fiery Holy Spirit sermons from the heart of the messenger. The ascended master will not only release a fiery vortex of light, but through our beloved messenger will provide specific and practical instruction in the art of waging spiritual warfare through the invocation of light by the power of the spoken Word. This is the great need of the hour.

In our hearts we know that time is running out for this planet. Armageddon is here. The battle lines are clearly drawn for the final titanic struggle between light and darkness—absolute God-good and deified evil. The clarion call must be sounded to the sleeping children of light: Wake up, sons and daughters of God, to your cosmic identity! Become the Christ and claim your divine inheritance. You can solve the problems of the age, realize your fiery destiny, and make your ascension in the light.

We also know that it is time—past time—for the free, spiritual people on earth to get together and to become united, nation by nation, to form a community of the Holy Spirit. It's time to mobilize the sons and daughters of God to challenge the conspiracies of the totalitarian forces of darkness that are threatening freedom all over the planet. It's time to contact and enlist all of our brothers and sisters on the path of the ascension to raise this planet into a new golden age of universal enlightenment. And that's why the eagles of Sanat Kumara are gathering to perform a mighty work of the ages—the saving of a planet and her people.

For we are one in the flame of the Holy Spirit and as lightbearers we share a common heritage and a cosmic purpose—to roll back and defeat the forces of darkness and their Luciferian culture of despair and death. As El Morya once said, "From the beginning we were winning." If we are faithful to the light and committed to the ascended masters and their strategy of victory—we shall overcome.

And that's what our Mission Amethyst Jewel is all about. That's why we are coming to visit you. Not only will we share the joy of communion and bask in the flame of the love-glow in the heart of the mother, but we will also learn the practical techniques that will allow us to gain the self-mastery of our own Christ consciousness. Our tutor and gurus, the ascended masters, will give us all that we need to fight through to the victory. Our armor is light and our sword is the sacred word of truth that will truly cleave asunder the real from the unreal.

We hold in our hearts a sacred vision for the earth—the dawn of a new day in a glorious sunburst of light when truth and beauty will reign supreme. Hearts will be one in the divine love of their Christ consciousness. The divinity in every soul will be treasured and respected, and every soul will bow in reverent adoration and praise to our beloved hierarch and gracious benefactor Sanat Kumara, the Ancient of Days, and to all of his mighty legions of light. This is the vision we hold for the earth and we can make it come true. But it will take the sacrifice, the love, and the light of the few to open the door of freedom for the many. Jesus said: "Are you ready for the sacrifices that the Great Law demands of you to transfer this light to the world? This is my question, and I expect that answer in action...Either we save the earth now or it is questionable that it can be saved at all."

We estimate that it will cost $26,500 to stump England, Ireland, Scotland, South Africa, Zimbabwe (Rhodesia), the Philippines, Australia, and New Zealand. I share this with you because Saint Germain has told Mother that he expects the chelas to sponsor the stumps financially in their areas. Much of the above amount can be raised through the sale of publications, offerings, and seminar fees, but it will still take a considerable number of sacrificial gifts to pay for our expenses.

As the central nucleus of lightbearers in your nation, you hold the key of opportunity for countless others who walk in ignorance of their God-identity, the I AM THAT I AM. Mother and the ascended masters are counting on you to help bring these lost sheep back to the fold of the true Church. And the stump and seminars will provide a tremendous impetus to that mission. Through the release of the Word, stumping accelerates light at the same time it gives the ascended masters opportunity to contact their chelas. Shiva has told us, "It will not take millions to hold the balance for the turning of the light, but thousands—a certain thousands of souls that I am calling forth, certain souls who are numbered. In fact, my very flame rests just above their head."

Mother has said that stumping is a very wise investment in the future of the ascended masters' teachings and in the future of world freedom. She likens it to the plowing of a field and the planting of seeds, many of which, after careful nurturing through the seasons, take root and eventually bring forth the fruit of God consciousness—an abundant harvest of souls of light.

And that is why we are sending this appeal to our friends in Europe as well as the countries to be stumped on this tour. Mother also desires to send a stump team to Europe in the spring of 1982, but wants to have *Studies in Alchemy* translated into French, German, Italian, and Swedish to accompany the tour. It is the dharma of the people of these nationalities to assume responsibility for seeing that these translations are accomplished—both with linguistic and financial support.

Archangel Jophiel and his Archeia Christine in "The Class of the Archangels" spoke of children of the light from America taking back to Europe "the fruits of God consciousness established in the New World from the very hearts of those pioneers who left Europe to establish a new flame and a new righteousness on the American continent."

And they concluded their mighty dictation with a stirring call to action:

> *With the raising up of teaching centers in the cities of the earth, there is hope to the entire Great White Brotherhood for miracles upon miracles to occur upon earth. I pray then that you will not count the personal cost in your life— not the cost of sacrifice or service or surrender or that selflessness which is the requirement of the hour. One and all, archangels send forth this call: Let us establish the coordinates of the Inner Retreat and the teaching centers! Let us raise up a body of lightbearers! And let us save the earth and her evolutions for the victory of the golden age! By this sign of the cosmic cross of white fire, we conquer! In His name, Pax vobiscum.*

This is our mission. This is our goal. This is the challenge of the hour. By your generous support of Saint Germain's eight-nation stump you can help make Archangel Jophiel and

Christine's call to action living reality.

Please understand that we need your gifts as soon as possible so that we can meet our immediate expenses and move swiftly ahead with our plans to take the stump message and our new seminars around the world this spring.

May Saint Germain's purple fiery heart inspire you with the fervor of his devotion to freedom. May Lanello's mighty blue cape infuse you with his devotion to the will of God. And through the radiant, joyous heart flame of our beloved Mother, may you experience the ruby-ray compassion of the Saviour of earth, Sanat Kumara—so that all lightbearers who come into the radiance of your soul's aura will be awakened and quickened to the truth that "sets the captives free."

I look forward to meeting you in the flame of the Buddha and the Mother.

Most sincerely,

Rev. E. Gene Vosseler

P.S. Please send your generous gift by return mail so we can continue stumping in 1981.

Golden Moments with Mark and Mother

Testimonies of Their Students
July 4, 2008

REV. LINDA WOROBEC: I would like to invite Reverend Gene Vosseler to come and share his golden moments with Mother. Gene is a long time devotee of Mother and the Buddha. He has been in our organization and church for thirty-one years. [Applause] His love for the flame of freedom is a moving spirit in his heart. He has delivered the teachings of the Ascended Masters worldwide, often preparing the way for Mother's stump lectures and conferences. He was ordained as a minister with Church Universal and Triumphant in 1984 and previous to that time he served as an ordained Lutheran and Unitarian Minister for seventeen years. He has had the privilege and joy to serve on the Board of Directors and currently serves as a member of the Council of Elders, the Ministerial Council, and on our Stewardship Team in our beloved church. I give you beloved Gene Vosseler. [*Audience Applause*]

REV. GENE VOSSELER: Grace be to you and peace from God the Father and our Lord Jesus Christ. Let the words of my mouth and the meditations of my heart be acceptable in thy sight, O Lord, my strength and my redeemer. Come Holy Spirit enlighten us. Come Holy Spirit enlighten us. Come Holy Spirit enlighten us.

I can't tell you what a great joy and pleasure it gives me to be up here this morning to share with you some thoughts and reflections of my time with our beloved Guru Ma. I feel deeply honored to share this with you. Many of you I've met on stumps around the world, and it's like old friends getting together. This is like my spiritual family. I feel no more at home in the world anywhere in the planetary body than right here in this court with you this day as we celebrate Saint Germain's freedom flame. Hail friends of freedom.

AUDIENCE: Hail friends of freedom. Hail friends of freedom. Hail friends of freedom.

REV. VOSSELER: First I have got to express my gratitude and thanks to two very special people in this organization. Robert and Linda Worobec, you have brought so much joy to this church and to these chelas over the many, many years. God has used your gifts so richly and so beautifully. And I simply had to say what I told Robert the other day. "Robert, Broadway's loss is Church Universal and Triumphant's gain. [*Laughter and clapping*]

You know I have to agree with my brother David Kravitz who spoke to you so eloquently yesterday afternoon. To prepare a five-minute speech is tougher than a half hour or two hour lecture. What are you going to say in five minutes that can encapsulate thirty-one years of experience with the blessed Guru Ma—who has given so much, who has given purpose and meaning to your life, who has been your Guru in the deepest, darkest moments of your life, who has given you the tender love your soul needs when it needs it, and gives you a little bit of tongue-lashing when your dweller-on-the-threshold needs it. We used to have a little sign that we'd put on that would say, "Pummel me." Pummel me. [*Laughter*] What, what do you mean. Yeah, pummel what? Pummel the dweller; pummel the not-self, that non-real thing that we have created which we are so deathly attached to because we have such a great investment in it, right? Has it been easy for anybody in this room to conquer the dweller-on-the-threshold?

AUDIENCE: No!

REV. VOSSELER: If it was easy, everyone would be here, right? [*Laughter*] That is just the way it is by the nature of light. So I want to simply say this; I am not going to be able to pack it in five minutes. [*Laughter*] There's no way I can do it. And I want to tell you something else. There's an autobiography coming out this fall. And it's really a biography of my experiences on this spiritual path. It's called *Wind of the Spirit.* And it's simply a spiritual odyssey. In there I will tell you things that I won't get into today that you will have an opportunity to hear. You can relax; it will not be a tell-all book. [*Laughter*]

Now, I want to simply say this. I thought David did so eloquent a job yesterday. I prepared something I was going to present to you today. You know what? I woke up this morning at about three o'clock and I thought, "No, I am not going to do that; I am going to wing it today, too." [*Laughter*] And I am going to wing it because I want to tell you the most important thing I can say from this platform to you today in terms of personal testimony to the Mother of the Flame. Do you know what that personal testimony is? The meaning of Mother in my life. And the meaning of these teachings and what she has brought to you and to me as chelas of the ascended masters. That's the greatest gift I can give to you.

Just a little bit of my background. I come out of a very orthodox Lutheran background. In fact, I was a fourth-generation Lutheran minister. Can you imagine—great-grandfather, grandfather, father. I wanted to be a coach at first, but I finally fell into line with the family plan and became a Lutheran minister. And I served for seventeen years in churches in British Guiana and then Hawaii. But there came a point in my life, spiritual questing, when I was no longer satisfied with the Lutheran doctrinal orthodoxy. The idea of original sin, for example. We used to say every Sunday morning the Apostles' Creed. We are by nature sinful and unclean. Now that is a heavy trip. [*Laughter*] If you believe that you are by nature sinful and unclean I guarantee you that is what you will manifest in your world. And so the doctrine of original sin, I thought about it and I said, "Well, if I am by nature sinful and unclean and I am created in the image of God, what does that make God?" [*Laughter*] Well, I will tell you a logical absurdity. It just takes some of us longer to figure it out. And some of you figured it out faster than I did. [*Laughter*] It took me fifty years to get out of that indoctrination.

And then I thought of another doctrine that I taught [which] was, "You only have one life to live." And that is orthodoxy position in every orthodox church—one life, one life to live? I thought of if a child dies of leukemia at the age of ten—one life? I thought of someone coming into life blind, deaf, and dumb—one life? I thought of thousands of young men who have been killed in war at the age of 21, 22 and 23 at the prime of life—one life? And all suffering as a result of God's will? I was teaching that, you know. And yet as I began to ponder and really think about it, the doctrine of reincarnation made sense. God gives us more than one opportunity to get it right. Because we all know earth is a schoolroom; and when we learn our lessons, we graduate. When we learn to balance our threefold flame and how to balance at least 51 percent of our karma, we will have the opportunity in fulfilling our sacred plan to make our great ascension in the light. To go back home to the source from which we came and the source to which we all yearn for in the deepest levels of our soul.

So I believe in the idea of reincarnation and I began my search spiritually. I looked and I searched. I actually spent a couple of years as a Unitarian minister. God bless the Unitarians, they are beautiful people. But it was a dry hole for me spiritually because of their very, very liberal religion, whereas orthodoxy is very tight and constrained. In a liberal religion you address God, "To Whom It May Concern." [*Laughter*] It's just a different ball game. It's a philosophical kind of thing. It's an intellectual kind of thing. And it just doesn't meet your deepest spiritual soul needs. So that didn't solve it. And I spent a couple years with a beautiful Buddhist master named Rinpoche Nippo Syaku. And I loved Rinpoche. He was a real Buddhist master. One of his profound insights was simply this, "Gene, if your big toe hurts, your whole world is your big toe." [*Laughter*] Very profound, right?

Anyhow, it was a very beautiful stay with him. But my soul was still hungering and longing for a more active path. One day someone whom I befriended—this is where when you cast your bread upon the waters sometimes it will return to you—I befriended this person. And this person came up to me and handed me a book. He said, "This book isn't for me but I am pretty sure it's for you, Gene." Do you know what the book was? *The Great White Brotherhood in the Culture, History and Religion of America*—which was my wife's first conference at Shasta. And so I took that book and I literally devoured it. I have to tell you I devoured it in one reading and I couldn't put it down. And the next day I'm on the phone calling to Pasadena. I said, "Tell me, do you folks ever have conferences?" They said, "Well, yes as a matter of fact we're having one in two days." [*Laughter*] "Great, I'll be there."

Two days later I attended my first conference, April 1977, Easter Conference. I walked into the door of this large conference hall and the usher that met me at the door was a fellow I knew. He was a fighter pilot named Ben Knudson. I baptized Ben and his wife and three children in Hawaii about five years before. [*Laughter*] He's the first person I met. You can imagine we had a joyous, joyous reunion. I have to go on very quickly now because I can tell my time is getting close.

I have to say this, that the first live dictation I heard confirmed my being in this church. I had a dream about a year before I found these teachings. And all I remember from the dream were two words, "eighth ray." Eighth ray, what is an eighth ray? I don't know anything about seven rays, but eighth ray? My first live dictation Mother announced, "I am going to give a dictation tomorrow morning at 9:30 and I want everyone to be in your seats promptly." I thought, I am going to miss it. I have to go down to the airport and pick up this girlfriend that's flying in. Nine thirty, I went down to the airport and picked her up and then came back to the chapel.

You and all the sons and daughters of God…You have an immortal divine destiny. God intends for you to rise up into the fullness of your Christhood.

It's 11:30 in the morning and the music starts for the dictation; and my first live dictation was Archangel Uzziel, the first dictation given on the eighth ray. I knew in the very depths of my soul that I was home. I knew I was with my spiritual family. I looked around and I saw my brothers and sisters and I knew my long search and quest, which I wasn't even aware of what was going on, was over. Just to add one thing, my beloved wife was decreeing from '75 to '77, two years almost constantly, night and day, between her job performance. I found out later from Mother that was to get me cut loose and set free. 1975 to 1977 has a very special meaning to us. I must say so long because I know time is getting close. [*Audience clapping; take your time. More. More.*] You are very kind but I've got a brother who is sitting in the front row who's got a freedom message he has to give, too, and I have to keep him very much in my consideration.

I wanted to give you that background because everyone here has a story and the basic message I want to get across to you today is the teachings of the ascended masters. You and all the sons and daughters of God, you are children of the sun; you are children of the light. You have an immortal divine destiny. God intends for you to rise up into the fullness of your Christhood. Christ Jesus was simply an example of what you and I are to become. Think of it for a moment. You have a divine destiny. You are sons and daughters of the Most High. You are meant to be pillars of light in the temple beautiful. Now I can't put it any more straight than that. You've got every tool you need. You've got the violet flame to transmute anything in the world that is not of the light. You've got the tools of the science of the spoken word. You can invoke that light and bring down the light into your four lower bodies that will consume all darkness, all that is not of the light, and elevate you and raise you into your full Christhood. That's why you are here. That is the mission of this church to introduce these teachings to the sons and daughters of God and the children of the light that are all over the world. And **you** have to do it. One of the requirements of your ascension is to be witnesses for the truth. You have to witness to the truth. And that is very, very important. This is what Jesus meant when he said, "feed my sheep." Or when he gave the commission, "Go ye into the world and preach the gospel to every creature, baptize them and teaching them. Thus forth I am commanding you and lo, I am with you always even unto the end of the age." That Everlasting Gospel has not changed. And if I can get across to you the meaning of Mother's life to me it's in that. She gave me the cosmic keys. She gave my soul what it needed in my darkest hours. We all know we go through those dark hours because we simply wrestle with our karma. And some of us have more karma than others. Some people think, "Oh my, he must have great attainment; you know you've been out lecturing for Mother." No, it probably means I had more karma than most of you. [*Laughter*] And you know I understand that and I am aware of it. And I am grateful for the opportunity that Mother gave me to teach these teachings around the world. I can't tell you the joy, it gladdens my heart when someone comes up and says, "Gene, I remember twenty-five years ago…" Just this morning I had a beautiful soul come up to me and remind me of something that took place twenty-one years ago. I had totally forgotten it. But that moment had meant something to him. So we all have these contacts along life's way. We simply have to be love in action. And that's what being a chela of the guru is all about. The guru is unconditional love. Those of us who have known her intimately are aware that unconditional love was always there. Unconditioned, she always had the immaculate concept for our souls. She knew who we were. And she always had that royal picture of us. That's what makes us so grateful and grateful for all that God has given us. Now I have overextended my leave; Sidney I apologize. I want to close with a very brief poem so I dedicate it to you this morning. It's called:

I AM White Light

"I AM" pure white light
a snow white dove
lighting the night
on wings of love.

"I AM" pure white light
ablaze with truth
lighting the night
with eternal youth.

"I AM" pure white light
    sending hope and peace
    lighting the night
    and sorrow's cease.

"I AM" pure white light
    singing freedom's call
    lighting the night
    bringing joy to all.

"I AM" pure white light
    with wisdom's ray
    lighting the night
    on your ascension day.

"I AM" pure white light
    a snow white dove
    lighting the night
    with cosmic love.

There is no death, I know, it's
True, for God's pure white light
Is the eternal you.

And that's what it is all about friends. You are pure white light. You are white stones in the temple of your being. And God has a mission and a plan for each and every one of you. God fulfill it! God-victory! Thank you. I bow to the Christ in you. God bless you all. God Victory. [*Clapping and cheers*]

11. THE PATH OF PERSONAL CHRISTHOOD BY MICHAEL UTTER

Author's Note:

I have asked my very dear friend and spiritual brother to share with you some of the rich spiritual insights that we hold in common. Michael Utter and his beloved wife, Kaylie, have been truest and dearest friends on this rugged adventure we call life. They are truly old souls and their love and dedication to our Gurus and to the path of the ascension and the ascended masters has been a never-failing inspiration to my soul. Their commitment to a life of loving, dedicated service to Native Americans, and before that, to refugees from Vietnam, Laos and Cambodia, Armenia and Afghanistan, reflects their obedience to Master Jesus' admonition to "love thy neighbor as thyself."

I joyfully share with you Michael's thoughts and deep spiritual understanding of the mission of the ascended masters and their call for us to be faithful warriors of the spirit. Michael's words are indeed a powerful clarion call for love in action and a challenge to invoke God's light over the forces of darkness, which are aligned against God's truth and light, that seek to destroy all that is beautiful and good on this planet.

On My Special Friendship with Brother Gene

My friendship with Gene Vosseler over the last thirty years is perhaps best understood in the context of our souls' journey together on a very challenging quest. I hold to the belief that planet Earth is a schoolroom where we are all given lessons in learning to become the Christ. We keep coming back again and again until we get our lessons right. I would further describe our journey together as the great quest for the Holy Grail itself. I have no doubt that the purpose of my friendship with Gene and the other close friends in our mandala has been to strengthen us on that inspiring but difficult spiritual passage.

Over three decades of friendship, there have been glorious times with Gene in the intensity of light and our shared love for our Guru, Elizabeth Clare Prophet, who we lovingly call Mother. There have been times of personal loss and sorrow. There have been intense political battles with Gene on the world stage in front of the national media. There have been long discussions about the meaning of life and the work of the Brotherhood of light in this dawning golden age. I am grateful this book is going to print and that from this book many souls may learn from Gene's life about the intensity of the inner fire and the dedication to the path of personal Christhood that he has demonstrated in this century. I hope this chapter will help to bring some further perspective on Gene's life from one friend's admittedly personal point of view.

The first time I remember meeting Gene was at the Albuquerque Summit Lighthouse Study Group in early February 1978. Gene was traveling, on a media tour prior to Mother's stumping for the Coming Revolution in Higher Consciousness. Mother was scheduled to stump at the University of New Mexico a month or so later. Gene, as usual, was humbly serving the cause of his Guru. I was serving to help coordinate arrangements and publicity for the stump in the Albuquerque area. When Gene and I first met, we spoke warmly about our mutual commitment to Mother and the Path. I was only twenty-seven years old at the time and was serving as vice president of the Albuquerque Study Group. Within a few months, Mother had appointed me president of the newly chartered Albuquerque Teaching Center. Gene's advice to me at that time was extremely important and meaningful. He advised I dedicate myself to fulfill the plans of hierarchy, pursue personal Christhood with passion, and seek humility before all.

As I recall my feelings when I met Gene for the first time, it was as if I had just met an old familiar friend. My conversations with Gene gave me great comfort on the Path then as they still do today, some thirty years later. I feel my life has been blessed by this friendship. I hope all our readers will come to understand the physical and tangible presence of Brotherhood, not only with the ascended masters beyond the veil, but with their fellow devotees on the path in the here and now. We all need stalwart friends on the path like Gene. If you don't have one, you are missing an important element of support on your path. When traveling on the path of the ascension, the principal of right association is very important.

Friendship and Community on the Path

In early 1980, I was working as the associate director of the Department of Community Development for the City of Albuquerque, New Mexico. My former wife, Sophie, and I were expecting our second child, our son Jay Lael Utter. Mother had requested that I join the staff of the Church at our Camelot headquarters in Malibu, California. After brief reflection on the matter, I resigned my budding career with the city, sold my property in New Mexico, and moved to Woodland Hills, California, with my two-year-old Uriel Raymond Utter and pregnant wife, Sophie.

Soon after arriving in California, I ran into my friend Gene, who counseled me about his experiences on staff with the Church and on making large, life-changing decisions to support the Brotherhood's work. He advised that when the motive of the heart is right, somehow these commitments always seemed to work out for the best, no matter the outer appearance of things. His instruction reminded me about Mother's teaching on the subject of friendship in our community. Real community can consist only in the shared love of friends.

Now to show how events turn on the wheel of life, a few short years later in 1982 I was working as executive director of the Hollywood Revitalization Committee, a non-profit community development agency sponsored by Los Angeles Mayor Tom Bradley's Office of Economic Development. For reasons known only to the Brotherhood, Mother had asked Gene and Wanda to take a leave from their staff assignments and work out in the world for a time. This change had occurred in Gene's life very suddenly. Gene found a small trailer to live in which was owned by Ralph and Lucille Yaney in Canoga Park. Gene called me up and asked if I possibly had a job or knew of one, as he had no immediate prospects for work. Immediately I became aware of a dramatic increase of fire and light around my heart—right during the phone call! I knew God wanted me to help my friend.

Naturally I said yes, that I had a job for brother Gene. I then had to figure out immediately how to create such a job and stay within my agency's previously board-approved budget. (It is always good to be the executive director in these moments.) As I recall, I hired Gene as a small business development specialist. While he had no particular prior training for the job, he performed the job very well. Gene has always had real skill in dealing with people from his heart. In Hollywood the revitalization corporation worked with thirty or so ethnic and language groups. Gene has always been well received by almost everyone he met. I never encountered a human relations problem Gene could not deal with fearlessly, promptly, and directly.

From our acquaintances in Hollywood and our subsequent jobs with the International Institute of Los Angeles, contacts were made with freedom fighters from ten or fifteen nations. These contacts and friendships became a key element in creating the Ban the Soviets Coalition during the 1984 Olympics in Los Angeles. From this experience, I relearned the well-worn truism—in our unity is our sole bulwark of success. You never quite know from which direction the Brotherhood will send reinforcements working for a worthy cause.

I would like to think that I have been supportive of my friend Gene in practical ways when he has needed my friendship. Likewise, I have been served by Gene as my minister in the Church for more than thirty years. I think friendships are nurtured through this reciprocity—trying to give a little more than we receive, but giving and receiving when we really need help. It is my observation that in this life, God will provide us all the opportunity we need to learn our lessons of love through mutual service and an occasional sacrifice.

I am reminded of our Lord Jesus, who said, "Thou shalt love the Lord thy God with all thy heart, and with all thy soul, and with all thy strength, and with all thy mind; and thy neighbor as thyself." I believe it is folly to think that we do not need to enjoy and celebrate our friendship with loyal friends in this life, yet somehow think that when we graduate from earth's schoolroom we will be loyal friends of the ascended masters in heaven. If you want direct contact with the Brotherhood of light, the best place to start is right here, right now, by being a true flesh and blood friend to your neighbor. When the masters see you are worthy to be a friend of their friends on earth, you will be given an opportunity to play a part in the work of the Brotherhood beyond the veil.

Respecting Our Elders

In 1989 I moved to Montana with the true love of my life, my beloved wife Kaylie. She and I have now been happily married for twenty years. Not only do we live together under the same roof, but we also jointly run a couple of small businesses. For the last decade I have been working with Native American communities running a non-profit corporation named RCI (Rural Community Innovations)—from Bozeman, Montana.

Fellow chelas on the Path sometimes ask me how I came to work almost exclusively in very impoverished Native American communities. The answer, in part, is that I never explicitly made that choice. It just seemed to happen on its own.

In 1997 when we began to work with Native communities, other indigenous clients began to approach RCI seeking the economic development services we offer. This change in our client base happened fairly quickly. The heart of our practice is to assist Native entrepreneurs to develop private businesses and to help increase private sector activity on Indian Reservations. Our focus in this work is to encourage proper use of the free enterprise system combined with the discovery and expansion of the flame of the heart. These keys help in overcoming dependence, alcoholism, depression, and substance abuse in communities experiencing long-term poverty.

The actual beginning of my work with Native Americans goes back to Mother's stump in Albuquerque in February 1978, which I mentioned earlier. After Mother finished her stump lecture well after midnight, she asked to be shown our new Albuquerque Study Group focus on Stanford Avenue, across the street from the University of New Mexico. I had only signed the rental papers for the building that very day. There was no electricity or working lights in the building. We went there and Mother, a few of her stump staff, and some members of the study group gathered in a large dining room area around the only furniture available—a metal outdoor patio table with a round hole in the center for an umbrella.

In this newly leased study group center, Mother gave a spontaneous dictation from the tall master from Venus, Mighty Victory. That night we seemed to have only one large flashlight available for illumination in the unlit building. Mother asked me to place the flashlight in the hole in the center of the table. During that dictation, Mighty Victory spoke of his altar on Venus. He described it as being a round altar, like our table, delineated with the twelve lines of the clock representing the twelve hierarchies of the sun. He further described the altar as being self-luminous from within. Mighty Victory stated, among other things, that he holds the line of victory on every line of the clock for this sector of cosmos. The dictation was at least ten to fifteen minutes in length. I experienced a tremendous release of energy standing right next to Mother and Mighty Victory. At the time I was absolutely sure I would remember every word of the dictation for the rest of my life. Not so. Five minutes later I could remember very little. Unfortunately, no one had a portable tape recorder available in the middle of the night. I would surely have brought one had I known Mighty Victory was dictating as part of the evening's program!

After the dictation, Mother asked me where the bookstore was to be located. I took her into an adjacent entry room. She asked everyone else except me to leave the room. Much to my surprise she spoke to me about the fall of the continent of Lemuria. She spoke about the souls of the fourth root race who had fallen from a higher state of consciousness under the damaging influence of the black priesthood of Lemuria. She spoke about some Native American people being from the fourth root race and having been the continuing victims of these false leaders and priests serving the cause of darkness from their stronghold in the astral plane. She also spoke about ancient warfare and human sacrifice that had occurred in the American Southwest and extending down into Mexico and Central and South America. She said these records must be cleared before Native peoples could achieve their freedom on this planet.

She asked if the Albuquerque Study Group and I would work on this spiritual clearance from Albuquerque using calls by Mighty Victory from the yellow pages of The Summit Lighthouse *Prayer, Meditation and Dynamic Decrees* (decrees number 22.02, 22.03, and 22.04). While the Albuquerque Study Group remained on Stanford Avenue for the next two years, we regularly gave the calls to Mighty Victory almost every day.

Years later in Bozeman, Montana, where I live with my family, I began to remember Mother's instructions for the clearing of the energies opposing the soul freedom of the indigenous peoples of the Americas. I have written a personal decree which I make for the clearing of these energies when I am visiting various Indian tribes across the western states. Usually I make these calls alone (all-One with the Brotherhood). I remain dedicated to soul freedom of these people and for the remainder of this embodiment I will continue to the work on this assignment given me by Guru Ma.

I have also learned a great deal from my Native clients. For example, on the Pine Ridge Reservation in South Dakota my Native friends have instructed me in what are known as the Seven Lakota Values. I like them for many reasons, not the least of which is that they remind me of the paramitas of Lord Gautama. One translation of the Seven Lakota Values is as follows:

- Woc'ekiya—Praying to the eternal spirit: finding spirituality by communication with your higher power; this is communication between you and Tunkasila (our Father God—literally grandfather in Lakota) without going through another person or spirit.

- Wa on' sila—Caring and Compassion: love; caring and/or concern for one another in a good way, especially for the family, the old ones, the young ones, the orphans, the one in mourning, the sick ones, and the ones working for the good of the people.
- Wowijake—Honesty and Truth: with yourself, with the higher power, and with others when given with sincerity.
- Wawókiye—Generosity and Helping: helping without expecting anything in return; giving from the heart.
- Wah' wala—Humility: we all partake of the one spirit of the universe; we are no better or less than others.
- Woksape—Wisdom: from consciously acting in life with knowledge comes wisdom.
- Wa o' bola—Respect: for self, for the higher power, for family, community, and for all life.

In Lakota culture the concept of respect (Wa o' bola) is particularly applied to our elders, especially in the spiritual sense. I think of my friend Gene as a respected elder. It is important for us all to learn from our elders who are truly ascending from out of our midst. In this unusual time in history, many old souls will be ascending to their eternal victory. I believe it is right association, as taught by the Buddha, to support, nurture, and learn from those ascending ones around us. Personal relationships with our elders who have faith and the Holy Spirit are a means for us to develop divine love. Before we finish our assignments, we will all need the support of our elders in heaven.

I am always surprised by those who disrespect our spiritual elders. Rather, I believe we should nurture a culture of respect, honoring true wisdom, helping our elders with generosity, caring and compassion. We should have the humility to listen and learn from our elders when we hear from them the voice of truth.

Gene's Three Biblical Quotes for Overcoming on the Path of Personal Christhood

Over these many years Gene and I have often spoken about the supreme importance of love as the one essential key on the path. As the ascended master beloved Rose of Light has instructed us, "Love will fulfill all the Laws. Love will overturn all tyrants and fallen angels. Love will seal you from all going astray and all temptation. Perfect love will cast out all unlike itself."[62]

In our many discussions on love and the path, Gene has often shared with me three Biblical quotes. Gene has said to me many times, "I strive to live my life in the Church and on the path by three biblical sayings." I hope if you will spend some time meditating deeply upon them you will see how they have shaped Gene's life and his work for the Brotherhood. They have the power to help you as well.

- I can do all things through Christ which strengtheneth me (Philippians 4:13).
- My grace is sufficient for thee: for my strength is made perfect in weakness. Most gladly therefore will I rather glory in my infirmities, that the power of Christ may rest upon me (Corinthians 12:9).
- As thy days, so shall thy strength be (Deut. 33:25).

---

[62] Rose of Light, "The Call to the Practice of Love," June 29, 1990, in *Pearls of Wisdom*, vol. 33, no. 22, (Gardiner, Mont.: The Summit Lighthouse, 1990).

Inspiration for the Path of Individual Christhood

When I meditate upon the teaching of the Indwelling Christ, I contact the eternal flame in the heart and I reflect on the great master Sanat Kumara's sacrifice to help each one of us personally with our Christhood. Sanat Kumara is the first and paramount Keeper of the Flame.

At a distant point in planetary history the evolutions of earth had fallen to the level of the caveman and had lost contact with the God flame and the mighty I AM Presence. Earth had become so dark there was not a single soul keeping the flame of the Christ consciousness alive.

Earth was at the point of being destroyed for the weight of its karma. This is when the great Lord Sanat Kumara volunteered to come to earth, to exile himself from his home in Venus, and to keep the flame of the Christ consciousness until such time that sufficient numbers among mankind would once again consciously tend the inner flame. The thought of him descending into the darkness of earth was so dire that 144,000 souls volunteered to assist him and accompany him to earth. Sanat Kumara describes in his own words this momentous event in cosmic history:

> The Cosmic Council had decreed the dissolution of earth and her evolutions because the souls of her children no longer worshiped the Trinity in the threefold flame of life burning upon the altar of the heart... Thus the light of the temples had gone out, and the purpose to which God had created man—to be the temple of the living God—was no longer being fulfilled. The hour of the judgment had come... [63]

---

[63] Sanat Kumara, "I Will Come When You Need Me, I place my Electronic Presence at the Gate of this City Foursquare: One Solution: Individual Christhood," *Pearls of Wisdom*, vol. 33 (1990), No. 44, (Gardiner, Montana: Summit University Press, 1990).

Was there a requirement of the Great Law that could save the earth? Yes, that requirement was that one who qualified as the Lamb, the embodied Guru, would reside in the earth to hold the balance and keep the flame of life for every living soul here.

Sanat Kumara says:

I chose to be that one. I volunteered to be a flaming son of righteousness unto earth and her evolutions.

After considerable deliberation, the Cosmic Council and the Nameless One gave their approval of my petition, and the dispensation for a new divine plan for earth and her evolutions came into being...

Thus I knelt before the great white throne of the Nameless One and he said unto me, "My son, Sanat Kumara, thou shalt sit upon the great white throne before the evolutions of earth. Thou shalt be to them the Lord God in the highest. Verily, thou shalt be the highest manifestation of the Deity which shall be given unto them until, through the path of initiation, their souls shall rise to thy throne of awareness and stand before thee in praise of the I AM THAT I AM which thou art. In that day when they shall rise up and say, "Blessing and honour and glory and power be unto him that sitteth upon the throne and unto the Lamb for ever and ever"—behold, their redemption draweth nigh.

That evening, the joy of opportunity was mingled with the sorrow that the sense of separation brings. I had chosen a voluntary exile upon a dark star. And though it was destined to be Freedom's Star, all knew it would be for me a long dark night of the soul.

Then all at once from the valleys and the mountains there appeared a great gathering of my children. It was the souls of the hundred and forty and four thousand approaching our palace of light. They spiraled nearer and nearer as twelve companies singing the song of freedom, of love, and of victory. Their mighty chorusing echoed throughout elemental life, and angelic choirs hovered nigh. As we watched from the balcony, Venus and I, we saw the thirteenth company robed in white. It was the royal priesthood of the Order of Melchizedek, the anointed ones who kept the flame and the law in the center of this hierarchical unit.

When all of their numbers had assembled, ring upon ring upon ring surrounding our home, and their hymn of praise and adoration to me was concluded, their spokesman stood before the balcony to address us on behalf of the great multitude. It was the soul of the one you know and love today as the Lord of the World, Gautama Buddha. And he addressed us, saying, "O Ancient of Days, we have heard of the covenant which God hath made with thee this day and of thy commitment to keep the flame of life until some among earth's evolutions should be quickened and once again renew their vow to be bearers of the flame. O Ancient of Days, thou art to us our Guru, our very life, our God. We will not leave thee comfortless. We will go with thee. We will not leave thee for one moment without the ring upon ring of our chelaship. We will come to earth. We will prepare the way. We will keep the flame in thy name."

We wept in joy, Venus and I and all of the hundred and forty and four thousand. And the tears that flowed on that memorable evening burned as the living sacred fire flowing as the water of life from the great white throne and the Cosmic Council, our sponsors.[64]

---

[64] Elizabeth Clare Prophet, *The Opening of the Seventh Seal: Sanat Kumara on the Path of the ruby Ray* (Gardiner, Mont.: Summit Lighthouse Library, 2001), pp. 11, 12–13, 14–15.

And so when Sanat Kumara came from Venus to make the earth his long but temporary home, he was accompanied by a retinue of many great beings of light. He established on an island in the Gobi Sea (now the Gobi desert) the focus of the threefold flame and there he resided with it until quite recently. Sanat Kumara anchored a ray of light from his heart to each and every one evolving on Earth to nourish the flame of the individual Christ Self. From that ancient time to the twenty-first century, Sanat Kumara has served the earth and her evolutions. His mission was completed on January 1, 1956, when his great disciple Gautama Buddha became Lord of the World and began to hold the balance for the planet and the focus of the threefold flame.

Without the love and assistance of Sanat Kumara, all evolutions of earth and the planet itself would have been recycled for their karma or rebellion. Because of his great service, Sanat Kumara is depicted in many religious traditions. In Hinduism he is revered as a Son of Brahma called Skanda or Karttikeya. The ascended masters teach us that in Zoroastrianism Sanat Kumara is the supreme God, called Ahura Mazda. In Buddhist tradition he embodied as Dipamkara, the lamp-lighting Buddha. In Judaism and Christianity he is the Ancient of Days.

I feel that Gene and others of our close-knit mandala are members of the 144,000. I have discovered that as I meditate on the great Father principle in my own heart it draws me again and again to the heart of our father Sanat Kumara. Although we are entering into an age of the Divine Mother, I trust there will always be an honored place for representatives of the Divine Father within the hierarchy of our Church. We must be very careful to keep a balance of the Father/Mother God. For me Gene Vosseler has been one of the first Fathers of the Church, following as best he can in the tradition of Sanat Kumara.

A Teaching from Gene on the Path Forward for Our Church

The Climb the Highest Mountain series has been outlined in thirty-three chapters by the ascended master El Morya and Mark L. and Elizabeth Clare Prophet, our messengers. This revelation of the Word is intended for the next two thousand-year dispensation in the Age of Aquarius. In the fourth book of the Climb series there is a chapter entitled "The Path of Brotherhood," which illumines the role of the apostle:

It was on the foundation of the apostles and the prophets that the Christian Church was built, with Jesus Christ himself as the chief cornerstone. The distinction between the two is that, while the prophet was God's spokesman to the believing Church, the apostle was his envoy to the unbelieving world. Prophets are lawgivers; they are God's spokesmen. It is to unbelievers, to those who know not the Christ within, that the apostle must have the courage to preach. There are many more apostles than prophets in the true Church, and we are all called to be apostles.[65]

Gene Vosseler has always advocated this principal of apostleship to me as a way to move our Church dynamically forward. Conversion by the Holy Spirit most often occurs from one fiery heart to another. Mother asked Gene to stump with the teachings of the ascended masters in some dozen or more countries around the world. As hard as it is to accept this calling of apostleship, it is this calling that was, and ever will be, an essential element in the archetypal pattern for our Christ self-mastery.

When Gene has passed on to his greater reward, it is my

---

[65] Mark L. Prophet and Elizabeth Clare Prophet, *The Path of Brotherhood,* Climb The Highest Mountain series Book 9, (Gardiner, Mont.: Summit University Library, 2003), p. 155

hope that this basic teaching of personal Christ mastery will be retained and practiced. In this unusual era between the age of Jesus and the age of Saint Germain, we have been privileged to have seen and heard the embodied Word in Mark and Elizabeth Clare Prophet. I believe it would behoove us to follow their instructions in this matter of apostleship. If Jesus Christ is indeed the same yesterday, today, and forever, so will be his sponsorship of new apostles. Gene taught a course that was approved by Mother on this subject for the Church many years ago.

Saint Francis Senior Resources—
Caring for Our Elderly

On Father's Day 2007, a group of chelas here in Bozeman was blessed to have Gene and Wanda share lunch with us after the Sunday Service at the Bozeman Community Teaching Center. Gene and Wanda were visiting from Texas, where they were residing at the time. After a wonderful fellowship over lunch, we all said our goodbyes. A number of community members that were present commented on how frail Gene appeared. The next morning, at a motel here in Bozeman, Gene suffered a mild heart attack, but fortunately he was only five minutes away from Bozeman Deaconess Hospital. Wanda's eagle eye for her beloved summoned medical help within seconds and he was delivered him to the hospital in minutes.

After some light surgery and a few days in the hospital, Gene and Wanda came to our home for a few weeks to recover from the mishap. Although the circumstances of Gene's extended visit were less than ideal, we had a wonderful time in our renewed communion. After my usual prayers one morning, I had the strongest presentment that the Master Kuthumi wanted us to form a new non-profit corporation to serve seniors in need. The name came through to us that the new corporation should be called Saint Francis Senior Resources, Inc. (St. Francis for short.) Immediately, I asked Gene if he would serve as its first president of the board of directors. Gene and I incorporated St. Francis that very same day.

At the turn of the twenty-first century, America is coming to grips with the retirement of our aging baby boomers, a term used to describe a large generation of people who were born during several years following World War II. This "graying of America" is also reflected within our spiritual community demographics as well. After decades of devoted and loving service to the Great White Brotherhood and the mission of the two witnesses, many of our senior members find themselves without adequate savings and resources for their old age.

Many of our apostles, monks, nuns, and pioneering devotees have worked selflessly for the Church for decades essentially as volunteers. After years of grateful service, some now faced poor health and financial hardships. Some have had to live out their final years with "heads white and eyes ready to close in this octave" in poor circumstances and lessened opportunity to engage in the mighty spiritual work assigned to their stage of life.

The mother Church has been appropriately focused on holding the balance for the planet, publishing the Word, fighting a variety of legal and government challenges, and preparing for Mother's transition. They have set up a charity fund, but more help is needed to care for this burgeoning elderly segment of our community. Therefore, individual chelas are now being inspired to pick up the torch. The necessity of serving this segment of stalwart and committed senior members has pressed heavily upon the heart of Rev. E. Margaret (Peggy) Keathley for more than a decade.

Mrs. Keathley owned property in Emigrant, Montana, near the entrance to North Glastonbury, which she named "Avalon" after the ancient mystical Isle of Avalon in England, where it is said that Jesus visited as a young man. It is also said that Joseph of Arimathea, Mother Mary, and early Christian followers, including many apostles and disciples, found refuge on Avalon during the years after Jesus' crucifixion. King Arthur and Guinevere were reputedly buried at Avalon, and Glastonbury enthusiasts say, "The veils between the worlds are thin here, opening doors of deepened perception. This seems to have existed since the beginnings of time." Students of the Avalon/Glastonbury mysteries even suggest that the original community was a remnant of the Atlantean civilization and that it was a center of teaching and initiation in ancient times.

Mrs. Keathley was indeed inspired by these views and sought to recreate this special focus for the release of light on the planet and she planned to leverage her property to this end. She and a team of initial investors attempted to build an assisted living facility and create a spiritual environment that would support the prophecy of "mass ascensions from the hillsides." They worked tirelessly through a company called Avalon Development, Inc., which set about to create a place for new age mystics to gather once again.

There has been formidable opposition to the Avalon project and to those who are determined to gather in one place to work together on the path of the ascension. After ten years of effort, Mrs. Keathley and her stalwart board of directors have decided that St. Francis Senior Resources, as a non-profit organization, was the only way to properly fulfill the vision. Avalon Development, Inc., has graciously donated the Avalon property and infrastructure to St. Francis. St. Francis is now working diligently to ensure the vision of Avalon in the Glastonbury community becomes a reality in the very near future.

St. Francis has created three programs that assist community members to focus their attention on service to our seniors. We hope St. Francis will grow to become a bright light of spiritual inspiration for the whole world as to how elders should be served. St. Francis' programs are also a means of demonstrating the culture of the Divine Mother to a hungry world. They will help us to become a beacon of love representing the ascended masters.

Three programs serve as the cornerstones of St. Francis Senior Resources: (1) Avalon Independent Living facility, (2)

St. Francis Adopt-an-Elder program, and (3) the St. Francis Care Corps volunteer program.

The Avalon Independent Living facility, now being constructed, is the first of several facilities to provide housing for low-income seniors. Seniors pay what they can and generous donations of community members fill in the gaps. It is a workable solution to help the aging monks and nuns of our activity to carry them through the initiations that they will face at the close of this life.

The Adopt-an-Elder program is designed to give people an opportunity to sponsor their elder friends at a vulnerable stage of life. It is meant to provide gap financing for core needs such as dentistry, glasses, and hearing aids, as well as other emergent needs such as construction of wheelchair ramps or home repairs. This program complements and supplements other less-adequate social services such as Medicaid and Social Security. Adoption can be long-term, with monthly support for those in need, or on an as-needed basis. It also provides a tax write-off for those who want to support a specific long-time devotee of God.

St. Francis Care Corps is an organized effort of capable and compassionate hearts who want to volunteer their services, rather than money, to the elderly in need. Seniors are matched with volunteers for services and skills that might include transportation, socialization, and end-of-life support.

Gene has asked that net proceeds from the sale of this book go to St. Francis Senior Resources, Inc. At the end of the book is some more information if you would like to support this worthy cause.

Questions for Those Who Are Striving on the Path of the Ascension

I have watched and listened to my friend Gene Vosseler for more than thirty years. I have watched him serve his Guru, his Church, his country, and his God. I sincerely believe my friend Gene is striving to walk the path of immortality. This is not to make an idol of Gene. My statement is not that he has been perfect, but to recognize his wonderful contribution to the collective life of our community.

In 2006, Summit University Press published a wonderful book titled *The Path to Immortality* as the seventh volume in the Climb the Highest Mountain series. On page 232 of that volume, there is a discussion about the examination of the soul before the court of the ascension at Luxor. I think it is useful to review a small portion of this ritual of the Last Judgment.

The ritual of the Last Judgment is an experience through which all sons and daughters of God must pass as their final test of the sacred fire before their ultimate reunion with their God Presence in the ritual of the ascension. It is our rite of passage to graduate from the schoolroom of earth. In this ritual the candidate is called for this test before the council of the twelve adepts at Luxor composed of twelve ascended masters presided over by Serapis Bey, the chohan of the fourth ray. In the book, Mother and Mark list the critical questions asked of each candidate.

One of the most important questions asked by the Council of Twelve is whether or not the example set by the disciple while in embodiment is one that would be desirable for all mankind to follow.

> *Has he openly proclaimed the teachings of the Christ and of the Brotherhood?*

Has he taken a stand for right in the midst of oppression and adversity, challenging the sinister force entrenched in the civilization of his time?

Has he left well-defined footprints on the sands of time that those who follow him may trace and thereby find their victory?

Or has he sown matrices of error as stones of stumbling in his brothers' pathway that will prevent their fulfilling the requirements of the Law?

If so, has he removed these barriers through subsequent service to life?[66]

It is my testimony about my friend Gene Vosseler that he can confidently and appropriately answer each of these final exam questions. May our brother Gene find his eternal Victory in the light according to God's own timetable. Thank you brother Gene, for a lifetime of friendship and for providing such a worthy example of striving for righteousness in our spiritual community.

---

[66] Mark L. Prophet and Elizabeth Clare Prophet, *The Path to Immortality*, Climb The Highest Mountain series Book 7, (Gardiner, Mont.: Summit University Press, 2006), pages 237-238.

12. EPILOGUE

As I conclude this epistle of my spiritual freedom odyssey in this life, there are several other things I wish to share with you, my beloved reader.

As we approached the Thanksgiving season in the year of our Lord 2008, I was asked to pen a brief article on the subject, and what I came to write was certainly different from what I intended. I'd like to share it with you at this time.

Thanksgiving Thoughts

As we near the day that we celebrate as a nation and a people—our Thanksgiving to God for all the material and spiritual blessings that we enjoy—we should pause to remember with grateful hearts our brothers and sisters who are currently overseas battling terrorists, suicide bombers, and fundamental Islamic extremists who would destroy our basic freedoms and all that we hold dear as a free people.

Many have laid down their lives and paid the supreme price of life itself. Others have suffered grave injuries that will affect their material, physical, and emotional well-being for the rest of their lives.

They have discovered that there is a price to be paid to insure that we as a free people can continue to enjoy freedom of worship, freedom of speech, freedom of the press, and the right to assembly. And for the chelas and our friends overseas, this battle for freedom is being fought for you as well, and some of your troops are fighting, too.

Now, I must confess that when I began to think about writing this article on Thanksgiving, I was thinking along more traditional lines of somewhat more standard thanksgiving thoughts. But after making calls to my gurus and other of my favorite ascended masters, the current of this article took a very different direction.

In the words of John the Beloved, "The wind bloweth where it listeth, and thou hearest the sound thereof, but canst not tell whence it cometh, and whither it goeth: so is everyone that is born of the Spirit" (John 3:8).

At this point I feel a bit like the minister who was noted for being somewhat long-winded, a fact certainly noted by members in his congregation. One Sunday in a spirit of agitated exasperation he remarked to his congregation, "I don't mind it when you take out your watches to check the time, but it upsets me when you begin to shake them." But since this indeed is the conclusion of my book, there are several more nuggets of information that I want to share with you.

First, as a nation we are currently blessed with a wonderful new crop of young people. These are the advanced souls, the ascended masters promised would be coming into embodiment after the year 1968. They have definitely arrived, very advanced and spiritually aware in their outlook and perceptions. And that is one reason why the forces of darkness are stepping up their attacks on them in the great cultural war—attacking their souls with drugs, alcohol, all manner of sex perversions, and anti-God, atheistic indoctrination in universities, etc.—the list goes on.

As parents of these beautiful souls we have great responsibility to train our children in the way they should go by living the exemplary lives that teach them right from wrong and those core values that will last a lifetime. I am thankful for those leaders in church and education that are keenly aware of this situation and who are dedicating their lives in the service of our blessed youth.

Second, an important thing I want to share is that as I approach my eighty-second birthday, I am spiritually reminded that, in this life of mine I have made mistakes, sins of commission and omission against other souls and parts of life. For all these errors of my past, I am truly sorry; I apologize, and beg forgiveness from all I have ever wronged or offended. I trust in the mercies of Almighty God and the transmuting Holy Spirit fires of the violet flame for absolution and transmutation.

And finally, yes this is finally, I want to, with a grateful heart, salute the beloved ascended masters who love and so generously serve our lives each day—particularly our great

Lord Sanat Kumara, the Ancient of Days, who at a critical time of earth's evolution stepped in to save our planet. And I am especially thankful to all the lineage of the ruby ray masters, including Gautama Buddha, Lord of the World; Lord Maitreya, Cosmic Christ; our Lord and Savior Jesus Christ; Padma Sambhava; and the two witnesses, our beloved messengers Elizabeth Clare Prophet and Mark L. Prophet (the ascended master Lanello). And of course we are grateful to the lords (chohans) of the rays, to the mighty Elohim, to the archangels and their archeiai, to the Lords of Karma, and to our beloved Bapu, Lord Morya El. O great beings of light out of the heart of our Father-Mother God, Alpha and Omega, we love you and we are One in your magnificent flame.

Your reverent servant,

Gene Vosseler
Pax vobiscum—all glory to God!

AFTERWORD

A Testimony to My Guru—My First Meeting with Elizabeth Clare Prophet

The date for this auspicious event was July 4, 1977. The place was the Ashram of the World Mother in Los Angeles, California. The time was during the July Freedom Conference of the ascended masters of the Great White Brotherhood.

There were no guarantees that we would be allowed to meet with the messenger of the ascended masters, who is Elizabeth Clare Prophet, since she was very busy giving lectures and dictations. But due to fortuitous circumstances, my beloved wife to be, Wanda Davidson, and I suddenly found ourselves face-to-face with Elizabeth Clare Prophet. After a few pleasantries, we stated the purpose of our interview, which was to ask for her blessing for the wedding that we were contemplating. Her response was, "Why didn't you get married today?" since she had performed a wedding ceremony for about twenty couples that day. I replied, "Mother, we wanted to be certain to get your blessing before taking that step." She replied, "I don't see any reason for you to wait. Why don't you get married here at the Ashram in front of the statue of Mother Mary?" And then to our amazement she added, "Would you like to honeymoon at Maitreya's Mountain up in Big Sur?" Our friend Dr. Ralph Yaney owned a piece of property called Maitreya's Mountain up in Big Sur country in northern California. Amazed at this response I blurted out, "Mother, Wanda and I have previously talked about doing that very thing. How did you know about it?" With an enigmatic smile and a twinkle in her eye she responded, "Well, Gene, after all I am your Guru."

To use the vernacular, the deal was sealed. She acknowledged herself as my Guru and I became a chela of the two messengers, who are the two witnesses written about in the biblical Book of Revelation. In the lineage of Sanat Kumara and the ruby ray masters, the two messengers have given us the Everlasting Gospel for the next two-thousand-year dispensation and the cosmic keys for the soul liberation of all those willing to walk the path of initiation to their victorious ascension in the light.

And for thirty-one years it has been my joyous privilege to walk this challenging path with my beloved Gurus who are a daily inspiration and comfort to my life.

Rev. E. Gene Vosseler

August 2008

How to Support St. Francis Senior Resources

In keeping with his mission in this life to promote soul freedom, the author has agreed to contribute the net proceeds of this book to St. Francis Senior Resources Center, for the construction and operation of the Avalon Independent Living Center, a place where many of our elderly and those in the larger community will live in preparation for their transition and their hoped-for and anticipated ascension in the light. Construction on Avalon is planned to begin in early 2009. It will be located near North Glastonbury, just 25 miles south of Livingston, Montana.

To contribute or for more information, please contact:
St. Francis Senior Resources
210 Cirque Drive
Bozeman, MT 59718
Ph 800.628.9184
Fx 406.587.8828
info@SupportOurElders.org

St. Francis Senior Resources, Inc. is a tax exempt under section 501(c)3 of the Internal Revenue Code. Your contribution is tax-deductible to the extent allowable by law.

www.ingramcontent.com/pod-product-compliance
Lightning Source LLC
Chambersburg PA
CBHW020347170426
43200CB00005B/73